On Puns

On Puns

The Foundation of Letters

Edited by
Jonathan Culler

Basil Blackwell

Copyright © Basil Blackwell 1988

First published 1988

Basil Blackwell Ltd
108 Cowley Road, Oxford, OX4 1JF, UK

Basil Blackwell Inc.
432 Park Avenue South, Suite 1503
New York, NY 10016, USA

British Library Cataloguing in Publication Data
On puns: the foundation of letters.
1. Puns and punning – History and
criticism
I. Culler, Jonathan
809.7   PN6149.P85
ISBN 0–631–15893–6
ISBN 0–631–15894–4 Pbk

Library of Congress Cataloging in Publication Data
On puns: the foundation of letters/edited by Jonathan Culler.
p.   cm.
Based on a conference sponsored by the Society for the Humanities,
Cornell University, in September 1985.
Includes index.
ISBN 0-631-15893-6
ISBN 0-631-15894-4 (pbk.)
1. Puns and punning – History and criticism.   I. Culler, Jonathan D.
II. Society for the Humanities.
PN6149.P8505   1988
809 – dc 19

Typeset in 10 on 12pt Ehrhardt
by Joshua Associates Limited, Oxford
Printed in Great Britain by
Page Bros Ltd., Norwich

Contents

Acknowledgements

This volume began as a conference, 'The Call of the Phoneme: Puns and the Foundation of Letters', sponsored by the Society for the Humanities, Cornell University ('Honi Soit Qui Mal Y Puns'), in September 1985. Substantial revisions and five additional papers – by Attridge, Czerniecki, Fineman, Meltzer and Shoaf – have since accreted to the original presentations. I am grateful to Frederick Ahl, who helped to conceive and organize the conference, and to other friends and colleagues who variously assisted with the conference or the volume: Mary Ahl, Cynthia Chase and William Levitan. A longer version of Derek Attridge's essay appears in his *Peculiar Language: Literature as Difference from the Renaissance to James Joyce*, © Derek Attridge (London: Routledge, and Ithaca: Cornell University Press, 1988). It appears here by permission of Cornell University Press and Routledge. Some material in Frederick Ahl's essay is adapted from his book *Metaformations: Soundplay and Wordplay in Ovid and Other Classical Poets* (Ithaca: Cornell University Press, 1985).

Jonathan Culler
Ithaca, New York

Contributors

Frederick Ahl, Professor of Classics at Cornell, has written *Metaformations: Soundplay and Wordplay in Ovid and Other Classical Poets* (Cornell) and translated Seneca's *Phaedra*, *Medea* and *Trojan Women* for the Cornell 'Masters of Latin Literature'.

Derek Attridge, Professor of English at the University of Strathclyde and Visiting Professor at Rutgers, is the author of *The Rhythms of English Poetry* (Longman) and *Peculiar Language: Literature as Difference from the Renaissance to James Joyce* (Cornell and Routledge).

Jonathan Culler, Director of the Society for the Humanities at Cornell, has written several works of literary theory, including *On Deconstruction* (Cornell and Routledge) and *Framing the Sign* (Blackwell and Oklahoma).

Krystian Czerniecki, a graduate student in English at Cornell, is writing a dissertation on Shakespeare.

Joel Fineman's *Shakespeare's Perjur'd Eye* (California) won the James Russell Lowell Prize for 1985. He teaches English at the University of California, Berkeley.

Debra Fried, Assistant Professor of English at Cornell, is at work on a book on poetic form, to which her essay in this volume belongs.

Françoise Meltzer, who teaches Comparative Literature at the University of Chicago, has published *Salomé and the Dance of Writing: Portraits of Mimesis in Literature* (Chicago).

Avital Ronell, Associate Professor of Comparative Literature at Berkeley, is the author of *Dictations: On Haunted Writing* (Indiana), an essay on Freud and Goethe, and *The Telephone Book* (Nebraska).

R. A. Shoaf, Professor of English at the University of Florida, has published *Dante, Chaucer, and the Currency of the Word* (Pilgrim) and *Milton: Poet of Duality* (Yale).

Gregory Ulmer, Professor of English at the University of Florida, is the author of *Applied Grammatology* (Hopkins) and co-author of *Glassary* (Nebraska), the companion to Derrida's *Glas*.

1

The Call of the Phoneme:
Introduction

Jonathan Culler

The Word *Pun* appears to be of Greek Originall. Some derive it from Πύνδαξ, which signifies either *Fundum*, a Bottom, or *Maniebrium gladij*, the handle of a Sword. From the former, because this kind of Wit is thought to *lye* deeper than any other. . . . Secondly, from the Handle of a Sword: Because whoever *wields* it will shew something *Bright* and *sharp* at the *End*: Another and more probable Opinion is that the word *Pun* comes from Πυνθάνομαι; because without *Knoledge* (sic), *hearing*, and *Enquiry*, this Gift is not to be obtained. There is a more modern Etymology which I cannot altogether approve, tho' it be highly ingenious: For, the Cantabrigians derive the Word from *Ponticulus* Quasi, *Pun tickle us*, which signifyes a *little Bridge*, as ours over the *Cam*, where this Art is in highest Perfection. Again; others derive it from *Pungo*; because whoever lets a *Pungo* will be sure to make his Adversary *smart*. And to include this Head, I shall not conceal one Originall of this Word assigned by our Adversaryes, from the French word *Punaise*, which signifyes a little stinking Insect that gets into the Skin, provokes continual *Itching* and is with great Difficulty removed.

Jonathan Swift[1]

Pun, my word here, is not a very old word. It appears, the *OED* tells us, soon after 1660, and is 'of undetermined origin'. 'It has been suggested,' the learned work continues, 'that *pun* might originally have been an abbreviation of Italian *puntiglio*, "small or fine point" . . . This appears not impossible, but nothing has been found in the early history of *pun*, or in the English uses of *punctilio*, to confirm the conjecture.'[2] A finer tale links our word to *pun* meaning 'to compact or pound', as in *Troilus and Cressida*: 'He would pun thee into shivers with his fist.' To pun, writes Skeat, 'is to pound

---

[1] Jonathan Swift, 'A Modest Defence of Punning', *Prose Works*, ed. Herbert Davis (Oxford, 1957), vol. 4, pp. 205–6.

[2] The *Oxford Dictionary of English Etymology* (Oxford, 1962), deems *pun* 'probably one of a group of clipped words which became fashionable in Restoration times, . . . apparently short for *pundigrion*', itself conjecturally 'a fanciful alteration of the Italian *puntiglio*'. The layers of conjecture emphasize the difficulty of distinguishing punning from etymologizing.

words, to beat them into new senses, to hammer at forced similies'.[3] Partridge reports, however, 'At one time, I entertained the idea that pun might afford an early example of blend: *puzzle* + *conundrum*, with *con-* pronounced *cun-*.'[4] The scholar of origins does not explain what displaced this entertaining suspicion.

It seems entirely appropriate that pun should be of uncertain origin and provoke etymological speculation, since this is the diachronic version of punning. The tradition of ancient etymologizing, in Plato's *Cratylus*, in Varro, in Isadore of Seville, was one of motivating the meaning of words through punning derivations.[5] Modern etymology has grown more historically circumspect, but in both etymologies and puns, Derek Attridge writes, 'two similar sounding but distinct signifiers are brought together, and the surface relationship between them invested with meaning through the inventiveness and rhetorical skill of the writer.'[6] In etymologies, a supposedly historical continuity between forms may stand in for the greater phonemic similarity of puns, but both use related forms to connect disaparate meanings, and, as in punning, the interest of etymologies lies in the surprising coupling of different meanings: *Stuart*, the Royal House, may come from *styward*, keeper of the pig sty. *Law* comes form *licgan*, 'to lie', so a lawyer is a liar. Etymologies – whether sanctioned or unsanctioned by current philology – are valued for the punlike quality, as they forge unexpected connections, whose suggestiveness shimmers on the borders of concepts, threatening to transform them: *christian* and *cretin* are the same word.

Frequently puns are thought justified if they have an etymological basis: discussing puns which Milton brings off 'with an air of learning and command of the language', so that they actually acquire dignity, William Empson remarks that his line in *Paradise Regained* about Elijah's ravens,

> Though ravenous, taught to abstain from what they brought,

'is ridiculous, though if it had been justified by derivation, as perhaps it claims to be, it would have been all right'.[7] Etymologies, we might say, give us respectable puns, endowing pun-like effects with the authority of science

[3] W. W. Skeat, *An Etymological Dictionary of the English Language* (Oxford, 1910).

[4] Eric Partridge, *Origins: A Short Etymological Dictionary of Modern English* (New York, 1966).

[5] See Frederick Ahl, *Metaformations: Soundplay and Wordplay in Ovid and Other Classical Poets* (Ithaca, 1985), pp. 22–5, 39–47.

[6] Derek Attridge, 'Language as History/History as Language: Saussure and the Romance of Etymology', in *Post-Structuralism and History*, eds Attridge et al. (Cambridge, 1987), p. 193. This valuable essay, to which I am much indebted, is reprinted in Attridge, *Peculiar Language: Literature as Difference from the Renaissance to James Joyce* (Ithaca and London, 1988).

[7] William Empson, *Seven Types of Ambiguity* (Harmondsworth, 1961), p. 104.

and even of truth, as when we say that *education* means 'to lead out' (*e-ducere*). Thus, the claim that 'history' has so far been 'his story' would gain critical force if etymologically supported. Etymologies show us what puns might be if taken seriously: illustrations of the inherent instability of language and the power of uncodified linguistic relations to produce meaning.

Although etymologists sniffily reject folk etymologies or popular etymologies in the same way they might reject puns – Skeat speaks of the 'unscrupulous inventions with which English "etymology" abounds, and which many people admire because they are "so clever" '[8] – they nevertheless succumb to their attraction, citing them and perpetuating the connections thereby established even as they deny their well-foundedness. Whatever linguists say about them, folk etymologies, like puns, are realities of language: both are instances of speakers intervening in language, articulating relations which, once identified, may be hard to banish. Linguists insist that *rage* and *outrage* have nothing to do with each other – *outrage* come from *ultra* plus the suffix *age*, and thus ought to be pronounced 'outrige' like other such formations (*coinage*) – but speakers pronounce the words so as to enforce the connection and treat *outrage* as the morally satisfying form of *rage*.[9] Folk etymologies and puns show speakers intently or playfully working to reveal the structures of language, motivating linguistic signs, allowing signifiers to affect meaning by generating new connections – in short, responding to the call of the phoneme, whose echoes tell of wild realms beyond the code and suggest new configurations of meaning: 'Even the stable boy will find / This life no stable thing.' Puns present the disquieting spectacle of a functioning of language where boundaries – between sounds, between sound and letter, between meanings – count for less than one might imagine and where supposedly discrete meanings threaten to sink into fluid subterranean signifieds too undefinable to call concepts: a commingling of 'stable' and 'stables'. The relations perceived by speakers affect meanings and thus the linguistic system, which must be taken to include the constant remotivation produced by impressions of connection or similarity.

Not surprisingly, in both the realm of puns – relations between signs in a language at a particular moment – and the realm of etymology – relations between signs from different periods – there is no dearth of people anxious to control relations, to enforce a distinction between real and false connections, true etymologies and folk etymologies, puns and valid conceptual relations. Etymological derivation has not escaped satire – Mark

---

[8] Skeat, *Etymological Dictionary*, p. xxviii.
[9] See Attridge, 'Language as History', p. 187.

Twain claimed that *Middletown* was derived from *Moses* by dropping *oses* and adding the *iddletown* – and folk etymologies are rejected by scholars, but puns have encountered broader hostility, from the claim Pope cites, that 'he that would pun would pick a pocket', and Sydney Smith's dismissal of 'a radically bad race of wit', to the categorization of one folktale type in Aarne and Thompson's massive, classic study as 'Stupid Stories Depending on Puns'.[10]

To sneer at puns as the lowest form of wit confirms Swift's derivation from *fundum*, 'bottom' or 'foundation', as in the foundation of letters, but also combines the gesture of rejection with the claim that if they are valued it should be as an amusing form of cleverness. If one were successfully to beat off this attack on puns, though, the outcome would be a punic victory – the defence of puns as a moderately higher form of wit, which would still make them supererogatory. To groan at puns, one might conjecture, is viscerally to reaffirm a distinction between essence and accident, between meaningful relations and coincidence, that has seemed fundamental to our thinking. The discussions in this volume explore various manifestations of that opposition and ways in which puns might challenge it. Committed to the view that puns are not a marginal form of wit but an exemplary product of language or mind, these essays share an interest in what puns show about the functioning of language, or literature, or the psyche. The pun is the foundation of letters, in that the exploitation of formal resemblance to establish connections of meaning seems the basic activity of literature; but this foundation is a foundation of letters only, a foundation of marks whose significance depends on relations, whose own significative status is a function of practices of reading, forms of attention, and social convention. Nowhere is the shakiness of the foundation clearer than in the shifty relation between letter and sound: the two meanings brought forth by a pun may be evoked by various similarities of sounds and letters. Most often, in English, different letters shadow forth the difference of meaning borne by similar sound sequences: *puns aren't just some antics*. Homophones are for us the very type of the pun ('They went and told the sexton / And the sexton tolled the bell'), but there are many other possible configurations, including the pure play of the letter in anagrams, which makes Ronald Wilson Reagan an *insane Anglo warlord* or suggests that in French the demon (*démon*) lies hidden in the world (*monde*).

Scholars have sought to define and classify puns, but the results have never met with much success.[11] Since the essays in this volume take pun as

---

[10] Antti Arne and Stith Thompson, *Types of the Folktale* (Helsinki, 1961), p. 399.

[11] See, for example, J. Brown, 'Eight Types of Pun', *PMLA* 71 (1956). Walter Redfern, whose *Puns* (Oxford, 1984) is the most informative and entertaining resource in this field, declines to categorize.

paradigm for the play of language, they do not seek to circumscribe it or discriminate it from other sorts of wordplay. Our nineteenth-century inheritance makes the pun a vehicle of humor, separating it from other verbal structures and excluding scholarship from this realm where lightness is all; but the essays here collected presume a continuity with wordplay that goes by other names, some of which we might briefly survey.

Depending on similarity of form and disparity of meaning, a pun evokes disparate meanings in contexts where each differently applies. But disparate meanings may be connected in numerous ways. *Paronomasia* or *adnominatio*, a broad figure of classical rhetoric closely related to the modern pun, 'is a figure in which, by means of a modification of sound, or change of letters, a close resemblance to a given verb or noun is produced, so that similar words express dissimilar things ... 'Hic quos homines alea vincit, eos ferro statim vinciit" ' (Those men who he beats at dice, he straightaway binds in chains).[12] Such wordplays, 'which depend on a slight change or lengthening or transposition of letters, and the like', put similar but not identical forms together in a sequence, as in Falstaff's 'Were it not here apparent that thou art heir apparent'. This sort of repetition is but an intensification of assonance, consonance or alliteration. Verlaine's famous comparison of a figurative weeping to an agentless raining, 'Il pleure dans mon coeur / Comme il pleut sur la ville', is not perhaps generally seen as a pun, but it belongs to paronomasia. Echoes that are particularly familiar in a language or a literature, such as *live* and *love* in English, or *amor* and *mors* in Latin, have lost the surprise of pun, which may mean only that the meanings are already felt to be related.

A more narrowly defined figure, *antanaclasis*, 'where the same word is used in two different meanings', is a homonymic pun: 'When Proculeus reproached his son with waiting for his death and the son replied that he was not waiting for it, the former retorted, "Well then, I ask you to wait for it".'[13] A compact instance from *Henry V* is 'To England will I steal, and there I'll steal'. By contrast, *syllepsis*, a type of pun singled out in the Renaissance but since then not generally distinguished from *zeugma*, produces a structure in which a single form (not repeated) must function in two senses: 'He bolted the door and his dinner.' Or again, 'Or stain her honour, or her new brocade, / Or lose her heart, or necklace, at a ball.'

Divergent meanings are also linked by other forms of repetition, of which anagrams are the clearest example: *live* and *evil*, *scared sacred*, *hated death*. Frederick Ahl, in his contribution to this volume, makes a strong case for the importance of anagrams and anagrammatic etymologizing as generative

---

[12] *Rhetorica ad Herennium*, IV. xxi. 29.
[13] Quintilian, *Institutio Oratoria*, IX. iii. 68.

principles of Latin poetry and habits of classical thinking. When Vergil writes that Saturn 'preferred the place to be called Latium because he had hidden safe on these shores' ('Latiumque vocari / Maluit, his quoniam latuisset tutus in oris'), the name *Latium* is derived not only from *latuisset* ('he had hidden') but also as an anagram of *maluit* ('he preferred'), 'which neatly complements the idea of Saturn's concealment in Latium.' Classical techniques also insist on the possibility of thinking of syllables as crucial units of language, which echo each other in ways that may produce meaning.

The echoing of syllables and morphemes is related to a modern device (though one also exploited by Rabelais), the portmanteau word, discussed by Derek Attridge. *Famillionarily*, *tighteousness*, *balmheartzyheat*, connect disparate meanings as puns do, and in impelling us to work out what words or parts thereof they sound like, they open a dizzying prospect of multilingual puns. In evoking *Barmherzigkeit* ('mercy'), just as forcibly as a balm of heart's heat, *balmheartzyheat* indicates that the effects of discourse may depend on the connections established with forms from other languages and thus that we cannot specify in advance, in a limited code, the relations that will produce meaning. With the portmanteau, Attridge writes, 'there is no escape from its insistence that meaning is an effect of language, not a presence within or behind language, and that the effect is unstable and uncontrollable.' Unstable like puns themselves.

The essays that follow do not attempt a survey or taxonomy of the pun. Although they range in their focus from the classical period to the post-modern, they do not provide a history; and while one chapter treats the Supreme Puntriarch, Joyce, they pass over other authors particularly associated with puns, such as Rabelais, Sterne, and Carroll – less interested, perhaps, in the virtuoso performance than in the steady punning of life, or what R. A. Shoaf calls the realm of juxtology, a world of yoking.

The majority of these essays focus on literature, although tradition has thought the pun an excrescence of literature, an obnoxious obtrusion from the source of genius, or a rhetorical device of questionable taste. If, as Auden says, 'Good poets have a weakness for bad puns', all the more reason for critical vigilance and stern condemnation. The terms of condemnation, however, may be suggestive. Samuel Johnson writes:

A quibble [i.e. pun] is to *Shakespeare* what luminous vapours are to the traveller; he follows it at all adventures; it is sure to lead him out of his way, and sure to engulf him in the mire. It has some malignant power over his mind, and its fascinations are irresistible. Whatever be the dignity or profundity of his disquisition, whether he be enlarging knowledge or exalting affection, whether he be amusing attention with incidents or enchaining it in suspense, let but a quibble spring up before him and he leaves his work unfinished. A quibble is the golden apple for which he will always turn aside from his career, or stoop from his elevation. A quibble, poor and barren as it is, gave him such delight, that he was content to purchase it by the sacrifice of reason, propriety, and truth. A quibble was to him the fatal *Cleopatra* for which he lost the world, and was content to lose it.[14]

The pun begins as luminous vapours, delusory and insubstantial, but ends as full-bodied Cleopatra, as though the process of exuberant writing had enforced the conclusion that language was an overpoweringly seductive alternative to 'the world', which initially seemed the only reality. The 'Cleopatra' here seems to be the powerful rhetorical disquisition that lures Johnson from his path, with its promise of a characteristic opportunity for affirmation of the priority of reason, propriety and truth.

Boswell remarks 'Johnson's general aversion to a pun', his 'great contempt for that species of wit'.[15] But he does report an incident in 1778, when Johnson led him to

a well-known toy-shop in St. James's street . . . to which he had been directed, but not clearly, for he searched about some time and could not find it at first; and said, 'To direct one only to a corner shop is *toying* with one.' I suppose he meant this as a play upon the word *toy*; it was the first time that I knew him stoop to such sport.[16]

Boswell appears to have missed the play of puns in Johnson's own poetry, where they seem neither a distraction nor low intrusion but a pure instantiation of the literary effect sought. In 'The Vanity of Human Wishes', for instance, the declining patriarch finds himself surrounded:

> The watchful Guests still hint the last Offence,
> The Daughter's Petulance, the Son's Expence,
> Improve his heady Rage with treacherous Skill,
> And mould his Passions till they make his will.

The witty condensation of the two wills, like the heady rage of the head of the family, seems the judicious identification of the intrications of life more than playful or ponderous stooping. If puns can be found working thus in the writings of declared enemies, they may well be presumed to lurk everywhere.

Shakespeare, of course, not only stooped to punning sport but positively wallowed with his fatal Cleopatra. In his work, and indeed, in his time, puns are bawdy, perhaps, but not frivolous: Shakespeare, notoriously, puns in the gravest circumstances. Mercutio, bleeding to death:

> Ask for me tomorrow and you shall find me a grave man.

---

[14] Samuel Johnson, 'Preface to Shakespeare', in *Poetry and Prose*, ed. Mona Wilson (London, 1970), p. 500.

[15] James Boswell, *Life of Johnson*, ed. R. W. Chapman (Oxford, 1976), pp. 1309 and 531.

[16] Ibid., p. 972.

Though critics generally deal with puns by relating them to characters' attitudes, the inclination to pun does not seem a feature of character; Lady Macbeth, not a funny woman, puns as she plots:

> If he do bleed
> I'll gild the faces of the grooms withal;
> For it must seem their guilt.

Puns also carry weight of solemn, sententious moments:

> The quality of mercy is not strain'd.
> It droppeth as the gentle rain from heav'n.

Punning frequently seems not so much the act of a character, expressive of attitude, as a structural, connecting device that delineates action or explores the world, helping the plays (and also the sonnets) to offer the mind a sense and an experience of an order that it does not master or comprehend. We do not know what is the relation between 'guilt' and 'gilding', or between the straining of exertion and of filtering, but we are urged to conceive an order in which they go together. Insofar as this is the goal or achievement of art, the pun seems an exemplary agent.

Recent work on Shakespeare has energetically explored the role of puns in other ways. Joel Fineman's *Shakespeare's Perju'd Eye: The Invention of Subjectivity in Shakespeare's Sonnets* links the pervasive play of *I* and *eye* in the sonnets to the production of a new subjectivity. In *Hamlet*, where puns do indeed seem connected to the perversities of the chief punster, Margaret Ferguson reads 'the connection between certain techniques of wordplay and a process of dramatic literalization that is associated in this play with the impulse to kill'.[17] Krystian Czerniecki, in this volume, also explores the link between puns and representation, specifically the quest of *Henry V* to recover and represent history. What in psychoanalytic terms is called the play between introjection and incorporation or mourning and melancholia is figured here in the word play of mockery and its undoing, of 'jest' and 'disgestion', of eating words.

Different sorts of claims are made for earlier English literature by R. A. Shoaf's essay, which portrays writers as juxtologists, devotees of juxtapositions achieved by language. 'Medieval poets,' he maintains, 'knew full well that language is "in charge".' His discussions of puns in Chaucer, in fifteenth-century lyrics, in *Gawain*, and in *Piers Plowman* argue for the power of language to create thought – for both critic and poet – suggestively linking the earliest English literature with twentieth-century experiments.

---

[17] Margaret Ferguson, '*Hamlet*: letters and spirits', in *Shakespeare and the Question of Theory*, ed. Patricia Parker and Geoffrey Hartman (London, 1985), p. 292.

The supreme juxtologist must be Joyce, whose *Wake*'s significance Derek Attridge expounds.

Punning can also serve as a basis of literary works in another way. In *The Language of Allegory* Maureen Quilligan argues that allegories, from Langland to Pynchon, are essentially narratives generated by wordplay, the expansion of puns into narratives or episodes, much as in Genesis a pun on evil (*malum*), led to the story of an apple tree from which Eve plucked the apple (*malum*). 'The plots of all allegorical narratives,' Quilligan writes, 'unfold as investigations into the literal truth inherent in individual words, considered in the context of their whole histories as words.' Thus, in the *Faerie Queene*, 'the basic plot of the book of holiness . . . unfolds as Spenser's investigation into the meaning of one particular word, "error".' Una and the Redcross Knight (knight errant) wander, lost in error's den, confronting its dragons. While sketching other factors involved, Quilligan argues that 'the basic mechanism that allows Spenser to raise and solve issues as disparate as the relationship between pagan and Christian ethics, the politics of Henry VIII, and the history of the church, is wordplay, and a kind of wordplay which, by its subliminal fluidity, resembles Freud's theory that the truth of the unconscious can be revealed through word association.'[18]

But the most general claim for puns as the foundation of letters would doubtless come from focusing on what Roman Jakobson called the poetic function of language: the projection of the principle of equivalence from the axis of selection onto the axis of combination, so that similarity becomes the constitutive device of the sequence. Similar items among which one ordinarily chooses are combined because of the pun-like productivity of their similarity, and the narrative or proposition or representation is generated from punning relations: 'Margaret, are you grieving / Over goldengrove unleaving?' not only puns on *leaving* but is produced by a punning transformation of *grieving* into *leaving*. Similarity of sound or grammatical structure passes into or gives rise to semantic relationships. Rhyme is one name for this principle, and Debra Fried's essay here discusses the relation between rhymes and puns – how attention to the play of sound encouraged by rhyme may effect or affect puns.[19]

Intriguing evidence for the importance of the principle of equivalence and the centrality of wordplay in literature comes from Frederick Ahl, whose essay here takes up themes of a recent full-scale study. His *Metaformations: Soundplay and Wordplay in Ovid and Other Classical Poets* argues that Latin poetry was constructed on the principle of motivating signs

---

[18] Maureen Quilligan, *The Language of Allegory* (Ithaca, 1979), pp. 33–5.

[19] R. A. Shoaf has also devoted a chapter to rhyme and puns in his book *Milton: Poet of Duality* (New Haven, 1985).

through the repetition of syllables, to link related signs to each other. Striking examples of wordplay in Vergil show that this was by no means a low or comic technique but a way of portraying significant relationships, and suggests that we need to begin a reinterpretation of Latin and Greek literature that will alter our notion of what is classical, or of what the 'classical' is.

Ahl also emphasizes the importance of anagrammatic play on proper names: the poem as a punning exfoliation of the proper name. Here antiquity only confirms a practice for which there is abundant later evidence. Shakespeare, whose sonnets ring the changes on *Will*, Francis Ponge, whose sponges Jacques Derrida has brought to the surface, or John Donne, whose name was always poised to become a participle, all illustrate what Derrida, writing of Jean Genet, has called 'the patient, stealthy, quasi-animal or vegetable, tireless, monumental, derisory transformation of one's name, a rebus, into a thing or name of a thing'.[20] From this vantage, literature can be seen not as an author's appropriation of the world but as a dissemination or dispersal of the proper name, the transformation of it into the elements of a world – in short, a foundation of letters.

Three of the chapters here – four including Czerniecki's – engage with psychoanalysis, the other region where pun surprises by its foundational role. If the unconscious, in that laconic saying, is structured like a language, it is not a transparent language where signifiers and signifieds are determinedly paired but a punning language, where the call of the phoneme and the foundation of letters serve as psychic relays. Since we think of dreams as sequences of images – visual rather than verbal representations – it is particularly striking, and remarkable evidence for the psychic centrality of punlike mechanisms when, as repeatedly happens in Freud's dream analyses, the link between a dream image and the day's residue turns out to be a word functioning as pun. For instance, a dream with a touch of absurdity about driving in a cab is linked with concerns about ancestry through the word *Vorfarhren* ('drive up' but also 'ancestry').[21] Joel Fineman here takes up a dream whose interpretation turns on puns on *pas* ('step', 'not', but also, in *Pas de Calais*, 'English Channel'), and especially on the gap or division that puns figure. Avital Ronell discusses, in distinctive style, the

---

[20] Jacques Derrida, *Glas* (Paris, 1972), p. 11. For Ponge, see Derrida, *Signéponge/Signsponge*, trans. Richard Rand (New York, 1984). In *Saving the Text* (Baltimore, 1981) Geoffrey Hartman discusses *Glas* and speculates on the possibility that literature may be the elaboration of what he calls a 'specular name' (pp. 97–117).

[21] Sigmund Freud, *The Interpretation of Dreams, Complete Psychological Works* (London, 1953), vol. 5, pp. 433–4.

Rat Man, whose obsessional neurosis and historic name come from the punning complex Freud elucidates: rats (*Ratten*) are linked to debt and installment payments (*Raten*) for both him and his father, who was a *Spielratte* ('compulsive gambler'), and to hesitations – again in both his case and his father's – about whether to marry (*Heiraten*). Puns are especially potent in the case of the Wolfman, who seems enmeshed in his 'Verbarium', the Joycean network of interlingual puns that structure the text of his life. In the dream from which his name comes there were six wolves:

Schematically: the *six* in the six wolves [*sechs*] . . . is translated into Russian (*chiest*: perch, mast, and perhaps sex, close to *chiestero* and *chiesterka*, 'the six', 'the lot of six people', close to *siestra*, sister, and its diminutive, *siesterka*, sissy, towards which the influence of the German *Schwester* had oriented the decipherment: thus, within the mother tongue, through an essentially verbal relay this time, the sister is associated with the phobic image of the wolf. But the relay is nevertheless not semantic; it comes from a lexical contiguity or a formal consonance.[22] ·

Thus, Abraham and Torok suggest, the word *sister* haunts the Wolfman, displaced into his eponymous phobia. Puns are a mechanism of the psyche and in numerous cases the connections of puns flagrantly structure a subject's experience. Less complex examples can also be imagined, such as the student from St Louis who obsessively took friends home with him during vacations. Why? Because he heard that 'Missouri loves company'. The unconscious, says Lacan, is the know-how of language.

Lacan's own know-how and its persistent deployment of puns, analyzed by Françoise Meltzer in her essay here, depends on an understanding of language which takes paronomasia as central rather than marginal. Approaches to the pun through literature and through dream-analysis or investigation of the mechanisms of the psyche contribute to the possibility of such an understanding but it remains for the most part to be worked out.

What the functioning of puns reveals about langauge is, first, the importance of the urge to motivate, which comes to seem a powerful mechanism of language rather than a corruption that might be excluded. Precisely because the linguistic sign is arbitrary, discourse works incessantly, deviously to motivate. Almost everyone who tries to recite the beginning of Lincoln's 'Gettysburg Address' introduces a punning echo – 'Four score and seven years ago, our *fore*fathers brought forth . . .' – as though discourse itself compulsively echoes when a pun is in reach. Bringing forth, in years involving fours, clearly requires forefathers. Studies

[22] Jacques Derrida, 'Fors', Introduction to Nicolas Abraham and Maria Torok, *Cryptonymie: Le Verbier de l'homme aux loups* (Paris, 1976), p. 60.

show a surprising proliferation of unintended punning effects in ordinary conversation, where one word seems to determine the selection of another in a punning way: 'So I hightailed it up to the market to get my turkey', or 'Baloney! you don't eat meat'.[23] The French linguist Pierre Guiraud speaks of 'retromotivation', illustrated above all in popular etymologizing, as 'an extremely general phenomenon which silently, and most often unbeknownst to us, works the entire linguistic system in its most popular as well as most learned forms.[24]

The question then becomes, what happens if we try to put this mechanism, or the practice of punning, at the center of thinking about language? Do we get a new understanding of language and what would it entail?

In Ferdinand de Saussure's account, the linguistic system consists of relational entities, signs defined by their relations with one another. Emphasis on new punning relationships disrupts the system: if *laconic* means both 'terse' and 'Lacanian', then the system of differences is functioning in a way that is difficult to predict or describe. If, as Saussure writes, the most precise characteristic of a linguistic unit is to be what the others are not, what happens when it seems to be another sign also?[25] Although linguistic tradition and its assumptions about language that we have made our own maintain that the structure of French or English is not affected by the potential suggestiveness or punning resemblances of signifiers, we should ask whether in fact the language one speaks or writes is not always exposed to the contamination of arbitrary signs by punning links – between the desire to write and to get it right, between the sound of music and sound argument; whether effects of motivation are not inseparable from – central to – the workings of language; and whether this does not trouble the framing gesture that seeks to separate in inside of the system from the outside of practice. What if the play of motivation and resemblance, Derrida asks, 'meant that the internal system of language does not exist, or ... at least that one only uses it by contaminating it, and that this contamination is inevitable and thus regular and "normal", belongs to the system and its functioning, *en fasse partie*, that is to say, both is a part of it and also makes the system, which is the whole, part of a whole larger than itself.'[26]

When Saussure defends the principle of the arbitrary nature of the sign against motivation, the sentence in which he dismisses onomatopoeia as a delusory appearance displays remarkable effects of motivation, suggesting

[23] See Joel Scherzer, 'Oh! That's a pun and I didn't mean it', *Semiotica* 22:3/4 (1978), p. 336.

[24] Pierre Guiraud, 'Etymologie et ethymologia (Motivation et rétro-motivation)', *Poétique* 11 (1972), p. 405.

[25] Ferdinand de Saussure, *Cours de linguistique générale* (Paris, 1967), p. 162.

[26] Derrida, *Glas*, p. 109.

that discourse may be deviously driven by precisely the sort of phenomena he wishes to exclude from language. 'Words such as *fouet* ["whip"] and *glas* ["knell"],' he writes, 'may strike [*peuvent frapper*] some ears as having a certain suggestive sonority; but to see that this is in no way intrinsic to the words themselves, it suffices to look at their Latin origins.'[27] *Fouet* and *glas* both strike the ear, perhaps, because whips and bells strike: the term for what words do as they make a noise seems punningly generated by the examples, or the choice of examples is generated by what words are said to do to the ear. This sentence, working to remotivate and thus link together supposedly arbitrary signs, displays a principle by which discourse frequently operates and suggests that arbitrary signs of the linguistic system may be part of a larger discursive system in which effects of motivation, demotivation, and remotivation are always occurring. Relations between signifiers or between signifiers and signifieds can always produce effects, whether conscious or unconscious, and this cannot be set aside as irrelevant to language.

In *Metaformations* Frederick Ahl speaks of the way highly inflected languages make the listener more aware of the constantly shifting shape of a word as it changes person or case and how they thus might produce a different sense of what language is and how it works.[28] For speakers of inflected languages, one might imagine, there is not so strong a Lockean inclination to take as the model of language the word, conceived as a particular phonological sequence (*dog*) that expresses or stands for a given idea ('dog'). Speakers of English tend to think of the single, self-identical sound sequence correlated with a distinct idea – the word – as the norm or essence of language, from which all else derives, and thus of homonyms, ambiguities, and so on as exceptions. This is, of course, an illusion; linguists find the term 'word' misleading and at the very least have to distinguish phonological words from grammatical words, if they do not abandon the concept altogether. The word is an abstraction from a complex play of sound and meaning that is more blantantly thrust upon speakers of a highly inflected language. They are continuously confronted not with autonomous 'words' but with signifiers that undergo various modifications to give rise to a series of meanings – I write, they were writing, it will have been written – in a complex play of similarity and difference. Such languages make the syllable a decisive unit for the construction of discourse and production of meaning.

If we try to imagine a model of language where the word is derived rather than primary and where combinations of syllables suddenly evoke meanings,

---

[27] Saussure, *Cours*, p. 102.
[28] Ahl, *Metaformations*, p. 21.

as a successful pun makes one suddenly 'recognize' two meanings, we may, as Derek Attridge suggests, draw examples from *Finnegans Wake*, which makes explicit a vision of language as sequences of syllables echoing other syllables that we have heard, in ways that sometimes but by no means always form codified signs. When 'The Mookse and the Gripes' begins 'Gentes and laitymen, fullstoppers and semicolonials, hybreds and lubberds!'[29] we find that reading becomes a punning assimilation of sequences to other sequences: *Mookse* suggests 'moose', 'fox' (because of the fable 'The Fox and the Grapes', or 'mock turtle' (*gripes* means 'gryphon', as in Lewis Carroll's 'The Mock Turtle and the Gryphon'), or perhaps 'mooc[ow]'. In *Gentes and laitymen* we find 'laity', 'gentles', and the inversion of 'Ladies and gentlemen', joined later by the high and low bred, as well as landlubbers and hybrids who mix the categories. The *Wake* presents what we are inclined to call 'echoes', a term that nicely conflates an automatic acoustic process with a willful mimetic one, but echoes whose signifying status is doubtful, connections which one hears or imagines but cannot demonstrate by any code or rule. This, I submit, is language.

Words, the *Wake* shows us, are rooted in other words, whose traces they bear. What is blatantly true for puns and portmanteaux also holds, Derek Attridge points out, for all linguistic sequences, which are composed of syllables from other sequences and refer obliquely to these sequences by their similarities and differences. Puns, like portmanteaux, limn for us a model of language where the word is derived rather than primary and combinations of letters suggest meanings while at the same time illustrating the instability of meanings, their as yet ungrasped or undefined relations to one another, relations which further discourse (further play of similarity and difference) can produce. When one thinks of how puns characteristically demonstrate the applicability of a single signifying sequence to two different contexts, with quite different meanings, one can see how puns both evoke prior formulations, with the meanings they have deployed, and demonstrate their instability, the mutability of meaning, the production of meaning by linguistic motivation. Puns present us with a model of language as phonemes or letters combining in various ways to evoke prior meaning and to produce effects of meaning – with a looseness, unpredictability, excessiveness, shall we say, that cannot but disrupt the model of language as nomenclature.

This conception of language which one must struggle to imagine is crucial to the exploration of what Gregory Ulmer calls the 'puncept': the relation-

[29] James Joyce, *Finnegans Wake* (London, 1962), p. 152.

ship between the pun and concept formation or the order of knowledge. Anyone who took seriously the groans at puns, the mockery of puns, would be surprised to discover that puns are at work in the central, formative structures of major conceptual systems. In Christianity, for example, they are to be found not only in the foundations but in the very designation of the foundation: 'Thou art *Petros*, and upon this *petra* I will build my church.' The Rock of Ages is a pun – a rocky foundation. Again, the establishment of Christianity in England is generated by a convergence of puns, according to Venerable Bede: encountering English slaves, Pope Gregory decided that these Angles should learn about angels; their province Deira should be saved *de ira*, 'from God's wrath', and the land of their king Aella should resound with alleluias.

Puns can inspire momentous action, as well as narrative. They may also become the instrument of knowledge. Pierre Guiraud argues that retro-motivation, by which the linguistic motivation of signs affects concepts and thus modifies the world, which in principle ought to be transparently denominated by language, 'is the general condition of all natural linguistic activity'.[30] One can accept this as an index of our unhappy state, or one can, as Varro and Ulmer urge, proceed on the premise that homonyms know something, interrogating, for example, the relation between *sense* and the *senses*, between *l'être* ('being') and *lettre*, between various sorts of *so-ing* (*sow*, *sew*), between (in Lacan's case) *le nom du père*, 'the name of the father', and the identical-sounding *non du père*, the paternal interdiction (not to mention *les non-dupes errent*, 'the clever ones err'). One might think of the pun, Ulmer suggests, as a research strategy: a signifying cluster works to bring together material for thought and to suggest structural relationships, curious turns. One can use such material for what Ulmer calls the 'systematic exploitation of the chance–necessity effects produced by the event of homophony or homonymy'.[31] The use of etymologies to generate or extend reflection has a long if not altogether respectable history. Puns work the same way – lively instances of lateral thinking, exploiting the fact that language has ideas of its own. Thinking that suspends familiar distinctions between the fortuitous or frivolous (accidental linguistic connections) and the serious of essential (substantive conceptual connections) arguably has a chance of productivity denied to other procedures. One might therefore be inclined to respond to the call of the phoneme by promoting punning thinking, were it not for a suspicion that any other kind of thinking works in the same way, directed, unconsciously, by punning relationships, verbal relays.

---

[30] Guiraud, 'Etymologie', p. 409.
[31] Gregory Ulmer, *Applied Grammatology* (Baltimore, 1985), p. 23.

What, then, does the pun teach? I have suggested that it foregrounds an opposition that we find difficult to evade or overcome: between accident or meaningless convergence and substance or meaningful relation. We treat this opposition as a given, presuming that any instance must be one or the other. But puns, or punning, may help us to displace the opposition by experiencing something like 'meaningful coincidence' or 'convergence that affects meaning', convergence that adumbrates an order *to be* comprehended or explored.

Our most authoritative declaration of the centrality of language, 'In the beginning was the Word', implies the priority of meaning to event, letter, or utterance, but the essays here assembled suggest that a post-modern age may find more apt the claim of Samuel Beckett's *Murphy*, which focuses on the coincidences of juxtology – neither code nor chaos: 'What but an imperfect sense of humor could have made such a mess out of chaos. In the beginning was the pun.'[32]

[32] Samuel Beckett, *Murphy* (New York, 1952), p. 65.

2

Ars Est Caelare Artem
(Art in Puns and Anagrams Engraved)

Frederick Ahl

In Flann O'Brien's satire of Irish Celticism, *The Poor Mouth*, a sickly English inspector comes to an Irish-speaking community, authorized to pay two pounds for every English-speaking child in a family.[1] In one cottage, he is greeted by a terrible stench and general filth. Desiring to get his business over quickly, he asks how many English-speaking children are in the household. 'Twalf, sor', he is told with apparent courtesy by the only person who can muster any English. Not a surprising number to one who assumes peasants breed like pigs. So when a young grunting creature responds to the question, 'Phwat is yer nam?' with an intelligible (but false) answer in English, the inspector enquires no more and pays up.[2]

There is, in fact, only one child. The sound and smell of the remainder comes from a herd of swine, given the semblance of human appearance and speech not so much by our rural Pygmalion, but by the inspector's disinterest in, and debased view of, the Irish.

The inspector probably misses the insulting bilingual pun in the deferential 'Twalf, sor'. 'Sor', in Irish, means 'louse'.[3] If he knows no Irish, he will be unmoved by the gales of laughter from O'Brien's bilingual reader, since 'sor' would suggest no more than an Irishman's quaint inability to pronounce English correctly. The special savor of this jest is its exclusion of the person mocked from understanding that (or at least how) he is being

---

[1] This chapter contains some excerpts adapted from my *Metaformations: Wordplay and Soundplay in Ovid and other Classical Poets* (Ithaca, 1985) and from my 'Statius' *Thebaid*: A Reconsideration', *Aufstieg und Niedergang der römischen Welt* 32.4 (1986), pp. 2803–912. Some modifications have been made after a reading of W. D. Redfern's *Puns* (Oxford, 1985).

[2] Myles na Gopaleen (Flann O'Brien), *The Poor Mouth*, trans. Patrick Power (London, 1975), p. 37; O'Brien's satire is based on *An t-Oileánach* (*The Islandman*) by Tomas O'Crohan (Thomás Ó Criomhthain) published in Dublin (1927) and translated into English by Robin Flower (Oxford, 1951). My thanks to Éamonn Ó Carrigáin and Seán Ó Coiléan of University College, Cork, for drawing my attention to these works.

[3] *The Poor Mouth*, p. 126 and n. 3 for Power's comment on the pun.

mocked – a common and necesary feature of humor among the underdogs in almost any society.

If O'Brien's inspector actually knew a little Irish, but had been university educated, he would probably have assumed the *double entendre* to be unintentional, since it is 'unthinkable' for a man who needs money to mock the giver. To convince a scholar that the pun was intentional, the Irishman would have had to say explicitly: 'Twalf, sor. And sor is the Irish for louse.'

The Assumption of Explicitness

Unless there is opposing 'evidence' from the same or contemporary contexts, we generally assume authorial intent does not extend much beyond what we consider explicit meaning. We cling to the utilitarian notion that language was 'born to facilitate men's mutual contacts' – a notion the surrealist Michel Leiris described as a 'monstrous aberration'.[4] We need to be reminded, as Osbert Burdett says Ruskin reminded us, that words have 'colour as well as meaning', that they can 'suggest as well as speak, and need not be condemned to the hodman's work of conveying information'.[5]

Such 'explicit' reading is less potentially dangerous for modern than for ancient literatures. When an octet of English capitalists in Act II of Gilbert and Sullivan's *Utopia Limited* assure the King of Utopia that 'Divorce is nearly obsolete in England', we know the observation is ironic in the bluntest sense Quintilian allows: the speaker means the opposite of what he says. But we do not have to use this observation as evidence for divorce in Victorian England. There is ample 'documentary' evidence for the increase of divorce in Victorian England. So we can rest content with an ironical reading of Gilbert and find our documents elsewhere.

An ancient comic writer like Aristophanes, however, may well be the principal – sometimes the *only* – 'source' of information on a given issue of Athenian life. And when a scholar's aim is to translate an Aristophanic text from poetic comedy into sociological or historical information, he is most likely to base his interpretation on an 'explicit' reading of the text. Aristophanes' statements will be taken at face value when there is no 'evidence' to demonstrate the opposite, although Aristophanes is as fond of topsy-turvydom as is W. S. Gilbert. The scholar knows how his colleagues will react if he uses a text that states the opposite of what it means as a basis

---

[4] Cited by L. Peeters, 'Pour une interpretation du jeu de mots', *Semitics* 2 (1971–2), p. 136 and n. 16; cf. M. Leiris, *Mots sans mémoire* (Paris, 1969), p. 110 and Redfern, *Puns*, pp. 78–9.
[5] Osbert Burdett, *The Beardsley Period* (New York, 1925), p. 46.

for a historical hypothesis. Besides, classical literature is primarily the province of a discipline that has, traditionally, had an arguably larger investment in conveying information than in discussion of the nuances of literary color and suggestion.

The Problem of Classicism

Ironical interpretations of Greek, and, more especially, Roman literature are resisted for other reasons too. There is a still widespread notion, formulated in response to romantic criticism of the classics, that 'classical' texts are (or should be) sincere, spare and restrained. We have accepted intellectually that classical statuary was gaudily painted, not renaissance white – though we don't restore the colors. But we are slower in acknowledging rhetorical color in classical literature. The more 'ornate' a text, the less classical it is judged to be. A Roman poet whose works are taken to be classical is approached on the most explicit possible level. If he resists explicit interpretation, he is decadent, post-classical, or, as we like to say nowadays, 'mannered'.

Here is David Vessey's assessment of 'mannered' Latin poetry:

Mannerism may, perhaps, be best described as a disease of classicism.... Mannered writers ... place *ars* above *ingenium*; they change virtues into vices and excellencies of style into specious artifices. Curtius has succinctly expressed the truth: 'the mannerist wants to say things not normally but abnormally. He prefers the artificial and affected to the natural. He wants to surprise, astonish, to dazzle. While there is only one way of saying things naturally, there are a thousand forms of unnatural-ness.'[6]

The observation on the 'naturalness' of expression is cited from Ernst Curtius' influential *European Literature and the Latin Middle Ages*. Even supposing that 'natural' literary expression were possible, Curtius' declaration that it has only one form is mistaken. Is it natural to express things in prose or in verse, in German or in French, in BBC English or in a Canadian dialect? Is anything other than the most literal possible expression 'unnatural'?

Curtius' ideal 'natural expression' suggests the language of the Yokuts Indians more than English, German or Latin. Peter Farb notes:

On his part the Yokuts speaker would undoubtedly have a low estimation of English because it lacks the restraint and consistency that he is proud to have achieved in his

---

[6] David Vessey, *Statius and the Thebaid* (Cambridge, 1973), pp. 8, 9. For a fairer sense of mannerism, see Gustav Hocke, *Manierismus in der Literatur* (Munich, 1959).

own language. . . . He would undoubtedly consider the most beautiful sentences in the English language to be freaks because of their feverish piling up of subordinate clauses, their qualifiers, their tricks of using words that mean one thing to express a metaphor about something completely different. Inevitably, he must conclude that English lacks the quiet dignity, balance, and restraint of Yokuts.[7]

Instead of disputing Curtius' notion of classicism and mannerism, we often try to save a Roman poet's claim to respectability by insisting that he really is simple and sincere, that his work is structured and unified. We assume that he is 'explicit' and deny that he uses such rhetorical techniques as would make him complex, devious and mannered. Only a handful of Roman poets can be adapted to fit these criteria, and their simplicity and sincerity are vigorously defended against critics who would drag them to their mannered doom.

Roman poets adjudged 'mannered' are often treated as an English poet would be by Farbs' hypothetical Yokuts speaker. Yet English is not 'stubbornly literal', as Yokuts is, according to Farb.[8] Neither is Latin. Nonetheless, R. T. Bruère described some powerful passages in Lucan's *Pharsalia*, for example, as a 'striving for bravura effect' which defies 'logic, precision, and restraint'.[9]

Bruère, like Curtius, has difficulty accepting that we are dealing with differences in figured usage, in conflicts of 'taste' between modern scholars concerned with conveying information, and poets reacting to ideas and expressing passions. Our reaction to Latin poetic passions often resembles that of the stereotypical Englishman to 'excessive' displays of emotion by an Italian.

Punning and Binary Thinking

Discomfort with figures of speech that pluralize meaning arises in part from desire to protect a writer within the classical canon from expulsion, or to reject a non-canonical writer. Such discomfort is reinforced by our universal scholarly desire to set boundaries upon the field of enquiry. Our egos fear the text may assume a life of its own and elude our investigative eyes. Yearning to define, we seek the unifying structure, the oneness that underlies the 'apparent' many. We impose the structure on works of art and literature, then re-shape, ignore or discard what is left over.

[7] Peter Farb, *Word Play: What Happens when People Talk* (London, 1973), p. 202.
[8] Ibid.
[9] R. T. Bruère, 'The Scope of Lucan's Historical Epic', *Classical Philology* 45 (1950), p. 230.

The damage done has had ripple effects on the criticism of all literature derived from or influenced by Roman poetry.

Our quest for structure and unity is justified not only at our universities, but at almost every level of our social conditioning. We take monistic reasoning for granted. Truthfulness is equated with simplicity, not complexity. Ours is a world of Marxist monism, of Islamic and Judaeo-Christian monism, of one god or no god, not of god or gods. We have, of course, been very successful in making this 'one or zero', 'true or false', thinking work for us. Computers thrive on such binary systems. The complexity of numbers, of sounds, and of theology, can be produced with the simple, binary one and zero, by 'either/or' thinking.

Figures of speech such as metaphor or irony confuse binary thought because they add the complexities of 'both/and' to 'either/or', thereby blurring the lines we like to draw between truth and falsehood, fact and non fact. It is no consolation to be told in W. S. Gilbert's *Utopia Limited* that ' "yes" is but another and a neater form of "no" ' since 'yes' is not *invariably* another form of 'no'. We have to decide whether its meaning is explicit or ironic from context.

Quintilian's irony, nonetheless, is one of the least disturbing figures of speech to scholars, although it inverts meaning and often defies conclusive detection. We are less willing to acknowledge two other forms of figured speech which ought to be easier to prove: puns and anagrams. I say 'ought' not because evidence for intentional punning and anagrammatizing is lacking, but because they are not treated *in extenso* by standard works on rhetoric, and are therefore not part of a scholar's 'required' work. He may 'safely' dismiss them as random or unintentional. But irony, though more difficult to handle, is an accepted figure in all conventional literary analysis.

If irony destablilizes a text by letting it mean both itself and its opposite, puns add an alien set of referends which multiply meaning and totally undermine the explicit. The ironical 'yes' is the opposite of 'no'; the punning 'know' adduces a new tension – and a different part of speech. When a third person inflects it, he finds 'no' running into 'nose'. Predictably no-nonsense scholars sniff their disapproval.

Besides, punning is not respectable. J. J. Glück tersely observes: 'Word-play, especially when called punning, is today regarded as the wit of crassitude.' Most Europeans, not just English speakers, are trained to admire irony but to disapprove of puns.[10] The socially expected response to a pun is a ritual protest: a groan. Hence our unwillingness to admit a writer might *consciously* employ puns unless he intends to elicit a (mockingly) protesting response.

---

[10] J. J. Glück, 'Paronomasia in Biblical Literature', *Semitics* 1 (1970), p. 52 and n. 8.

Our negative assessment of punning leaves orthodox critics reluctant to discuss wordplay in ancient literature, not just because it undermines the 'classical' simplicity of a text, but because critics who work with puns (justly) fear scholarly attack for 'devaluing' authors (and themselves). Since punning is considered crass, the critic has no scholarly obligation to look for puns and full license to explain them away if efforts to avoid acknowledging their odious presence fail. Few scholars are so Oedipal as to seek what they do not consciously wish to find.

Taste and Subversion

Not all ages and cultures respond to wordplay as we do. When Shakespeare's Antony declares: 'O judgment, thou art fled to brutish beast' (*Julius Caesar*, III. ii. 104), 'brutish' is clearly a pun – and an old Latin pun – on Brutus' name. Cicero makes it in a letter to his friend Atticus about Brutus, during Brutus' lifetime (*Letters to Atticus* 6.1.25). Further, Shakespeare's Hamlet makes essentially the same pun (and adds two others) in the context of Julius Caesar's theatrical death (*Hamlet* Act III ii):

> *Polonius*   I did enact Julius Caesar. I was killed i' the Capitol; Brutus killed me.
>
> *Hamlet*   It was a brute part of him to kill so capital a calf there.

While Antony's 'brutish' pun is rarely denied, it is often passed over without comment. Such omission does not mean the pun is too obvious to need pointing out. Shakespearian commentators routinely point out heavily underscored puns. No, Antony, unlike Hamlet, does not explicitly say Brutus is brutish. So anyone who wishes to ignore the pun may, by scholarly convention, feel free to ignore it. And many scholars would like to. William Empson feels punning is effeminate and remarks that 'many of us could wish the Bard had been more manly in his literary habits'.[11]

Similarly, critics are often uncomfortable with John Donne's blatant pun on his own name in 'A Hymne to God the Father': 'When thou has done thou has not done'. John Shawcross, among others, reacts cautiously: 'perhaps a pun is intended on his name'.[12] He discreetly leaves open the possibility that the author may not have realized that he had punned, that the play may be accidental.

---

[11] William Empson, *Seven Types of Ambiguity* (Harmondsworth, 1973), pp. 110–11; cf. Redfern, *Puns*, p. 46.

[12] John Shawcross, *The Complete Poetry of John Donne* (New York, 1967), p. 392 n.

Punning triggers responses of fear as well as ritual groans and laughter. Peter Farb observes:

English-speaking communities nowadays regard the pun as a very low form of humor – and they are particularly fearful of the obscene pun, which is a major variety of the form. The obscene pun is dangerous because it cleverly attacks the sacredness of taboo words, and it manages to do so with an innocent appearance. A dirty story usually leads up to the punchline by the use of taboo words, but a well-fashioned obscene pun never overtly uses obscene words. Rather, the pun allows two different words, which are pronounced in the same way, to be substituted for each other. Usually one of the two ambiguous words is taboo, but the teller of the pun claims innocence by leaving it up to the listener to connect the innocent and the taboo meanings.[13]

Farb recognizes that the punster, like Flann O'Brien's, may be a subversive who wants listeners (or critics) to imagine that the wordplay exists in their own minds, not in the speaker's or writer's realm of intention. The punster may need the facade of innocence, to gain the help of the very victims whose literal-mindedness he mocks against the potentially dangerous explicators of his meaning. Writers protect themselves during political and moral censorship by making it dangerous or embarrassing for others to prove their subversion. They leave their readers helpless to explain what they have noticed without appearing to indict themselves for suggesting the taboo meaning.

When scholars insist on the intentionality of the explicit, they miss this literary ploy. They dismiss the possibility of the writer's disguised utterance, and generate good and nasty copy, if not sound argument, by attributing the wordplay to the reader's deviant mind not the writer's subversive intent. Larry Benson, for example, observes: 'In all charity we must tolerate the punsters as best we can. Let us not deny them their private pleasures.'[14]

The 'protected pun' is a dimension of literary rhetoric the English-speaking world is reluctant to acknowledge: the writer's feigning of ignorance about what his text might mean. Czeslaw Milosz's Polish poet, to whom he gives the pseudonym Delta, claimed the only thing he disliked about post-war Moscow was the smell of oranges. In those days oranges could not be bought for money in Moscow's shops or even for love at the US Embassy. But, officially, there were no shortages. The odor of non-existent oranges, of official lies, is what the poet cannot stand.[15] Yet what party official would risk the labor of taking him to task?

[13] Farb, *Word Play*, p. 88.
[14] Larry Benson, 'The "Queynte" Punnings of Chaucer's Critics', *Studies in the Age of Chaucer: Proceedings no. 1, 1984: Reconstructing Chaucer*, eds P. Strohm and T. J. Heffernan (Knoxville, 1985), p. 47.
[15] Czeslaw Milosz, *The Captive Mind* (New York, 1953), pp. 180–1.

The term for such usage in antiquity was *emphasis*, which, in Quintilian's description, meant 'leaving something latent for the listener to, as it were, discover.'[16] Its forcefulness and pungency are enhanced, Quintilian continues, if the listener thinks that he has discovered this hidden meaning himself and that the speaker does not intend him to draw any such conclusion (*Instructing the Orator* 9.2.64). So concerned is Quintilian about the correct use of *emphasis* that he warns his reader to avoid unintentional multiple meanings. *Cacemphaton*, 'unintentional *double entendre*', was in his judgment a severe blemish of style (8.3.47).

Scholars often prefer to charge a writer with *cacemphaton* than allow for intentional punning or ambiguity – unless the writer announces his intention to be ambiguous. We ignore Quintilian's warning in *Instructing the Orator* 9.2.69–70 that we should not rely too much on ambiguous words and *double entendres* or on syntactical ambiguity: figured speech should not be obvious: '*ne manifestae sint!*' If obvious, he adds, it ceases to be figured. Rather, we acknowledge emphasis only when a phenomenon explodes in undeniable, Joycean profusion. To us 'emphasis' is the proclamation of an idea in a text, not its subtle and covert suggestion, as it was to the ancients.

Criticism of ancient literature remains shackled by a tradition that despises (and disposes of) wordplay, and assumes that 'meaning' is simple unless there is proof of ambiguity – in which case our task is to resolve the ambiguity back to simplicity. Our surveys of Greek and (more devastatingly) of Roman literature often offer a crudely explicit reading of writers who had good political as well as artistic reason to dissimulate their intention to indulge themselves in other emphatic (in Quintilian's sense) figures of speech.

The Assumption of Random Wordplay

If a pun that the critic does not wish to acknowledge oscillates relentlessly before his reluctant eyes, he predictably asserts that the writer cannot be proved to have intended it, that he was, perhaps, unaware of its existence. It is an accident of language, a random occurrence of no particular significance.

Those who argue strongly that we cannot show with clarity what a writer intended to say are often no less strongly convinced about what a writer could *not* have intended. Thus Jacques Derrida, in the oral proceedings of our conference, argued that Baudelaire did not mean us to understand his

---

[16] For ancient *emphasis* see my 'The Art of Safe Criticism in Greece and Rome', *American Journal of Philology* 105 (1984), pp. 174–208 and the sources cited there.

expression *plein chant* (full song) as a pun on *plain-chant*. A 'non-intentionalist' fallacy, it appears, is rising even as the intentionalists withdraw.

If we maintain that the generation of puns and other wordplays is accidental unless proved otherwise, we are following the popular tendency to exaggerate the power of chance. As Kevin McKean points out, the computer has shown us that the opposite is the case: 'In a world as crazy as this one, it ought to be easy to find something that happens solely by chance. It isn't.'[17] Hence the large expenditures of money to design computers which generate random sequences of numbers to protect the transmission of banking information, coded messages and so forth.

Why should one assume that a pun is accidental – and thus *cacemphaton* – rather than the opposite: that the pun is likely to be intentional unless one can demonstrate that it is not? Works of art, as of architecture, stand by design rather than by accident. Scholars rarely suggest that similes or metaphors in a great poet, much less the ornate supports of a baroque building, are accidental. We consider puns accidental, wherever possible, because most of us would prefer them not to be there, and certainly do not regard them as art's building blocks. They are the rooms in the great poetic palace that the architect (O we pray!) did not know he had included in his design.

Such an assumption of unintentional punning may be justified in some modern writers because our academic culture rejects puns, and often shows its moral antipathy to figures of speech which say one thing and mean something else. So it is not implausible that even careful modern writers might generate unintentional puns. But it would be wiser, I think, to leave the onus of proof on those who argue for unintentionality. A pun is a phoneme or series of phonemes which *has* no simple meaning. Before concluding that a writer intends only one of its meanings, we should carefully examine the possibility that he intends more.

Since our culture 'objects to' puns, we are desensitized to their presence. Blindness to multiple *entendre* is only one dimension of our education which trains us to think (and to express ourselves) dissociatively, not associatively – to suppose, that is, that the speaker or writer does not intend us to construe his or her words too carefully: to assume carelessness not ambiguous intent. Wiser, perhaps, to follow Walter Redfern and J. Vendryès: the pun is not natural, it is an art form and thus not careless.[18]

In considering the works of writers who either eccentrically or in accordance with their cultures think associatively, we must be careful. In Shakespeare, for instance, arguments against the intentionality of a given

[17] Kevin McKean, 'The Orderly Pursuit of Pure Disorder', *Discover* 8.1 (1987), p. 72.
[18] Redfern, *Puns*, p. 15; J. Vendryès, *Le Language* (Paris, 1921), p. 209.

pun are little more than a Yokutsian declaration that our dissociative usage is the norm and that pluralizing, associative meaning needs to be proved. Much the same is true of Greek and Latin literature.

Creative punning is, after all, fundamental to the evolution and development of literacy in many areas of the ancient world. Johannes Friedrich comments thus on Egyptian hieroglyphs:

It occurred to the Egyptians very early, probably way back in the initial stage of the develpment of the art of writing, that a concept difficult to represent pictorially could be symbolized by the picture of *something phonetically quite similar, but conceptually unrelated*. This was as if we wanted to represent, say, the concept underlying the verb *beat* by a picture of a *bit*, or the concept of *bad* by the picture of a *bed*.[19]

Friedrich underscores his contention that the words which sound alike are 'conceptually unrelated'. He assumes the dissociative thinking characteristic of much modern scholarship. But for the ancients, as we will see, the reverse seems to be the case: if two words (or syllables) were phonetically similar, they felt obliged to postulate some relationship between them.

The Anagram

If Quintilianic irony is the least demonstrable but most acceptable figure of speech among the three we have alluded to (irony, pun, anagram), the anagram is without doubt the most demonstrable and least acceptable. To understand O'Brien's pun on *sor*, we must know what this combination of letters means in both Irish (English) usage and Irish (Gaelic). To grasp the presence of an anagram, we need not necessarily understand the language – only the writing system. To explain its presence, we can simply say that it is an accident, or we can search for an explanation.

The juggling of letters in the topsy-turvy names of Samuel Butler's Antipodean counter-Utopia makes an easy starting-place. Whereas Thomas More's *Utopia* is 'Nowhere' translated into a new word whose Greekness suggests a certain flavor of the political ideal, Butler's 'Erewhon' is an inverted 'Nowhere', whose inhabitants have reversed names such as Yram and Mr Nosnibor, and whose life is hardly ideal. Dylan Thomas' Llareggub in *Under Milk Wood* is, ostensibly, an insignificant, apolitical Welsh town. But, though Llareggub begins with a double 'L', it is in origin a rude English expression for 'Nothingness' which, when reversed, will seem Welsh enough to the casual glance. The intentionality of these reversed words is generally taken to be deliberate.

[19] Johannes Friedrich, *Extinct Languages*, trans. F. Gaynor (New York, 1957), p. 10.

Some modern writers engage in more complex anagrammatizing that extends beyond words into numbers. In Jorge Borges' *Tlön, Uqbar, Orbis Tertius*, numbers translated from the decimal to the duodecimal system or from arabic to roman assume different appearances, properties and significance. XLVI is not simply 46 but a curious variant on the palindrome: 1 ten from 5 tens + 5 plus 1. And in *The Library of Babel*, Borges plays with the notion of knowledge emerging from an infinite shuffling of the finite symbols of the 'original' alphabet. Other novelists and poets have commented on Borges' anagrammatizing tendencies, and paid him tribute by introducing him anagrammatically into their own works. Vladimir Nabokov anagrammatizes him into the wonderfully Nordic Osberg. Umberto Eco makes Borges (an Anglo-Saxonist as well as a poet and artist of short stories) the nicely medieval Jorge de Burgos, a distorted anagram of his distorted mirror image of the Anglo-Saxon friar, William of Baskerville. These are suitable metamorphoses for a poet and essayist who loved anagrams and riddles.

The classicist, employing more stringent rules of evidence, requires explicit assurance by the author before accepting that an Osberg could be intended as the anagram of a Borges. Yet we should begin our remarks on Greek and Roman anagrams by noting that numerous ancient writers preceded Borges in treating the alphabet as the element of language which could be rearranged, just as the natural elements which make up substance can be rearranged, to form a new being. The letters are the building blocks of much ancient linguistic reality.

The most familiar example of this theory is Plato's *Cratylus*, a dialogue Platonic scholars approach gingerly because it touches on so many features of language which they prefer to regard as not serious. The Platonic Socrates himself is aware (*Cratylus* 425D) that his statements may appear laughable: 'I think it will appear ludicrous that reality becomes evident through imitation in letters and syllables'. But nonetheless he does set forth precisely such a theory. Writing is (*Cratylus* 423E) 'imitating this very essence of each thing in letters and syllables'. He continues (424E–425A):

So then we apply individual letters to reality, on a one on one basis, wherever that seems to be required. We also apply many, making what we call syllables. We put syllables together, and with them we put nouns and verbs together. And with nouns and verbs we put together something that is already large, beautiful and complete.

By the end of the dialogue he has repeatedly underscored the notion that writing is not (as we might see it) the *recording* of reality in words, but the *imitation* of reality in letters and syllables.

The importance of learning syllables as well as letters in school is stressed by even such an educational conservative as the Roman rhetorician

Quintilian. Quintilian insists that children should learn not just the alphabet, then words, but the alphabet, then *syllables*, and finally words. In *Instructing the Orator* 1.1.30–2, he points out that there is no easy way to solve the problem of teaching syllables; they must be learned by heart and by constant repetition. Once the syllables are learned, *then* the student can go on to words and sentences. This same progression from letters to syllables and then to words can be found in Greek grammarians. But when *we* discuss Latin poetry, we progress from individual letters directly to words. We tend not to consider the syllable as a sense unit.

The *Cratylus* above all examines the appropriateness of names. And the 'appropriateness' of a name may often be discovered by examining and rearranging the letters within it. Such transposition of letters and syllables sometimes occurs, Plato says, for the purpose of *disguise*, as in the case of Tantalus (Greek Tantalos). Hidden anagrammatically within Tantalos' name is his suffering, for he is *talantotatos*, 'most unfortunate'. His name also tells us that he is punished by having an (anagrammatical) weight – *talanteia* – poised over his head in the world of the dead (*Cratylus* 395D–E). The syllable *tal*, then, moves from second position to first, giving us a syllabic anagram within the word. The syllable *tan* has its constituent letters shuffled to generate a different-sounding syllable: *ant*.

Anagrammatizing etymologies are not restricted to proper names. The explanation Socrates offers for *phronesis* (wisdom) is that it is comprised of *phora* (motion) and either *noesis* (perceiving) or *onesis* (enjoyment) (411D)). Even truth, *aletheia*, could be an anagram: *aletheia* is 'divine wandering', *theia . . . ale* (421B). This last example is particularly interesting, because Socrates could have reversed the word order to avoid an anagram: *ale theia*. We should probably have this etymology in mind at the end of Plato's *Republic*, in the myth of Er. For Er, after wandering through the Elysian fields, arrives at the river Lethe, where everyone who drinks forgets all he knew. Er does not drink; he is non-Lethed, he has the absence of forgetfulness, which is itself the truth, *a-letheia*, as the result of his divine wandering.[20]

We should add that such etymologies based on anagrammatized letters or syllables are common enough in the Roman as well as in the Greek world. Quintilian, in fact, complains in *Instructing the Orator* that etymologists routinely 'change letters or syllables around: *permutatis litteris syllabisve*' (1.6.32).

---

[20] For *aletheia* and Lethe, see Marcel Detienne, 'La notion mythique d'*aletheia*', *Revue des études grecques* 73 (1960), pp. 27–35; F. M. Ahl, 'Amber, Avallon, and Apollo's Singing Swan', *American Journal of Philology* 103 (1982), pp. 373–411; W. G. Thalmann, *Conventions of Form and Thought in Early Greek Poetry* (Baltimore, 1984), pp. 147–9.

The Intelligibility of Anagrams

Anagrams would have been more immediately intelligible to ancient Greeks than to most of us. We have separate notation systems for numbers and letters. Not many of us could recite the alphabet backwards as readily as forwards, much less count through it in two or threes, add B to G, subtract M from X, or speedily rearrange a sequence of seven letters into various permutations. The ancient Greeks almost certainly could perform such maneuvers with ease, since their numerical system was a slightly amplified version of their alphabet. Alpha was 1 as well as 'a' and beta 2 as well as 'b'. Each letter was a number as well as a sound. Not only do we find jokes which play on the relationship, as in Suetonius' *Life of Nero* 39, where the total numerical value of the letters in Nero's name can also be represented by the expression 'he killed his mother', but there are also poems built on the same kind of system. Nor was such manipulation of letters and numbers restricted to the educated. Plutarch (*Symposiaka* 5 (673A)) points out that even ordinary people who have no literary interests engage in after-dinner games involving names and numbers – the enumeration of matricide in Nero, for example – not to mention riddles and conundrums.

Classical scholars are even less comfortable with anagrams than with puns. They can (and usually do) ignore them (since there is no scholarly tradition which requires us to acknowledge them). We do not regard anagrams as proper figures of speech, and we are less trained to recognize or generate them than to create puns or sophisticated patterns of metrics and rhyme. What we do not do, we tend to assume our predecessors either did not do, or were silly to have done. If forced to acknowledge anagrams, we resort to the knee-jerk response that they are not meaningful, or are accidental. Yet the odds against the random production of even short intelligible words are substantial. McKean, reporting on George Marsaglia's work on random numbers, notes that the odds that 'those famous monkeys that, if given enough time, will type all of Shakespeare ... will produce a simple word, like cat are one in 17,576'.[21]

Let us look at some instances where the odds against randomness are astronomical: juxtaposed, intelligible anagrams of five and seven letters. I do not know of any systematic attempt to determine the frequency of their occurrence in Latin literature, but a computer program which reduces words to alphabetical order would help.

In Cicero's *De Natura Deorum* 3.67, Balbus talks of 'the same Medea running away from father and fatherland: *eadem Medea patrem patriamque*

---

[21] McKean, 'Orderly Pursuit', p. 19.

fugiens'. The situation is, in all its ingredients, the same. Medea is present in the Latin word for 'same': *eadem*. And the sameness of sound is picked up in the phrase by the juxtaposition of *patrem* and *patriam*.

Often, however, juxtaposed anagrams suggest more complex effects. In *Metamorphoses* 4.293, Ovid juxtaposes *altrice* to its perfect anagram *relicta*. Similarly Vergil in *Aeneid* 7.702 juxtaposes *pulsa* and *palus* – in fact, these last are the only words in one abbreviated poetic line. What made me suspect they were not random was the fact that *altrice* and *relicta*, *pulsa* and *palus* were not just intelligible anagrams of one another, but complemented each other's meaning: *altrice* means 'nurse' and *relicta* 'left behind'; *pulsa* 'beaten' and *palus* 'lake'.

The first anagram occurs when the child of Hermes (the god of language) and Aphrodite sets out on a journey that will culminate in the physical rearrangement of his own being. He will be combined with the nymph Salmacis into one creature (part male, part female), and become not the product, but the *fusion* of male and female: Hermaphroditus. He parts from the female force that nurtures him, but will be reabsorbed into it. Finally, our poor Hermaphroditus is ensnared in a pool without reeds – *calamis* by a nymph named *Salmacis* who attacks him like an octopus and fuses with him in a curiously asexual rape.

The second anagram describes the rippling upon the surface of a lake (*palus*) caused by the beating (*pulsa*) of swans' wings upon it as they take off. The anagrams occur at *Aeneid* 7.702, a line composed of only these two words. *Palus* further suggests a pun on *palus* 'whipping-post, execution post', which enhances the reader's sense of 'beating' in 'lake'. Further, Vergil plays with *palus* and *pulsus* (beating) at the ends of *Georgics* 4, in lines 48 and 49 respectively, and follows with *pulsam* (beaten) in line 51.

Not all Latin anagrams, of course, are juxtaposed as are the examples I have given from Cicero, Ovid and Vergil. Others are, like Shakespearian puns, separated by intervening text, or left emphatically (in the ancient sense) for the reader to deduce. You have to train your eye to detect anagrams, as you must train your ear to catch the sophisticated pun or spoonerism – the latter a limited kind of anagram itself. Something must lead you to suspect that there is more than first meets the eye in the words before you.

Such was the case when I noticed *Aeneid* 8.322–3, where Vergil tells us why Latium was so called: 'He (Saturn) preferred (*maluit*) the place to be called *Latium* because he had hidden (*latuisset*) safe on these shores.' Critics often note the punning etymology, *latuisset*, but no one, as far as I know, had spotted that *maluit* is a perfect anagram of *Latium*, which neatly complements the idea of Saturn's concealment in Latium.

Anagrams are frequently used by Roman writers (as by Plato in the

Cratylus) to suggest that something is concealed within something else. A particular favorite is the play on *ignis*, 'fire', and *cinis*, 'ash' – 'c' and 'g' were regarded as etymologically interchangeable by Roman poets from Ennius onwards. Seneca's Ulysses in *Trojan Women* 544 knows that *cinis* can be stirred back into *ignis* even after a great conflagration. Statius (*Thebaid* 10.155) knows that *cinis*, as it rises suddenly from below, can take away fire, *ignis* (*subitus cinis abstulit ignis*). Water can similarly be anagrammatized away, as in Seneca *Oedipus* 44, where shallows have no water, *unda*, and are therefore *nuda*: *nuda vix unda vada*: nude shallows, almost void of water. I suspect that for the Roman the anagram may have had something of the reinforcing sense we attribute to the rhyme: we use rhyme to suggest that 'might is right'; Seneca uses an anagram. In *Hercules in his Madness* right – *iure* – can be replaced by might – *vires*: *pro iure vires*. (It is our convention, not a Roman convention, that differentiates 'u' from 'v'.)

The anagram belongs to a world of visual wordplay, a world that seems to us to pertain more to the eye than to the ear, intensifying at a visual level the ideas the text conveys. It is a Looking Glass world where Ovid's Narcissus falls in love with his own perfect reflection. His passion for himself is *sitis*, 'thirst' – a palindrome capturing self-love in a verbal mirror-image (*Metamorphoses* 3.415). But when the surface is ruffled, as in Vergil, the letters may shift: *pulsa palus*, just as they may when Borges becomes distorted in the mirror of Eco's library.

The Potter's Wheel

Is anything other than a certain 'color' lost if we neglect the anagram in Latin poetry? The answer is very clearly 'yes' in many instances. Horace, in *Ars Poetica* 212, describes how a vessel intended to be an amphora ended up as a pitcher on the potter's wheel:

> amphora coepit
> institui: currente rota cur urceus exit?

Here is the Loeb translation of H. R. Fairclough, followed by some modern discussion of the dilemma:

That was a wine-jar, when the moulding began: why, as the wheel turns round, does it turn out a pitcher?[22]

C. O. Brink discusses this line and a half in detail, on the assumption that Horace is distinguishing between an *amphora* and an *urceus* as: 'How do they

---

[22] H. R. Fairclough, *Horace: Satires, Epistles and Ars Poetica* (London, 1926).

differ? Commentators are divided. A majority of them think a comment on size is intended.'[23] But if he had considered the *syllabic* structure of the last part of line 22, the dilemma would have been largely resolved:

CURrente rota CUR URCeus exit?

The syllable *CUR* is the sole ingredient of Latin *CUR*, 'why'; it is also the first syllable of *CURrente*, 'running, turning'. The first syllable of *URCeus*, 'pitcher', is an anagram of *CUR*, 'why'. The combination of *CUR URCeus* echoes the sound of *CURre-*, 'running'. So Horace partially answers his own question. Further, *amphora*, what the *urn* was supposed to be, is a Greek word, derived from a verb meaning to turn around: *amphipheromai*. The Greek *amphora*, put on the Roman potter's wheel, 'turns into' a Latin urn. We have a conundrum, the product of linguistic metamorphosis. The poetic art imitates the potter's:

It started out as a casserole; can you diSCERN why it comes out an URN when the wheel RUNs?

If we ignore the anagram, we surely miss Horace's point.

The Problem of Seriousness

The presence of many 'serious' puns and other wordplays in studied literary contexts casts doubt on the common prejudice that puns are necessarily, or even primarily, humorous – much less casual – throughout literary history. When the grieving Antony laments over Caesar's body (*Julius Caesar* III. i. 207–8), his punning is no more the stuff of laughter than is Donne's play on his own name:

O world, though wast the forest to this hart;
And this indeed, O world, the heart of thee!

If we impose modern judgments of wordplay on Shakespeare or the ancients, and insist that the pun is a low form of humor, the wit of crassitude, a serious pun becomes a contradiction in terms. That is why scholars of Plato are uneasy with the *Cratylus*, replete with etymologizing puns and anagrams. We regard them as ridiculous and unscholarly. So Socrates (who is neither ridiculous nor unscholarly) cannot be 'serious' about them.

Seriousness has become, as it were, the default drive of the Western mind. For the ancients it was not. Pluralistic thinking has a tendency to discover humor because it is ever aware that a given word or idea does not belong

---

[23] C. O. Brink, *Horace on Poetry II: The 'Ars Poetica'* (Cambridge, 1971), p. 103.

exclusively to one field of reference or to one context. In fact, ancient critics would probably criticize our monistic thinking for generating too many artificial boundaries between things, words and ideas, for maintaining seriousness by pretending that a word or term exists in quarantined isolation and for refusing to tolerate the intrusion of levity or of rhetorical paradox.

To many critics a work's seriousness is a measure of its importance. Good tragedy, we reckon, is serious. But many of Euripides' later tragedies, *Orestes* for instance, strike modern critics as too full of bizarre or humorous elements to be genuinely 'serious' tragedy.[24] And here we are often at odds with ancient critics. Aristotle, for example, defends Euripides against charges by contemporaries that the tone of his tragedies was inappropriate because 'many of his plays end in misfortune'; he even wickedly accuses such critics of *hamartia* (*Poetics* 1453a 8–9): 'they are in (tragic) error: *hamartanousin*'.

If we would simply jettison the unsmilingly puritan notion of seriousness from our critical vocabularies, we could allow texts, as we could allow God (or gods) to laugh without any diminution of 'divinity'. In the pluralism of words, sounds, and their meaning the poet within us finds freedom from the restrictions that the theologian would apply. In *City of God* 19.23 St Augustine, who struggled to establish Christian monism in a dominantly pluralist society, argued that Christians must sacrifice to no god *nisi Domino soli*, 'except solely to the Lord', as Exodus 22.20 states. Unfortunately the Latin text does not help his argument because it contains a (possibly unintentional) pun. *Soli* means not just 'alone' or 'solely' but 'Sun'. And some Christians chose to interpret the passage as meaning: 'Except to our Lord Sol'. This pun was not just risible hearsay to Augustine. It was heresy. 'The worship of the word,' as W. Gass observes, 'must be pagan and polytheistic. It cannot endure one god.'[25]

Robbed of a response by the Protean ambiguity of Latin, Augustine urged his readers, if they would not accept his assurance, to look at the Greek.

A modern scholar would simply snort and dismiss the problem as another instance of 'folk etymology'. Augustine could not. He knew that etymologizing explanations were not the ramblings of illiterate peasants but ideas of language maintained by important ancient thinkers. Cicero has the Stoic Balbus argue in *On the Nature of the Gods* 2.68, that *Sol*, the Sun, was so named because he was the sole (*solus*) star of its size. More important, the great Roman scholar, Varro, argued in his *Lingua Latina* (5.68) that *sol* was so

---

called because he was the sole light of day. And such punning etymologies continued to be used, not only in Stoic and Academic circles, but even among Christians, for many years. The most famous etymologizer of them all was to arise a couple of centuries *after* Augustine: Isidore of Seville, a Christian bishop of the early seventh century AD. The battle was far from over, and Augustine knew it.

We have alluded, in passing, to the major etymologist of this kind in the Roman world, Marcus Terentius Varro. Varro, a theologian, linguist, polymath and satirist of the first century BC was, Augustine himself admits (*City of God* 4.1), 'a very learned man among the pagans and of the most weighty authority'. Cicero, Seneca, Quintilian and countless other Roman men of letters agree: Varro was the most learned of the Romans. And, even though he did write three books on farming among the 700 or so he published, it is not right to call him 'folksy'.[26]

Imagine that a respected emeritus scholar who had held a joint appointment as Professor of Poetry, Linguistics, Natural Sciences and the History of Religion wrote, at the age of 80, a three-part, technical guide to farming which included a listing of all the major critical sources he had drawn upon – something of note in and of itself. Imagine his book took the form of a Platonic dialogue. Imagine that the chief interlocutors were all real persons with real names, but that, by some curious coincidence, the names were Mr Field (Agrius), Mr Fielding (Agrasius), Mr Ranch (Fundanius), Mr Rootsucker (Stolo), Mr Cowey (Vacca), and Mr Hogg (Scrofa). Mr Hogg, of course, discusses, among other things, pig-raising. Mr Cowey refuses to remain silent when the conversation runs to cattle (Varro, *Res Rusticae* 2.5.2–3) because this is a field, he says, in which he is specially qualified. Cowey, however, is warned by the narrator to steer clear of bulls and not be too presumptuous.

If this agrarian punning seems ludicrously corny, brows will furrow further on learning that Varro dedicated this opus, his *Res Rusticae*, to his wife, named Ranchy (Fundania). Yet the resulting work was read, used and praised for its usefulness for a millenium. Imagine this, and you glimpse something of how Varro felt he could address his pluralistic audience in a work on farming.

Numerous other ancient writers were non less happy to spice their works with etymologizing plays, often just for fun. Cicero's learned Academic, Cotta, in *On the Nature of the Gods* (1.80) unabashedly returns, after a digression, to his divine subject with the remark: *redeo ad deos* (I go back to the gods), which puns on *deus* (god), *redeo* (go back), *ad deos* (to the gods) and *adeo* (to go). And when he confesses (ironically) to defeat in argument

---

[26] On Varro see my *Metaformations*, pp. 22–3, n. 5.

(*concedo*) he anagrammatically asks his interlocutor to teach him (*doce*) (1.65). For Cicero's Stoic Balbus, however, wordplay is a matter of theological etymologizing. For his Cotta it is a matter of stylistic elegance.

But etymologizing does not always have a humorous purpose. In Sophocles' *Oedipus* 1036, a messenger etymologizes Oedipus' name as *oidi* (swollen) and *pous* (foot) to substantiate his own connection with the naming of the child. Jocasta in Euripides' *Phoenician Women* 21 offers the same 'swollen foot' etymology, as does Apollodorus (3.5.7). Significantly Seneca's Corinthian messenger (*Oedipus* 811–13) reproduces 'Oedipus' from a Latin anagram *iopedum* (which my translation only approximates) as well as a translation of the Greek etymology:

Oedipus   Now say what distinguishing marks were on my body.

Old Man   The trace of footprints pierced with steel: From the swelling you
          got your name and from your piteous feet (vit*io pedum*).

Modern commentators, almost without exception, also detect play on OIDa 'know' and POUS 'foot' in OIDiPOUS. But they never reproduce it in translation.

While it may still seem ridiculous to many of us that a man's fate is in his name, the idea of the *omen* within the *nomen* ('name'), or, as the Greeks put it, *onoma* ('name') in an *ornis* ('bird of omen'), is commonplace in antiquity.[27] Although Quintilian (*Instructing the Orator*, 5.10) condemns the practice among orators, we find it taken much for granted not only by Plato, but by Aristotle, as, for example, in *Topics* 2.6.2. In *Rhetoric* 1400b it concludes Aristotle's discussion of the enthymeme – the figure of reason that is to rhetoric what the syllogism is to dialectic. And his first example of it is drawn from Sophocles' now lost play, *Tyro*:

Another topic (*topos* of the enthymeme) is from names, as when Sophocles says: 'You are obviously Steele (*Sidero*); you have it as your name.' People habitually do this sort of thing in praising the gods. Similarly Conon used to call Thrasybulus 'rash (*thrasy*) in advising (*boulos*)', Herodicus used to say Thrasymachus was 'always rash (*thrasy*) in fighting (*machos*)', and Polus 'always horsing around (*polos* = young horse, colt)'. He said of the lawgiver Draco (= snake, dragon): 'His laws are not human but dragonian' because they were severe. So too Euripides' *Hecuba* (*Trojan Women* 990) says of Aphrodite (born from the foam, *aphro*): 'The goddess' name rightly begins with mindlessness (*aphrosyne*).' And Chaeremon: 'Pentheus (*penthos*: suffering): a proper name (*eponymos*) for the catastrophe to come.'

---

[27] See Max Sulzberger, ' "Onoma Eponymon", Les noms propres chez Homère et dans la mythologie grecque', *Revue des études grecques* 39 (1926), pp. 381–447.

The same phenomenon is so common throughout Greek literature that, as Sulzberger long ago pointed out, it is useless to list all the examples.[28] A few suffice.

Plato plays off Thrasymachus' name (bold [*thrasy*] in fighting [*machos*]). Thrasymachus makes the case that might is right in the *Republic*. The punning etymology of Pentheus' name is better known to us from Euripides' *Bacchae* 508, where Dionysus says: 'You are fitted for suffering by your name.' But such etymologizing is not primarily a Euripidean phenomenon, as Quintilian (*Instructing the Orator*, 5.10) seems to suggest. In Sophocles' *Ajax*, Ajax (Greek Aias) has no difficulty in finding his grief (*aiai*) in his name (*Aias*), 430–3: 'Aiai! Who would ever have thought my name would be such a proper name (*eponymos*) and fit with my misfortunes! So now it's time for me to cry out aiai twice and yet a third time.'[29]

However gauche and folksy such punning, anagrammatizing, and punning etymologies appear to some of us now, they figure 'in early juridical works the world over' as D. A. Binchy writes.[30] Etymologizing 'was classed as a special branch of Irish, called by the early grammarians "the language of separation", and the jurists were among its leading exponents'. But Binchy, like other Irish scholars, disapproves of it, even though he realizes that it was a highly Academic practice. He also recognizes that Irish legal practice was founded on Latin. Tomás Ó Máille has demonstrated that Isidore of Seville's early seventh-century *Etymologiae* 'was regarded as the last word in human knowledge, and it increased in importance as time went on. . . . Throughout the middle ages it was the text-book most in use. Its adoption in Ireland in the seventh century is evidence of the desire of the Irish to be in touch with the learning of the time.'[31]

Again, modern scholars cannot conceal their contempt. 'From Isidore,' Osborn Bergin remarks, 'the Irish learnt that *equus* "horse" comes from *aequus* "equal" . . ., that *beatus* "blessed" is a contraction of *bene auctus* "well-increased"; and so on. The same fantastic analysis was applied to Irish words.'[32]

---

[28] Ibid., p. 431.

[29] On etymological figures in the *Ajax*, see W. B. Stanford, *Sophocles 'Ajax'* (London and New York, 1983), pp. 270–1 and his notes on *Ajax*, pp. 308–9, 317–18, 430–3, 574, 606–7, 685–6.

[30] D. A. Binchy, *Celtic Law Papers* 42 (Brussels, 1973), pp. 90–1.

[31] Tomás Ó Máille, 'The Authorship of the Culmen', *Eriú* 9 (1921), pp. 71–6, esp. p. 76.

[32] Osborn Bergin, 'The Native Irish Grammarian', *Proceedings of the British Academy* 24 (1938), p. 4.

Divining Wit

We *know*, of course, that interpreters of the law, like our own constitutional experts, are concerned with reconciling old laws and legal principles with what contemporaries want to do, not necessarily with what the original lawgivers meant. As often as not interpreters of the law are revising – their critics would say subverting – the laws under the guise of interpreting them. In short, they seek not 'true' origins or scholarly, Indo-European etymologies, but origins or etymologies which will give a basis upon which to justify whatever they want to argue. Take the instance of Numa, king of Rome and legendary founder of the Roman legal system.

In Ovid's *Fasti* 3.309–94 the god Jupiter and King Numa converse. The latter is trying to find the proper religious acts to avert the wrath of the heavens which is shown when a thunderbolt falls. Jupiter, in answering, 'hid the truth in obscure ambiguity' (337–8), Ovid states. Laws and oracles are, of course, often ambiguous, and luckily so. For their ambiguity allows humanizing interpretation. But despite Ovid's assurance of ambiguity here, the 'explicit' meaning is clear: Jupiter is asking for a human sacrifice. But Numa does not want to give him it, so he tries to pun his way out of the dilemma (339–40):

'Cut me a head (*caput*)', Jupiter said. The king replied: 'We will obey: 'A head (*cepa*) must torn away and cut from my garden onion patch.'

Isidore explains this vegetable dilemma in *Etymologiae* 17.10.12: 'The *cepa* (onion-head) is so called because it's nothing else but a head (*caput*)'. Our use of 'head' for garlic or cabbage is much the same.

Jupiter, however, is not put off by elementary etymologies (line 341): 'Jupiter added: "a human head".' Numa replies with another wordplay on the *cap* (head) base: *capillos*, 'hair', which even grows upon the *caput*: 'You'll get,' he said, 'a head of hair (*capillos*).' Jupiter's reference to a *hum*an head is itself a witticism, given Numa's statement that the onion head will come from his garden. We see this from Isidore 11.1.4: 'he is called a *hum*an because he is made of *hum*us, as in Genesis 2.7.'

Jupiter now specifies that the head must have a soul (line 342): 'He asks for an animate one; and Numa suggested a fish'. The Elder Cato resolves part of this riddle in *On Agriculture* 158.1. Among the suggested ingredients in his recipe for a purgative is 'a fish called the *capito*' ('Headfish'). And *capito* is also the term for a large head.

Numa wittily uses language to subvert the tradition that the falling of a thunderbolt requires expiation with a human victim. The god, fortunately, does not become angry. He enjoys Numa's humor and his jesting, he admires his competitor. He is not, like Hesiod's Zeus, enraged at being swindled out of the best part of the sacrifice by a wily Prometheus. Numa is playing court jester to Jupiter. Since he is, quite literally, playing with fire, he approaches the interview with fear. If something goes wrong, his life is forfeit.

We may compare with Numa's sleight of tongue Ovid's explanation of how the sacrifice of humans in the days of our elders – *priscorum* – was changed into offerings of rush figures – *scirpea* (*Fasti* 6.621–2):

Then too the Vestal virgin customarily throws rush images [*scirpea*] of men of old [*priscorum*] from the oak bridge.

Ovid suggests the substitution of the rush images for the men of old by anagrammatizing *prisc*orum into *scirp*ea. But he also goes on to note various traditions as to the origins of this curious practice. Two human bodies, according to one tradition, were used as sacrifice to the 'old god who carries the sickle' (*Fasti* 5.626). Another tradition suggested that 'weak old men were once thrown from the bridges (*pontibus*)' (line 634). Vestal virgins, aided by the *pontifices*, the 'bridge-builder' priests, threw them from the Sublician Bridge (*Pons*). The Tiber himself, a mainstream authority on river-appeasing sacrifices, denies human sacrifice was ever allowed, and argues that 'rush images', not people, were thrown into his waters.[33]

Numa's success, and that of Ovid's Tiber, is vital to the humanizing of society. As Numa's relationship is to the gods, so the poet's is to the king. His task is to direct the destructive power of tyrants and gods away from humans onto lesser ritual objects – to pluralize what appears to be the unitary and fixed meaning of a text. So Numa and Ovid use etymologies and anagrams to shuffle traditions their predecessors have bequeathed them, to subvert, reshape and redirect the reader's thoughts. They are trying to change their societies' perspectives on reality, and thus change reality itself.

For many moralists, however, the lawyer (rhetorician) is of dubious morality, ready to argue both sides of a case, to search for exceptions to the rule, to corrupt monism with pluralism. The moralist does not want religious rules changed or made susceptible to change. Not surprisingly, then, the pluralizing, punning Varro is for Augustine in *City of God* a major intellectual opponent, a stumbling-block to Latin Christianity. And Varro was no trivial rival. Although much of what he writes seems to us unconventional, revolutionary, bizarre, silly, or obviously wrong, in antiquity it was not considered even avant-garde; he was the voice of the learned establishment for several centuries.

[33] For the Argei, see L. A. Holland, *Janus and the Bridge*, Papers and Monographs of the American Academy at Rome, 21 (Rome, 1961), pp. 313–42.

Varro was a resolute pluralist in theology and in language. Like most of his contemporaries, he had no difficulty in seeing that a Greek, Egyptian or Gallic god was essentially the equivalent of such and such a Roman god. The existence of one did not preclude the existence of another. Similarly in language, he argues for one etymology, then contends that an opposing explanation is equally true, along with several others. The Roman, legally minded, trained in rhetoric, knows that truth is not absolute. If A is arguably true, its opposite B is arguably true as well. Scholars in the humanities, however, like Christian theologians, are less flexible, and insist on a quest for absolute truth rather than for what may be arguably true.

An example or two is in order. Varro gives us several etymologies of the Latin word *caelum*, 'sky, for example'. In *Lingua Latina* 5.20 he says it derives from *cavum*, 'hollow', and, ultimately from *chaos*. 'Sky' is created from primeval 'Chaos' – a derivation which fits with the ancient ideas of the origin of the universe found in the book of Genesis and in Hesiod's *Theogony*. As words are derived, so worlds are born, and vice versa.

But this is not Varro's only suggested etymology for *caelum*. He also suggests (5.18) that it derives from *caelare*, which, when spelled with an 'a', means 'to engrave' and, when spelled without an 'a', 'to conceal'.

Aelius writes that *caelum* is so named because it is *caelatum*, 'engraved', or from the opposite of what it appears to say – *celatum*, 'concealed' – because it is there to be seen. It was no bad idea when someone suggested that *caelare*, 'to engrave', came from *caelum* rather than *caelum* from *caelando*, 'engraving'. But this alternative etymology could just as well be made from *celando*, 'concealing', because it is concealed during the day and is not concealed at night.

In a fragment of his *Menippeae* he notes: '*caelum* (sky) is so called from *caelatura* (engraving)'. The natural historian Pliny concurs: 'sky (*caelum*) indeed is so named, doubtless, from the sense of "engraving", (*caelati*) as Marcus Varro explains' (*Natural History* 2.8). And *caelum*, we may add, also means a sculptor's chisel.

Varro, then, *expands* etymological possibilities rather than contracting them, as we tend to. Although *caelare* describes the *creation* of art, it stimultaneously describes the concealment of art. We may glimpse the meaning of the famous adage: *ars ets c(a)elare artem*. Art is not generated simply by burying something: art is the simultaneous creation and concealment of itself – art engraved.

Ovid takes Varro's idea further. It was god, or nature, that with artistic eye, forced shape upon the world, thereby dividing up the oneness of *chaos* (1.21–88). We will note, incidentally, that unity and oneness are not, for Ovid, ideals to be striven for. They make for chaos, a kind of primeval black hole. The deity, Ovid continues, separated earth from sky and then *hid* (*secrevit*) sky (*C(A)ELum*) away from air (1.22–3). That is why Jupiter, the lord of heaven, is such an outstanding master of disguise, and why water nymphs stayed on the run from Jupiter's love.

As life emerges, Prometheus molds a model of man, he engages in *caelatura* (1.76–88). Not only does his creature retain 'seeds of the igneous sky (*caeli*) that was born with it' (line 81) – but it is ordered to look up to the sky (*caelum*), to contemplate god's other handiwork (lines 85–6). Up in the sky, hidden from untrained eyes, are the mythical shapes of the constellations. One, the Dolphin, Ovid describes in *Fasti* 2.79 as: 'etched in stars (*caelatum*) upon the sky'. God (or Nature) has made the sky something other than a confused and hidden covering for things. It is a masterwork that Prometheus creates man to contemplate. Man is created in the divine image so he can contemplate the divine, in the *Metamorphoses* as in the Old Testament. At the same time, the constellations etched upon the sky are concealed from the eyes of the uninformed. 'That's not a dolphin, it's just a clump of stars,' our apostle of the explicit will observe. 'You are reading into it something that is not there.'

Varro saw poets as chiefly responsible for renewing language by making it carry fresh meaning, and he fiercely attacks people who try to 'regularize' language and freeze expression:

These new 'inflections' of the word, which have been introduced with good reasoning behind them, the world of officialdom and public life spits out in disgust. It is the duty of good poets, especially dramatists, to accustom people's ears to them. Poets have a lot of power in this process. . . . For the customs we are used to in speech are always moving.

As the 'creative' user of language, the poet may select individual words, decide how to use them, and inflect them as he wishes. He controls the 'declension' of a word just as he controls the context into which he places it. In short, the meaning of a word is not absolute and fixed, in Varro's view, but is determined by context (*Lingua Latina* 8.40): 'If a sound has to be like another sound when uttered, it does not make any difference whether it signifies a male or female being, whether it is someone's name or just a common noun.' The poet, as maker of contexts, controls the multiple possibilities of language. In 'real life', of course, control lies, depending on one's beliefs, with nature, god(s), or random chance.

It would be easy, I suppose, to classify one of the most famous Roman *double entendres* as random: the curious story of a fig-seller's cry, mentioned by Cicero in *On Divination* (2.84). '*Cauneas*! Carian figs!' the merchant cried; but his words sounded like '*Cave ne eas*! Take care not to go!' to the Roman general Crassus, about to set out on a military expedition. The fig-seller was not aware of his *double entendre*. But the ancient science of divination lay precisely in understanding that apparent coincidence of sound and meaning that the speaker does not himself notice might well be obvious to the listener. Two different meanings intersect when different lives with different areas of concern cross each others' paths. One is trying to sell his fruit. The other is buried in thoughts of war in Syria. Is the fig-seller's pun random, or is it a divine warning spoken in oracular fashion through an uncomprehending medium? Crassus goes on to his death, and Jupiter does not proclaim an answer. The answer supplied, then, depends largely on whether one views the world as a determinist or as an apostle of free will.

But Ovid's description of the bird of ill-omen, the screech-owl (*bubo*), that presided over the ill-fated wedding of Procne and Tereus is a different matter (*Fasti* 6.433–4):

> haC AVE coniuncti Procne Tereusque, parentes
> haC AVE sunt facti.

Under this bird (AVE) would BE WHERE Procne and Tereus coupled, under this bird (AVE) would BE WHERE they became parents.

The owl, reported by Ovid's sounds (not its own), warns the couple to BEWARE (*A, CAVE!*) just as the fig-seller warns Crassus not to go to war.

The Roman poet often claims the title of *vates*, 'seer' or 'prophet', and with that title the ability to speak in oracular *double entendre*. Yet he routinely disavows that he is speaking for himself. Vergil calls upon the muse to speak in him and through him, much as his Sibyl calls upon her god to do so. If we take the poet at his word, nothing he says is really his; it is the god's. But the poet's ignorance has qualities of Socratic dissimulation. The fig-seller may not have realized his pun, but surely Ovid realized his. For a poet who shows the evolution of a divine order is likely to be deterministic with his puns. Yet, being a poet, he would probably deny that he intended the *double entendre* if you actually asked him about it.

The Tale of the Dog

And now a final, mundane illustration of how Varro would explain a lowlier problem of semantics: why *canis* means both 'a dog' and 'you sing'. We treat the *double entendre* as coincidence, but Varro did not. If *canis* means 'you sing' and 'dog', there is a *reason* for the resemblance. And he gives it (*Lingua Latina* 5.99): 'The trumpet and the dog are said to sing *canere*; the latter is likewise called a *canis* because, when on night watch duty and when hunting, he gives the alert with his voice'. . . . 'They are called hounds (*canes*) because they sound (*canunt*) warning with their bark (*latratu*) of arcane happenings (*quae latent*)' (*Lingua Latina* 7.32).

At this point the scholarly mind dissolves into quivering spasms. The petulant response is to flee to an etymological dictionary to show dog, *canis*, and sing, *canis*, are not interrelated. Varro is barking up the wrong tree, we conclude, and bow out of the argument. But if we do so, we are guarding our own dogma to the detriment of Latin poetry. It is in large measure irrelevant whether Varro is right or wrong. We don't laugh, at least openly, at the absurdities of Aristotle's physics or biology, because if we are to grasp Aristotle's thought and times, we know we must see why he thought as he did, not make fun of him for doing so. Besides, most of us humanists don't know enough science to make fun of Aristotle. But we are all, at heart, grammarians. We know we know better than Varro.

Not all forms of *canere*, 'to sing', resound with dogs. There must be something about the context which unleashes the canine *entendre*. *Can* may suggest whiteness and age as well as singing and dogginess. Vergil employs this play in *Aeneid* 10.191–2 when he is describing the metamorphosis of the Ligurian prince CYCnus, 'Swan':

While lightly singing (*canit*) and solacing his sad love with song, he whitely aged (*canentem*) with soft feathers.

The vowel in *cano*, when extended, physically transforms the singer to old age and long-necked whiteness in mid-song, and so makes him a swan. Old, prophetic bards are often compared to swans in Greek and Latin poetry: to be swanlike is to greet one's death with a song of exceptional beauty, as in a famous passage of Plato (*Phaedo* 84D–85B), where Socrates hopes his own prophecy will match that of swans, 'who sing especially well when on the point of death, because they are about to go off to the god whose servant they are'. Their god is Apollo, famous for his associations with singing swans and their distant northern retreat is the land of the Hyperboreans.[34]

The play on *can*, then, suggestive of cycnic singing, is a far remove from a dog's cynic howling. But the possibility always lurks that someone will find a way of making even these planes intersect. Ovid, in the *Metamorphoses*, offers his own venture into singing and dogs. He compares the musical Phoebus, usually linked with singing and northern swans, to a dog (*canis*) in *Metamorphoses* 1.533, when the god is hot in unsuccessful pursuit of Daphne, who keeps Apollo at bay by turning into a laurel tree. In this case the Latin suggests not a Celtic or Ligurian singer but a Gallic dog.

The reverberations continue, for the combination of *Gallicus* and *canis* also suggests the music of different kinds of creatures: the falsetto shrieks of the castrated priests of Cybele, the Galli; the *gallus*, 'rooster'; and *gallicinium*, 'cock crow'. Suetonius (*Nero* 45) records a jest about Nero,

---

[34] See my 'Amber, Avallon, and Apollo's Singing Swan'.

notorious for his singing, his troubles with the Gauls, and his marriage to his castrated boyfriend Sporus, which captures several of these innuendos: 'It was written on pillars that his singing aroused even Gallic cocks'.

There is also a visual dimension to these plays on *gallus*: the funerary urn of a deceased high priest of Cybele, an *archigallus* or 'head cock', is shaped like a rooster.[35] Whether this association was meant to appear funny is hard to say. Even if it was, it was doubtless meant to honor, not insult, the dead.

Conclusion

Ancient texts in which we find literary myths and other narratives, be they philosophical or poetical, are a complex fabric of meanings, sounds, syllables, and words which the writer weaves together. The elements of wordplay are not, I suggest, an occasional, much less random, ornament of his art; they *are* his art. Greek and Roman writers were more sensitive to the possibilities – including what they took to be the scientific, even divine possibilities – of wordplay than we are. Through them they make language sustain all the meanings its phonemes are capable of evoking. Like sound assimilates to like sound. The result is the generation of extended and paradoxical phonemic families where a syllable may signify a number of different, but not distinct concepts.

Once we become comfortable with these larger and more complex associations we will be ready, I think, to relish the multiplicity and complexity of what we have so long taken to be, at heart, simple, sincere and classical. We should answer the call of the phoneme without fear that it may ring false.

[35] See my *Metaformations*, pp. 34–5 and nn. 12 and 14.

3

The Play of Puns in Late Middle English Poetry: Concerning Juxtology

R. A. Shoaf

> Be subtle, various, ornamental, clever,
> And do not listen to those critics ever
> Whose crude provincial gullets crave in books
> Plain cooking made still plainer by plain cooks,
> As though the Muse preferred her half-wit sons;
> Good poets have a weakness for bad puns.
> ('The Truest Poetry is the Most Feigning',
> W. H. Auden)

> He had to choose. But it was not a choice
> Between excluding things. It was not a choice
>
> Between, but of. He chose to include the things
> That in each other are included, the whole,
> The complicate, the amassing harmony.
> ('Notes Toward a Supreme Fiction',
> Wallace Stevens)

Auden's and Stevens's wisdom and their patience are often forgotten. The burden of this essay, however, will be to remember them, to keep them fresh in mind as various poets and their poetry are discussed. Their wisdom and patience are often forgotten because in fact they frustrate many critics who (be their palates as they may) are interested in power and who, therefore, fear puns and the choices puns exact, for puns are about power – puns *are* power[1] – and they unsettle those who want to be in control, who want to be on top of things. A pun, like Bottom's dream, often 'hath no bottom' and therefore no top either (no 'inside' or 'outside', for that matter, too), and this indeterminacy and uncertainty vex most critics, leave them uncomfortable as to who's in charge. After all, what *would* they do if, in fact, language itself were 'in charge'?

---

[1] See R. A. Shoaf, *Milton, Poet of Duality: A Study of Semiosis in the Poetry and the Prose* (New Haven, 1985), pp. 60–71.

Medieval poets, I will argue in these few pages, knew full well that language is 'in charge'. Juxtologists, as I like to think of them, they recognized that words yoke themselves together, and together with things, in the most unpredictable ways. Medieval poets – especially Chaucer, the *Gawain*-poet, and Langland – knew that, as Scripture has it, 'the Spirit blows where it will, and you hear its voice, but you do not know whence it comes or where it goes' (John 3:8) – they understood that language exceeds man's grasp and that that's what heaven is for.[2]

In the first part of this essay, I will examine puns in four of Chaucer's poems – *Troilus and Criseyde*, *The Franklin's Tale*, *The Miller's Tale* and *The General Prologue*. I will then consider, in passing, the role of puns in an early fifteenth-century lyric (anonymous), and, finally, I will look briefly at crucial puns in *Sir Gawain and the Green Knight* and in *Piers Plowman*. The summary goal will be to see that, different as these various poems are from each other, they still share an isomorphism in the structure of the pun and its multiple effects.

In Chaucer's poetry, the pun is a device for delaying, interrupting, or otherwise frustrating closure.[3] Often when a character insists on closure and its unisemy, a restriction of meaning, a pun emerges to suggest polysemy and a ludic re-opening of the text. Thus the pun also serves as a device for questioning motivation in poetic discourse; a pun often transgresses motivation and exposes it as asymptotic with its context. A pun is a hole, so to speak, that makes the whole of the discourse possible – even as the orifices of the body make life itself possible.

Let me begin with a relatively simple example. In Book 1 of *Troilus and Criseyde*, the Narrator remarks of Troilus, after the latter has seen and fallen in love with Criseyde:

> And over al this, yet muchel more he thoughte
> What for to speke, and what to holden inne;
> And what to *arten* hire to love he soughte,
> And on a song anon-right to bygynne,
> And gan loude on his sorwe for to wynne.[4]

---

[2] I discuss this and related issues at length in my paper 'Medieval Studies after Derrida after Heidegger', forthcoming in *Essays on the Theme of Language in Medieval Thought and Literature: Sign, Sentence, Discourse*, eds Julian Wasserman and Lois Roney (Syracuse, 1988).

[3] A recent discussion of closure or, as the case may be, the lack thereof, in Chaucer's poetry is Larry Sklute, *Virtue of Necessity: Incompletion and Narrative Form in Chaucer's Poetry* (Columbus, 1984); this book, however, is to be used with caution – consult my review in *Journal of English and Germanic Philology* 85 (1986), pp. 443–5.

[4] *Troilus and Criseyde* 1.386–90 (emphasis added); the text of Chaucer's poetry cited here and elsewhere is that of *The Riverside Chaucer*, gen. ed. Larry D. Benson, based on *The Works of Geoffrey Chaucer*, ed. F. N. Robinson (Cambridge, Mass., 1987).

The word *arten* means *direct* or *urge on*,[5] but it is also a pun, *art-en*; and the pun plays havoc with the Narrator's presumptions at this point in the narrative.[6] *Art* will induce (and seduce) Criseyde to love: she will succumb to the *art* of Troilus's *canticus*, which follows immediately upon this passage, and to the *art* of Pandarus's mediation.[7] But it is just this *art*, the *art* of the go-between or the 'Galeotto', which the Narrator in the early part of the poem is pleased to think he is innocent of.[8] In fact, however, this art will prove to contaminate his entire project, so much so that he will have, in the end, to expose his hand, lest his words, too, prove to be, like Pandarus's, 'wordes white' (*Troilus and Criseyde* 3.1567), words of deceit.[9]

Chaucer the poet plays the pun on *arten* in Book 1 to subvert the Narrator's presumption of innocent instrumentality, and in doing so, he provokes us to realize that the Narrator is already saying more than he is aware of. Love is inseparable from art, language from desire, rhetoric from eros, and the Narrator, we gradually perceive, has to (and does) learn the coincidence of language and desire in the course of 'translating' the book of Lollius. Thus his motives change by poem's end, and art, especially the art of puns, has had much to do with the change. The Narrator at poem's end knows that he cannot 'circumscribe' (*Troilus and Criseyde* 5.1865) the word *arten* in the way he presumed he could at poem's beginning. The Narrator at the end knows and fears the price of such closure.[10]

Another example now, more complicated, from *The Franklin's Tale*.[11] One particularly vexed problem which Chaucer addressed time and again in his

---

[5] See Norman Davis et al., *A Chaucer Glossary* (Oxford, 1979), *sub voce*, p. 7.

[6] Dante uses a similar pun, on Italian *arte*, in *Purgatorio*, canto 1, line 126; for discussion, see R. A. Shoaf, *Dante, Chaucer, and the Currency of the Word: Money, Images and Reference in Late Medieval Poetry* (Norman, Oklahoma, 1983), pp. 56–7; Dante's poem is cited from Giorgio Petrocchi, ed., *Il Commedia secondo l'antica vulgata* (Milan, 1966–7).

[7] See *Troilus and Criseyde* 3.253–5: 'for the [Troilus] am I bicomen, / Betwixen game and ernest, swich a meene / As maken wommen unto men to comen'.

[8] See, e.g., the very next stanza in Book 1 (393–8):

> And of his song naught only the sentence,
> As writ myn auctour called Lollius,
> But pleinly, save oure tonges difference,
> I dar wel seyn, in al, that Troilus
> Seyde in his song, loo, every word right thus
> As I shal seyn –

in other words, his mediation, so he thinks, does not interfere with his text of Troilus's song; just the contrary, however, he soon learns, is the case – see *Troilus and Criseyde* 2.22–49.

[9] See, further, Shoaf, *Dante*, p. 132, and Michel Serres, *The Parasite*, trans. L. R. Schehr (Baltimore, 1982), pp. 160 and 194, on the 'white domino'.

[10] For an extended discussion of this issue, see Shoaf, *Dante*, pp. 142–57.

[11] For the complete version of this argument, see my 'Chaucer and Medusa: *The Franklin's Tale*', *Chaucer Review* 21, 2 (Fall, 1986), pp. 274–90.

poetry is the question of the relation between the letter and the spirit, the literal and the metaphoric. His reading of Dante, in particular, sharpened his awareness of this problem, and especially his reading of *Inferno*, cantos 9 and 10. These cantos, which are the cantos of the heretics, especially the Epicureans, are also the cantos of Medusa. And in Dante's figure of the Medusa, Chaucer found an adequate image for his own understanding of the dynamics of the letter and the spirit. This image and the understanding resolved in it help to articulate, in particular, the structure of *The Franklin's Tale*, and it is possible, therefore, in this tale to recover an especially informative moment of Chaucer's reading of Dante. In fact, *The Franklin's Tale* in certain ways is a palimpsest of *Inferno*, cantos 9 and 10, especially in its concern with Epicureanism, petrification, illusion, surfaces and magic; it is also a crucial example of the power of the pun in Chaucer's poetry – of the way he responded to the call of the phoneme.

After Aurelius has told Dorigen that 'the rokkes been aweye',

> He taketh his leve, and she *astoned* stood;
> In al hir face nas a drope of blood.
> She wende nevere han come in swich a trappe.
> 'Allas', quod she, 'that evere this sholde happe!
> For wende I nevere by possibilitee
> That swich a *monstre* or merveille myghte be!
> It is agayns the proces of nature.'

V (F) 1339–45 (emphasis added)

The word 'monstre', which occurs only three times in *The Canterbury Tales*, only 11 in all of Chaucer's works,[12] authorizes our understanding here a pun in *astoned* – namely, *a—stoned*, that is, 'turned to stone'. The *monstre* which Dorigen 'sees' is the Medusa, she who turns to stone those who look on her.[13] *The Franklin's Tale* is precisely an essay in the astonishment/a–stone–ishment of surfaces. Dorigen is so *astoned* by the *surface* of Aurelius's words that she does not even bother to go look at the coast, to see, to investigate, the truth of his claim. She is *astoned* by the *monstre* of the letter, and this Medusa inhibits her asking (really, a simple question), what does it mean?

In *The Franklin's Tale*, Chaucer explores the effects, uniformly ambiguous and problematic, of appearances or illusions on those who cannot penetrate the rhetoric of either or both, and the end of his exploration is to recommend, however obliquely, a certain moral vigilance to his readers, an attitude of preparedness which never shrinks from going beneath the

[12] I rely for my statistics on J. S. P. Tatlock and A. G. Kennedy, *A Concordance to the Complete Works of Geoffrey Chaucer* (1927; rpt Gloucester, Mass., 1963) *sub voce*.

[13] For Medusa as *monster*, see Ovid's *Metamorphoses* 5.216–17, ed. G. Lafaye, 3 vols (1930; rpt Paris, 1972).

surfaces, or literal meanings, of texts, to isolate and identify the hidden motives which mobilize their rhetoric – especially the drive for originality.

I depend for my arguments to a certain extent on the role of the Medusa in Dante's *Commedia*: there, she is a figure of literalism, of the letter that kills (2 Corinthians 3:6), and, correspondingly, of that kind of reading which insists on the letter and resists figuration, that reading which refuses to lift the veil or, indeed, if need be, to rend the veil, to see underneath.[14] The crucial moment in the *Commedia*, which Chaucer must have known intimately, occurs in the ninth canto of *Inferno*.

After the Furies have threatened Vergil and Dante with Medusa (*Inferno* 9.49–54),[15] Vergil hides the pilgrim's eyes (*Inferno* 9.55–60), lest he be turned to stone, and then, in one of his famous addresses to the reader,[16] Dante exclaims:

> O voi ch'avete li 'ntelletti sani,
> mirate la dottrina che s'asconde
> sotto 'l velame de li versi strani.
> (*Inferno* 9.61–3)

(O you possessed of sturdy intellects, / observe the teaching that is hidden here / beneath the veil of verses so obscure.)

Dante does not, in other words, want his text to astonish his readers; he does not want it to be stony (*petrosa* – as were his rhymes to the *donna petrosa*[17]) or to turn others to stone; he does not want it to inhibit the necessary penetration of the letter which reading requires of 'sani intelletti'; he does not want his text, Medusa-like, to induce either *oblivio* or blindness.[18] Quite the contrary, he wants his text to awaken vigilance in his readers; he wants it to open their eyes, that they not be blind to the significances beyond the letter. Hence he urges his readers to lift the veil, to penetrate the text, to see underneath – all of which are procedures of right reading which Chaucer's

---

[14] See John Freccero, 'Medusa: The Letter and the Spirit', *Yearbook of Italian Studies* (1972), pp. 1–18; also in *Dante: The Poetics of Conversion*, ed. Rachel Jacoff (Cambridge, Mass., 1986), pp. 119–35.

[15] The translation used here and elsewhere is Allen Mandelbaum, *The Divine Comedy of Dante Alighieri, 'Inferno'* (New York, 1982); this particular passage is found on p. 79.

[16] See Erich Auerbach, 'Dante's Addresses to the Reader', *Romance Philology* 3 (1949), pp. 1–26; also Leo Spitzer, 'The Addresses to the Reader in the *Commedia*', in *Romanische Literaturstudien 1936–1956* (Tübingen, 1959), pp. 574–95.

[17] Freccero, 'Medusa', has shown that *Inferno*, canto 9, is a palimpsest of Dante's earlier *rime* to the 'stony lady' (pp. 11–13); for further helpful comment, see Giuseppe Mazzotta, *Dante, Poet of the Desert* (Princeton, 1979), pp. 275–95.

[18] See the *Enciclopedia Dantesca*, 3: 883, *sub voce*, for the common gloss *oblivio* on Medusa. For the etymology, 'quasi *mèidesan*, quod videre non possit', see the sources in Freccero, 'Medusa', p. 7, and Mazzotta, *Dante*, pp. 277–9 and pp. 277–8 n. 1.

Dorigen omits because she cannot, does not, and will not see – because Aurelius and the Clerk of Orleans's 'text' has 'astoned' her, turned her to stone.

Following the lead in Dante's text, I want to propose that Chaucer wrote *The Franklin's Tale* as an exposure or penetration of literalism, the word *monstre* and the pun in *astoned* being two of the many clues to this design. Hence the importance, now clearly evident, of the fact that Dorigen never *sees* the illusion on the coast of Brittany: all she 'sees' is Aurelius's *word*, his narrated 'text' – that is, the letter – and this letter, a Medusa, so blinds her, so astonishes her, that she cannot even bother, once under its literalistic, gorgonic spell, to test whether it refers to any reality. She cannot bother even to try to read.

As the Franklin observes, she is already like a stone in that she is easily engraved or impressed:

> By proces, as ye knowen everichoon,
> Men may so longe graven in a stoon
> *Til som figure therinne emprented be.*
> So longe han they conforted hire til she
> Receyved hath, by hope and by resoun,
> The emprentyng of hire consolacioun,
> Thurgh which hir grete sorwe gan aswage;
> She may nat alwey duren in swich rage.
>
> V (F) 829–36 (emphasis added)

This likeness to a stone only hardens as events develop. And such stoniness is Chaucer's target in the tale. He would isolate it and circumscribe it so as to purge it from his reading and also from his readers' reading. The tale is written, in short, and is to be read as an instance of how writers and readers should *not* read and write. It is a figure of the abuses of figuration.

The pun in *astoned* is one of the means at Chaucer's disposal to cross the Franklin's motives and expose him for the hollow man he really is – a status-anxious parvenu.[19] We first realize his status anxiety during the exchange between him and Harry Bailey right after *The Squire's Tale*:

> 'Straw for youre gentillesse!' quod oure Hoost.
> 'What, Frankeleyn! Pardee, sire, wel thou woost
> That ech of yow moot tellen atte leste
> A tale or two, or breken his biheste.'
> 'That knowe I wel, sire,' quod the Frankeleyn.

[19] On the debate concerning the Franklin's moral character, see *Chaucer Review* 21, 2 (1986), pp. 288 n. 12.

'I prey yow, *haveth me nat in desdeyn*,
Though to this man I speke a word or two.'

V (F) 695–702 (emphasis added)

The words 'haveth me nat in desdeyn' are crucial; they are just the over-reaction, just the exaggeration, one would expect from the guy on the make, the man with too much at stake in how he appears before those whom he feels he must at all costs impress. Everything the Franklin does hereafter is intended to make sure, as sure as possible, that the pilgrims do *not* 'have him in disdain'. From this point on, he will concentrate all his efforts on presenting as smooth and glossy a surface as he can, for if we are *astoned* by the surface, we will not be moved to investigate the depths.

We can explain his behavior, in part, at this point, by recourse to his Epicureanism.[20] As we learn in *The General Prologue*, the Franklin is 'Epicurus owene sone' (I A 336), and for the present argument, the most important consequence of this genealogy is his implication in Epicurean epistemology. Epicurus taught that 'all sensations are true'. Only reasoning or judgment can err.[21] The importance of this position for understanding *The Franklin's Tale* is obvious; it is a major source of the irony in the poem. In fact, the characters rely principally if not exclusively on the evidence of their senses, especially the sense of sight, but that evidence and those senses are almost always unreliable. Moreover, the judgment of each character and finally of the Franklin himself in one way or another at one time or another errs. Furthermore, this reliance on the senses is also a dependence obviously on surfaces – again, especially in regard to sight – and thus the Epicurean genealogy of the Franklin serves Chaucer's exposure or penetration of his superficiality, of his status-anxious flight from all depths.

Of course, there are depths in *The Franklin's Tale*. But the depths are themselves illusions – paradoxically, they too are surfaces. I refer, I should perhaps make clear, to the Franklin's depths, not Chaucer's; Chaucer's depths are not Medusa – this is one reason why we read him so closely: he does not turn us to stone. But the Franklin does, or would if he could.

His depths, or say profundities, are illusions which he masks to appear as profundities, and these masks are visages of Medusa: if we look into them, we will be petrified, afraid to question the Franklin, convinced rather that he is *right*. The most important instance of the paradox of illusory depths, depths that are surfaces and Medusas, is the sleight of hand by means of

[20] Two recent studies of Epicureanism pertinent to my argument are: Robert P. Miller, 'The Epicurean Homily on Marriage by Chaucer's Franklin', *Mediaevalia* 6 (1980), pp. 151–86; and Emerson Brown, Jr, 'Epicurus and Voluptas in Late Antiquity: The Curious Testimony of Martianus Capella', *Traditio* 38 (1982), pp. 75–106.

[21] J. M. Rist, *Epicurus: An Introduction* (Cambridge, 1972), p. 19 and pp. 37–40.

which the Franklin tries to deflect attention away from Arveragus's desperate expediency:

> Paraventure an heep of yow, ywis,
> Wol holden hym a lewed man in this
> That he wol putte his wyf in jupartie.
> Herkneth the tale er ye upon hire crie.
> She may have bettre fortune than yow semeth;
> And whan that ye han herd the tale, demeth.
>
> V F 1493–8

The perfect Epicurean gesture. Wait until all the evidence is in, let your senses collect all the *idols*, and then judge (*demeth*).[22] But while we are thus on hold, playing this waiting game – while we are gazing at this Medusa, petrified by the illusion of honor, *gentillesse*, and noble self-sacrifice – precisely what we are *not* doing in our petrification is investigating, penetrating, prodding the tale, its text, to ask the one question sure to betray the Franklin's hand if he fails to keep the Gorgon in our faces: why does Arveragus threaten Dorigen's life if she reveals to anyone what has happened to her?

In one breath, Arveragus claims, in lordly fashion, 'Trouthe is the hyeste thyng that man may kepe', but no sooner is that out than 'he brast anon to wepe' (V F 1479–80); then, in the very next breath, as if this were not bad enough, he goes on, compounding his expediency and hyprocrisy, to command her:

> I yow forbede, *up peyne of deeth*,
> That nevere, whil thee lasteth lyf ne breeth,
> To no wight telle thou of this aventure –
> As I may best, I wol my wo endure –
> Ne make no contenance of hevynesse,
> That folk of yow may demen harm or gesse.
>
> V F 1481–6

These speeches issue from the desperation of a moral adolescent whose principal concern is to save his face, no matter what the cost – even if the cost should be the life of his wife. But the Franklin has managed to create with his aside the illusion of a depth – there's more here, he implies with this Medusa, than meets the eye – in order, paradoxically, to keep us from lifting the veil (the veil of his rhetoric) at this point. If we *were* to lift the veil at this point, if we were to awaken from the stony silence in which the Franklin has cast us, the game would be up – we would see Arveragus for what he is. Hence, we are promised a depth, but the promise of a depth is

---

[22] On the *eïdola*, see ibid., pp. 83–8.

only a surface, a Gorgon, which astonishes us. And thus *astoned* we will not, the Franklin presumes, expose Arveragus or him. However, this depth, despite all the Franklin's prestidigitation, does prove, inevitably, to be just one more surface – like the depth of Arveragus's *soveraynetee* which in fact is only the name thereof (V F 751), a Medusa of a name to astonish all who look on the marriage between Dorigen and him.

From the position we have just achieved, we can expose the Franklin for the hollow man he really is. He distracts us from Arveragus's moral compromise – he cannot supress it, of course, since one or more of the pilgrims may have already heard the *lai* elsewhere – in order to secure his own *name of gentillesse*. For if he can bring the tale to its bizarre conclusion, with its improbable reconciliations, then he can pose his *demande d'amour* or *questione d'amore* – 'Which was the mooste fre, as thynketh yow?' (V F 1622) – in emulation of the Knight (I A 1347–8), and this will be to suggest his parity with the Knight (whose son, incidentally, he has interrupted in order to tell his tale) and thus it will also imply that the quality and degree of his *gentillesse* are as good as the Knight's. Moreover, having thus slyly sidled up alongside the Knight, he also and just as slyly takes center stage since his *demande d'amour* also asks 'Which was the most *frank* [free]?' – that is, which is the most like *me*, the *Frank*leyn? All of the Franklin's rhetorical strategies, in brief, conspire to set him before our eyes: we never do *not* see the Franklin. Like his disclaimer of familiarity with the colors of rhetoric (V F 726–7), which instantly assures us that he is very familiar with them, and like his interruption of his tale to gloss his own figures ('th'orisonte hath reft the sonne his lyght – / This is as muche to seye as it was nyght' – V F 1017–18), his *demande d'amour* tells us that the Franklin is quite up on the *gentle* art of *fin'amors*. His *sauce* is always *poynaunt*.

The Franklin's Tale, his interpretation of the *lai*, is an idolatry of sorts.[23] The Franklin would intercept and misdirect the substitutionality of inter-pretation.[24] The Franklin would detour our interrogation of the signifier, by which we constantly substitute a later signifier for an earlier one in our search for the momentary probability of meaning, because he knows that, in his case, the signifier has hardened, has petrified, into the idolatrous signified of his own self-aggrandizement. If he does not intercept and misdirect our interrogation of the signifier, he knows we will discover, to our (not to mention his) dismay, that he does not signify, having long since ceased signifying, already forever signified in the *eîdola* of his senses. An idolator, he has petrified the process of signifying, prematurely arrested it,

<hr/>

[23] On the Medusa and idolatry, see Freccero, 'Medusa', esp. pp. 6–10.
[24] Derrida would perhaps use in place of this phrase the term 'supplementation'; see Jacques Derrida, *Of Grammatology*, trans. Gayatri Spivak (Baltimore, 1976), pp. 144–5.

wresting the probability of meaning into an illusory and self-serving certainty. Think of his table which 'dormant in his halle alway / Stood redy covered al the longe day' (I A 353–4) – *fixed*, in other words, or *frozen* in place to be an icon of his wealth. The Franklin is all surface – what you see is what you get, 'poynaunt sauce'. Hence his desperate attempt to persuade us that his surface, a finished signified, is a depth, a mysterious signifier, crying out for interpretation. The Franklin must, in short, sign us up as co-conspirators in his literalism.

He must astonish us. Even as Aurelius astonishes Dorigen, causing a sight which she sees *only* in his words to petrify her. Aurelius turns her to stone, by forcing her not to probe the surface – the surface, note well, of his words (which is the surface of the letter) – for its probable meaning; rather she invents meanings, pseudo-depths, astonished as she is by the Medusa of Aurelius's letter, which, in turn, terrify her even further by their gorgonic aspect, moving her to contemplate suicide (V F 1360–6; 1458). In both cases, the necessary intelligence to convert signifiers into other signifiers – to ask, in short, what does it mean? – is inhibited. In both cases, questioning is intercepted and either suppressed altogether or purposely misdirected. In both cases, signification and interpretation alike are petrified.

Because the Franklin seeks to astonish his audience, to 'petrify' them, Chaucer interrupts his rhetoric and exposes his ploy by the play of the pun in 'she astoned stood'. When we hear the pun, we realize, beyond the Franklin's control of our responses, that 'a-stone-ishment' is a very real peril in acts of interpretation, and we are thus awakened to new vigilance. But this is also to say that the signifier *astoned* in Chaucer's text is precisely *not* the kind of signifier which the Franklin deploys: it is not stony or petrifying; quite the contrary, because it is a *pun*, it is flexible, vivifying, in no way hardening – it is an openness or (w)hole in the text whose fissure promises the gift of gap, or our deepened understanding of the Franklin and his motives.[25]

From this position we can consider the final two puns from Chaucer's texts which I wish to examine in the present essay. They are 'Nowelis flood' in *The Miller's Tale* and (much more notorious a crux) 'cosyn' from *The General Prologue*. Together, these two puns will lead us to some tentative conclusions about the play of puns, the gift of gap, in Chaucer's poetry and on towards some observations about various puns in the poetry of his major contemporaries.

Carpenter John's famous pun would, of course, be news to him:

---

[25] If memory serves me, my student Amie Williams first used the phrase 'the gift of gap' in my seminar on Dante and Chaucer in Yale College in the spring of 1982. I have since that time appropriated the phrase to my own, multifarious uses.

This carpenter out of his slomber sterte,
And herde oon crien 'water!' as he were wood,
And thoughte, 'Allas, now comth Nowelis flood!'

The Miller's Tale I A 3816–18

He is hardly aware of what he is really saying or of the way it serves to expose him. On the contrary, he is confused, unable to hear what he has said (Noah and Nöel); the dual and duel of sounds in the word issue in a pun which does not so much transgress intention (questionable, anyway) as it opens a (w)hole in the text for the reader to enter into the play of the poetry.

The duel of sounds in 'Nowelis' produces a dual of new senses, and the poet accepts the duel to enjoy the dual ('It was not a choice / Between, but of' – Stevens).[26] This is to say, he welcomes the differences or contraries within the pun and, as within a field of play, he lets them duel in order to dual (it is in play that our instinct to duel can become the imagination to dual), knowing that in this way the dual may redeem the duel: the dual, the poet knows, will remain always open, never closed, as a mere duel alone inevitably is.

We may cast this a different way, in other terms also arising from the text. The poet does not cover the (w)holes that, however troublingly, constitute our life. It is the (w)hole between 'Noe' and 'Nowelis' – such that the one falls into the other ('Noe' is [and, of course, is not] 'inside' 'Nowelis') – that constitutes the brilliant pun. And the poet must leave this (w)hole open if he would benefit from the gift of gap. Only so can the gift of gap open the text to the heady parody that makes it at once so very funny and so very profound.[27]

This practice, however, is not without its perils, as Chaucer well knew. Hence the part played by (w)holes in *The Miller's Tale*. The most famous holes in *The Canterbury Tales*, in fact, are in *The Miller's Tale*, most notably Carpenter John's window and Alison's 'naked ers' (I A 3734). 'And at the wyndow out she putte hir hole' (I A 3732) not only marks one of the funniest moments in *The Canterbury Tales* but also one of the most significant, for when Absalon kisses Alison's 'naked ers' through John's window, Chaucer acknowledges in these three holes (and in the fourth, soon to be mentioned, of Nicholas's anus) the inescapable if sometimes dismaying dependency of relationships (of all sorts) on gaps – we cannot make wholes without holes (another way of saying, we are always in debt, like it or not).

[26] On the terms *duel* and *dual* and their importance to the interpretation of puns, see Shoaf, *Milton, Poet of Duality*, pp. 66–71.

[27] For a helpful introduction to the parody of the story of Christ's incarnation (the Christmas story) in *The Miller's Tale*, see Beryl Rowland, 'Chaucer's Blasphemous Churl: A New Interpretation of the *Miller's Tale*', in *Chaucer and Middle English Studies: In Honor of Rossell Hope Robbins*, ed. Beryl Rowland (London, 1974), pp. 43–55.

Hence, just as without the (w)hole between 'Noe' and '*No*(w)*el*', there would be no pun in 'Nowelis flood', so without the (w)hole between *The Knight's Tale* and *The Miller's Tale*, there would be no parody pointing the crucial difference as well as extensive identity between the two tales.[28] Similarly, without the (w)hole (or gap) between one leaf and another, no reader could 'turne over the leef and chese another tale' (I A 3177); and in that case, a large part of Chaucer's irony would be lost, for the reader who turns over the leaf from *The Knight's Tale* to another tale, covering the (w)hole or gap between it and *The Miller's Tale* by *not* reading *The Miller's Tale*, is the reader who makes Chaucer's point: his or her flight from the hole, in this case from 'harlotrie' (I A 3184), proves the importance of the hole to the whole – by protesting too much, he or she acknowledges that the whole is impossible without the hole. The reader, on the other hand, who happily turns over the leaf to *read The Miller's Tale* also, of course, makes Chaucer's point – only this is a good deal easier: his or her ready delight in holes tells the whole story.

And the whole story would be incomplete without the realization that *The Miller's Tale* is, in effect, a pun on *The Knight's Tale* (*The Knight's Tale* is [and is not] 'inside' *The Miller's Tale*). The pun enables Chaucer to interrupt and to check the pretensions of the Knight to define and determine the nature and the course of the tale-telling contest. When the Miller cries out, 'I kan a noble tale for the nones, / With which I wol now quite the Knyghtes tale' (I A 3126–7), Chaucer initiates a process of duelling and dual-ling which will constantly interrupt each pilgrim's efforts at closure on the contest, closure which would give him or her the upper hand.

Puns are only one part but certainly an important part of this process since the very nature of the pun is to be both a duel and a dual. The pun interrupts premature closure by calling attention to the open hole in a word or a phrase or a structure which betrays the facile and self-aggrandizing whole which the pilgrim has all too often been attempting to assert. And, finally, we can see the importance of this process and of the role which puns play in it by observing Chaucer apply it to himself, to the pilgrim-narrator in *The General Prologue*, in one of the most difficult as it is also one of the most important puns in *The Canterbury Tales*.

The narrator is Chaucer's solution to the problem of fiction, or the lie that tells the truth.[29] One crucial question facing every artist who does not want to deceive and seduce but must perforce use many of the same devices as the 'con'-artist does, is, how to tell the audience how to tell the difference

---

[28] See Shoaf, *Dante*, pp. 163–72 and the bibliography cited there on the complex relationsihp between the two tales.

[29] See Shoaf, *Dante*, pp. 34 and 247 n. 27 for discussion and documentation on this issue.

while he is telling a tale, the difference between a 'con' and a true lie? In answering this question, Chaucer discovered his originality.

The artist tells his audience how to tell the difference by regularly calling attention to his mediation, by systematically interrupting – that is, fragmenting or gapping – his narration, by opening holes in the whole of the fiction through which the audience can always see the difference between fiction and reality, by inscribing himself, in short, as narrator within the narrative such that the audience cannot forget his mediation.

Chaucer is nowhere more adept at this practice than in the pun on 'cosyn' ('cousin' and 'cozen') in *The General Prologue*:

> For this ye knowen al so wel as I:
> Whoso shal telle a tale after a man,
> He moot reherce as ny as evere he kan ·
> Everich a word, if it be in his charge,
> Al speke he never so rudeliche and large,
> Or ellis he moot telle his tale untrewe,
> Or feyne thyng, or fynde wordes newe. . . .
> Eek Plato seith, whoso that kan hym rede,
> The wordes moote be *cosyn* to the dede.
>
> I A 730–6; 741–2 (emphasis added)

Let a narrator tell the audience that he is telling someone else's tale and the illusion of the tale will always be checked by the illusion of the narrator re-telling the tale. No matter how he protests the accuracy of his retelling, the protest will always acknowledge, call attention to, the difference between his words and the truth. We can never forget that he is creating an illusion, and he, therefore, can never astonish us with one.

Let him, moreover, protest the accuracy of his report with a pun, whether or not he, the narrator, 'intends' the pun, and we will be all the more sensitive to his mediation of the words of others – it is *he* who is mediating them. Next, let the pun occur in a sentence which is protesting the fidelity of words to deeds, and we can only wonder – be *astoned* without being *a-stoned* – at the play of consciousness in the poet's artistry – we can only join with him in the game, playing with the illusion even as he does.

Finally, in addition to all this, let the pun be 'The wordes moote be *cosyn* to the dede' and we see with the poet the (w)hole of his art. On the one hand, before the pun is heard, we realize that cousinage is a distant relationship, a relationship of greater difference than brother or sister or, especially, father or mother. And, therefore, the word insists on the distance and disparity between words and deeds. Even as it argues for a relationship, it concedes that the relationship is one of greater difference than similarity. On the other hand, hearing the pun, we realize that *cosyn* is a dual arising from the duel between the senses 'related by blood' and 'deceive',[30] and Chaucer is acknowledging, we know, that words can cozen or cheat or deceive the deed – even as, here, *cosyn* is *cosyn* to the deed of 'cousining' (it 'cozens' that deed) by conceding difference in the very claim of similarity. The whole of the meaning in this line can never deny or conceal the hole from which it emerges, and the emptiness of language is here the occasion for the truth to trace its devious way to the fullness of the light.

The pun in *cosyn* insists on the duel and the dual between words and deeds. In a line like 'The wordes moote be cosyn to the dede', the difference between words and deeds can never be forgotten – the pun prohibits a-stone-ishment. But even as it does so, it condemns the artist to the deferral of closure and of the pleasures of its innocence. It exiles him to the middled and muddled estate of mediation where interpretation is endless and closure is always a fiction. In such an estate the artist may insist on the truth of his fictions but only if he first acknowledges that they *are* fictions – not real, just cousins to the deed. After all, his wit is short, we do understand (*General Prologue* I A 746).

In an essay of this nature, I cannot include all the material that would be ideally wanted in my argument. I must omit, for example, any detailed consideration of the fifteenth-century lyric, 'While thou hast gode and getest gode', where there is an obvious pun on *good* and *God* (as, for example, in line 35: 'Ken thy gode and know thy gode') and where the *V* and *I* refrain – 'With an "V" and an "I" gode will come and go' (lines 9, 19, 29, 39) – probably plays with the *vi* of the grammatical expression, 'ex vi transicionis' ('by the power of transitivity'), which is so important, we know, to *Piers Plowman* and which may be the lyric's way of articulating the *transition* from one sense of *gode* to another.[31] But if I must omit this and other fascinating examples, I would disappoint obvious expectation by not discussing examples from Chaucer's two greatest contemporaries, the *Gawain*-poet and William Langland.

The *Gawain*-poet's play with puns and play of puns I have studied

---

[30] See Davis, *A Chaucer Glossary*, p. 28; see, further, Ruth M. Fisher, ' "Cosyn" and "Cosynage": Complicated Punning in Chaucer's "Shipman's Tale"?', *Notes and Queries* 210 (1965), pp. 168–70.

[31] The lyric is conveniently found in *Middle English Lyrics*, eds Maxwell S. Luria and Richard L. Hoffman (New York, 1974), no. 14, pp. 14–15; it is no. 4083 in *The Index of Middle English Verse*, eds Carleton Brown and R. S. Robbins (New York, 1943). On the crucial phrase, 'ex vi transicionis' in *Piers Plowman* (B. 13. 151), see Robert E. Kaske, '*Ex vi transicionis* and its Passage in *Piers Plowman*', in *Style and Symbolism in 'Piers Plowman': A Modern Critical Anthology*, ed. Robert J. Blanch (Knoxville, 1969), pp. 228–63; and Edward C. Schweitzer, ' "Half a laumpe lyne in Latyne" and Patience's Riddle in *Piers Plowman*', *JEGP* 73 (1974), pp. 313–27.

elsewhere, as part of a monograph on *Sir Gawain and the Green Knight*.[32] Here, them, I will only call attention to one of the most obvious of his puns in that poem, namely *cost*.[33] This word, of Old Norse derivation (*kostr*), means 'quality' or 'characteristic', but it is also obviously homophonic with *cost*, as in 'what one pays for a thing'.[34] And out of this and similar puns, the *Gawain*-poet generates a vision of exchange in human life – exchange, which always puts closure in question – equalled only by the vision of exchange entertained by Langland, a vision predicated on *redde quod debes*.[35]

Piers Plowman is concerned, of course, with more than just exchange, and I am making no brief here for the poem's ultimate theme. However, like the works of the *Gawain*-poet and of Chaucer, it pursues its concerns in part by means of puns, and I would like to conclude my remarks in this essay by examining one of these puns in light of my argument to this point.[36]

The pun is spoken by Wit during a conversation between him and Will:

> [Tynynge] of tyme, truþe woot þe soþe,
> Is moost yhated vpon erþe of hem þat ben in heuene;
> And siþþe to spille speche, þat [spire] is of grace
> And goddes gleman and a game of heuene.
> Wolde neuere þe feiþful fader [h]is fiþele were vntempred
> Ne his gleman a gedelyng, a goere to tauernes.
>
> *Piers Plowman* B. 9. 99–104

This is remarkable poetry, conscious of its medium, language, in a highly personal way. And we can locate the self-consciousness exactly, in this case, in the pun on *spire*, both 'shoot' or 'sprout'[37] and also, I will argue, 'breath', as in the *spiration* of the Holy Spirit.[38] In fact, in this pun and its context, we find an attitude toward language highly characteristic of Langland – in effect, almost a signature.

[32] See R. A. Shoaf, *The Poem as Green Girdle: 'Commercium' in 'Sir Gawain and the Green Knight'*, Humanities Monograph no. 55 (Gainesville, Fla., 1984), esp. pp. 1 and 42–5.
[33] *Sir Gawain and the Green Knight*, eds J. R. R. Tolkein and E. V. Gordon, 2nd edn ed. Norman Davis (Oxford, 1968; rpt with corrections 1968), line 1849, p. 51, for one of several (for a total of eight) examples.
[34] Shoaf, *Green Girdle*, pp. 5, 34–5.
[35] See, e.g., Passus B. 19. 261 and B. 20. 309. The text of the poem cited here and elsewhere is that of the B-version edited by George Kane and E. T. Donaldson (London, 1975).
[36] Here I am drawing on my study, ' "Speche þat spire is of grace": A Note on *Piers Plowman* B. 9. 104', forthcoming in *The Yearbook of Langland Studies* 1987.
[37] These are, for example, the glosses offered by A. V. C. Schmidt in his edition of the poem, *The Vision of Piers Plowman* (London, 1978), p. 95.
[38] On this complex issue, see Ronald L. Martinez, 'The Pilgram's Answer to Bonagiunta and the Poetics of the Spirit', *Stanford Italian Review* (Spring 1983), pp. 37–63; see also Mazzotta, *Dante*, pp. 192–226 and his earlier 'Dante's Literary Typology', *MLN* 87 (1972), pp. 1–19.

If speech is not only the 'shoot' or 'offspring' of grace but also the 'breath', the 'spiration', of grace, then Wit expresses a simultaneity of senses which communicates precise theological information. Speech, in Langland's Christian context, is the shoot of grace *because* it is the breath of grace. Speech as the breath of grace makes it possible to say that speech is the shoot of grace.

If the grace of the Holy Spirit did not breathe in men, the speech of men could not say that speech is a shoot or offspring of grace. The pun, in effect, is the gift of grace: the 'spire of grace' makes such multiple senses possible ('the Spirit blows [*spirat*] where it will and you hear its voice, but you do not know whence it comes or where it goes' – John 3.8). The 'spire of grace' issuing from the Holy Spirit inspires the speech of men to say, for example, that speech is 'spire of grace'. Without such in*spira*tion, the speech of men could not be 'Goddes gleman and a game of hevene', for 'spire' (sense: 'shoot') is *already* 'spire(d)' (sense: 'breath[ed]', 'inspire[d]') in that it is an improper or metaphoric or catechrestic usage. Speech, in other words, is definitely *not* a 'shoot' *properly* speaking. And this very impropriety is the effect of *spiration*, the breath of the grace of the Holy Spirit. The first sense is an effect of the other, the indeterminate but nonetheless true spiration of grace, and thus Langland's line enacts what it says: 'speche, that spire is of grace' is(/as)[39] speech that is inspired of grace.

By the very same token, however – and here the pun exceeds Wit's intention if it does not actually transgress it – speech *can* be *spilled*, can become a 'fiþele vntempred' and 'a gedelyng, a goere to tauernes'. Precisely because speech is 'spire' (shoot and breath), it is capable of multiple meanings; and these can be, all too easily, perverted – into frivolity, or worse. Langland knows as well as Chaucer and the *Gawain*-poet do how difficult it is to control the direction of the spirit (so to speak) – witness his attempt to define 'treasure' in *Passus* 1 (lines 45, 56, 70, 83, 85, 137) or his bold appropriation of 'coveitise' to positive significance.[40] Langland understands that to be able to say at all that 'speche . . . spire is of grace' is also to risk speech's becoming 'a gedelyng, a goere to tauernes'.

Important support for this argument can be found in a passage from Gregory the Great's *Moralia in Iob* (on Job 33.4), a passage which Langland could easily have known:

---

[39] We could write this 'is' *sous rature* precisely to mark the impropriety of its copula; see Jacques Derrida, 'Différance', in *Margins of Philosophy*, trans. Alan Bass (Chicago, 1982), pp. 1–27, esp. p. 6.

[40] See B. 5. 52: 'lat Truþe be youre coveitise' and B. 13. 150: 'Kynde love coveiteþ noȝt no catel but speche'.

For what are our words but seed? And when this is poured forth in due measure, the mind of the hearer, as the womb of her who conceives, is made fruitful for an offspring of good works. But if it escapes at improper times, polluting him that emits it, it loses its generating power. . . . Seed, then, which is intended for the purpose of procreation, when it escapes in an improper manner, pollutes the other members; and speech also, by which learning ought to be implanted in the hearts of the hearers, if uttered out of due order, brings disgrace even on the truths it utters.[41]

In other words, precisely because speech is seminal, it can also be onanistic and polluting. Note also that we have in Gregory's words a possible if not probable source (doubtless among others) for understanding Langland's verb 'spille': because speech is seminal, it can also be *spilled*. In short, the possibility of multiplicity in language is necessarily also the possibility of promiscuity in language ('a gedelyng, a goere to tavernes'): because language is always potentially improper (that is, metaphoric[42]), it is also always potentially impure.

The whole among multiple senses, then, can degenerate into merely a hole. The labor of the poet, therefore, must be to prevent this from happening, to preserve the whole. To preserve the whole, however, the poet cannot simply close the hole. Death will ensue upon such (de)termination. He must rather flow with the play of language and especially of puns; even if the flow flows through flaws, he must go with the flow or never be free. He must enter the spoiled garden (though garden still) of unpredictable and indeterminate flowers, his rhetoric subject ever to duality and mutability.

The critic, following the poet, who seeks the power of determinacy, to determine the meaning of a given text, walks in the garden with 'low breathings coming after him' (*The Prelude* I.323). Like the young Wordsworth, he must be furtive because his borrowings may actually be thefts. His determination that this word or image or figure means one thing and not another, founded upon profound philology, may not be 'love of words' at all but rather fear that the 'love of words', like all desire, is transgressive and transumptive, provocative of change. To overcome this fear, to re-enter the garden, the critic would do well to become something of a juxtologist himself, a reader for whom even random juxtaposition of terms is sufficient logic to initiate discovery. The juxtological critic is not afraid of coincidence, does not seek (Cartesian) certitude, is always suspicious of

---

[41] *Morals on the Book of Job*, trans. by Members of the English Church (Oxford, 1848), 3: 1: 24; the Latin text is found in J.-P. Migne, ed., *Patrologia Latina* 76: 267CD. For other examples and a stimulating discussion of their importance to understanding later medieval poetry, see Eugene Vance, 'The Differing Seed: Dante's Brunetto Latini', in *Mervelous Signals: Poetics and Sign Theory in the Middle Ages* (Lincoln, Neb., 1986), pp. 230–55, esp. pp. 239–41.

[42] In medieval Latin, the words for 'literal' and 'metaphoric' were *proprie* and *improprie* respectively; see Shoaf, *Dante*, pp. 33–4 and 247 nn. 25–7.

'clarity' (whose ideology, he asks, is served by this 'clarity'?). The juxto-logical critic, in fact, resembles the poet, learning his patience – the *weakness* Auden reminds us of, the *choice* Stevens reminds us of:

> He chose to include the things
> That in each other are included, the whole,
> The complicate, the amassing harmony.

4

The Jest Disgested: Perspectives on History in *Henry V*

Krystian Czerniecki

> our history shall with full mouth
> Speak freely of our acts.
> (I.ii.230–1)[1]

Of all Shakespeare's histories, none is more insistently self-reflexive, more obsessively concerned with the conditions of the possibility of its own representation, than *Henry V*. An explicitly articulated concern of the prologue, epilogue and choruses, this preoccupation comes, through various techniques of verbal repetition and the strategic and/or fantasmatic deploying of puns, to inhabit the mimetic enterprise itself. My epigram, which comes from the mouth of King Henry, from the mouth, so to speak, of Monmouth, may be taken as a figure for this enterprise. I will be concerned with the metadramatic and metapsychological significance of the pun implicit in Henry's boast. What it is to speak freely with full mouth, not just loudly, as the line is usually glossed, but literally, in an oxymoronic breach of etiquette, with one's mouth full, and why this is the only way one can speak in a history play of history – this is the burden of what follows.

I

When the chorus first takes the stage in *Henry V*, Shakespeare identifies his project in terms, not of plenitude, but of loss or deprivation:

> O for a Muse of fire, that would ascend
> The brightest heaven of invention!

---

[1] Unless otherwise indicated, references are to *The Riverside Shakespeare* (Boston, 1974) and will be indicated in the text. All emphasis will be my own.

A kingdom for a stage, princes to act,
And monarchs to behold the swelling scene!
Then should the warlike Harry, like himself,
Assume the port of Mars, and at his heels,
(Leashed in, like hounds) should famine, sword and, fire
Crouch for employment. But pardon, gentles all,
The flat unraised spirits that hath dar'd
On this unworthy scaffold to bring forth
So great an object.

(Pro.1–11)

The opening O of the chorus is situated in a rhetorical tradition in which it would customarily indicate the invocation of a muse, an apostrophe which claims the presence of the addressee (even if it draws attention, at least implicitly, to the pure rhetoricity of that claim). But this O, an O which will punningly become both stage and mouth, does not yield, as we might have expected, to apostrophe. Instead we begin with a wish ('O for a Muse of fire' rather than 'O Muse of fire') explicitly recognized as such, a wish which modulates into the lamented impossibility of a representation of history entirely adequate to its object.

The privative mode, evoked in the articulation of the wish, locates the dramatic project in the belated economy, not of grace or gift, but of labor.[2] This labor is the work of mourning engaged in by the play in its attempt to recover or recuperate (from) the loss of referential guarantee, the loss we might say, speculatively to be sure, of history. I will argue in what follows that two opposed strategies are at work in this recuperative project. On the one hand there is the work of mourning itself, the metaphorical representation of the lost object that in a certain psychoanalytic vocabulary would be called its introjection.[3] On the other hand, there is the fantasmatic incorporation of that object, a response to loss that is radically anti-metaphorical, marking the failure of any purely mimetic strategy, and associated not with mourning but with melancholia. Though the explicit project of the play privileges the first strategy, these two responses to loss are in constant competition. The play comes finally, I suggest, to subvert its authorized recuperative strategy by revealing the irreducibility of an incorporative moment in the face of loss.

As a prelude to the reading of *Henry V*, however, a further specification of the status of these concepts within the psychoanalytic discourse I have alluded to is in order. Abraham and Torok define introjection as a

---

[2] Rather than the gift of a benevolent muse, the success of the dramatic project will depend on work: 'Work, work your thoughts, and therein see a siege' (III.Cho.25). Much of this chapter will be concerned with the specific modality of this labor.

[3] See especially N. Abraham and M. Torok, 'Deuil *ou* mélancolie: introjecter – incorporer' in *L'Écorce et le noyau* (Paris, 1978), pp. 259–75.

dialectical process governing the passage from literal to figural, particular to general, from object- to intersubjective relations. Introjection begins with the experience of an empty mouth: the (absent) satisfactions of the mouth full of the maternal object are eventually replaced by those of the mouth empty of that object but filled with words addressed to a subject. One passes thus from the presence of the object to an 'auto-apprehension of its absence', language, insofar as it functions as determinate negation, affirming the absence of the object while, or rather, by *figuring* its presence, a figuration that can only have meaning in 'a community of empty mouths' and is guaranteed by the presence of the mother already possessing language.[4] It is this dialectical strategy that underlies the work of mourning. Forced by reality-testing to acknowledge the loss of a loved object, the subject introjects it, affirming its loss in the passage through language, while preserving it as figure in the self, 'dead *save in me*'.[5] The personal experience of loss becomes in this manner a collective, communicable one, an experience that can be known, and in some sense shared, the possibility of articulating the nature of a loss being the prerequisite of the piecemeal withdrawal of libidinal energy from the lost object which constitutes the working through of grief. The part of the self that had been invested in the object is freed from it, gathered back into the self and made available for new investment.

Incorporation, according to Abraham and Torok, is introjection's catastrophic reversal. In it the oral metaphor governing introjection is taken literally and thereby destroyed, the object itself, or a part of it, rather than some substitutive supplement, being introduced fantasmatically into the body.[6] In the event of the failure or impossibility of introjection – a function of the (perceived) abuse of the subject by its ego-ideal (the indispensable object of narcissistic identification) – the object and associated cathexes are vomited to the inside, swallowed (so that the loss does not have to be borne or

[4] Ibid., p. 263.

[5] J. Derrida, 'Fors', *The Georgia Review* 31 (1977), p. 71. This essay, which appeared in French as the introduction to Abraham and Torok, *Cryptonomie: Le Verbier de l'homme aux loups* (Paris, 1976), informs my reading of introjection and incorporation.

[6] The difference between introjection and incorporation is compared in Abraham and Torok, 'Deuil *ou* mélancolie' (p. 262) to the difference between learning a language and buying a dictionary. Here the essentially Hegelian provenance of these concepts is clear. Introjection would be analogous to the type of interiorizing memory or recollection Hegel understands by the term *Erinnerung*; incorporation would be associated with *Gedächtnis*, typified by the rote learning of lists. In Abraham and Torok, as in Hegel, the special privilege accorded the dialectics of internalization is problematized by its dependence on the non-dialectical modality with which it is contrasted. On this matter in Hegel, see Paul de Man, 'Sign and Symbol in Hegel's *Aesthetics*' in *Critical Inquiry* 8 (Summer 1982), pp. 761–75, esp. pp. 771–3. My chapter will address this question through the reading of *Henry V*.

stomached, 'digest[ed]' as *Henry V* will put it), encrypted in a space within, yet radically other than the ego. In this manner the fact of loss is obliterated – indeed the denial of loss may extend to a denial that there ever was anything to lose – and the necessity of any libidinal reorganization is obviated. Whereas in mourning loss is determinately negated in order to be recuperated, in melancholia, which has as its operative mechanism this magical incorporative moment, loss is foreclosed – but it is not therefore done away with. The aggression originally directed at the object felt to have betrayed the subject now appears to be directed towards the self, as the continued identification of the subject with the lost object turns the subject into the object of its own violence – this self-vilification being, in Abraham and Torok's account, the fantasmatic attempt to stage the *mourning* of the lost, encrypted object for the subject, in what would be the re-affirmation of the object's love for and dependence on that subject.

I would like now to turn back to *Henry V* in order to allow the play to evoke in its own way the two strategies of recuperation I have been discussing. They are first adumbrated in the prologue in the lines immediately succeeding the introductory evocation of the absent muse to which I have already referred:

> But pardon, gentles all,
> The flat unraised spirits that hath dar'd
> On this unworthy scaffold to bring forth
> So great an object. Can this cockpit hold
> The vasty fields of France? Or may we cram
> Within this wooden O the very casques
> That did affright the air at Agincourt?
> O pardon! since a crooked figure may
> Attest in little place a million,
> And let us, ciphers to this great accompt,
> On your imaginary forces work.
> Suppose within the girdle of these walls
> Are now confin'd two mighty monarchies,
> Whose high, upreared, and abutting fronts
> The perilous narrow ocean parts asunder.
>
> (Pro. 8–22)

This passage sets up an opposition, occulted as one of its terms is obscured by a somewhat duplicitous appeal to common sense, between mimesis as a literal (though it thereby ceases to be mimesis in any conventional sense), and mimesis as a figurative cramming or stuffing. Having acknowledged the absence of a muse that would in some sense have guaranteed the relation between subject and historical object, the chorus indulges momentarily in a curious fantasy, displaced (and thereby defensively obscured) in the form of rhetorical questions:

> Can this cockpit hold
> The vasty fields of France? Or may we cram
> Within this wooden O the very casques
> That did affright the air at Agincourt?

Ostensibly providing a justification of the metaphorical project in which 'flat unraised spirits' 'bring forth' or represent an object far greater than they, these lines would seem to locate the necessary recourse to that mimetic strategy in the contingent characteristics of a specific stage, thereby positing, or holding in reserve, the fantasmatic possibility of a literal recovery of the past, of bringing the 'very casques' of Agincourt into, say, James's court. It is as if the 'it goes without answering' of the rhetorical questions here permits, and disguises, a perverse ambiguity: 'might we not effect this cramming after all?' What we have then as the first of the two opposed projects in the play is an occulted fantasy of literal incorporation, a cramming whose privileged locus for *Henry V* will come to be, as it is for Abraham and Torok, the O of the bereaved mouth.

If the chorus is able to reject what remains in a sense its secret project (to the rhetorical questions referred to above, the answer that goes without saying is presumably 'no'), this is to be attributed to the efficacy of the recuperative strategy explicitly invoked by the chorus. For though the 'very casques' of Agincourt can't be crammed, except fantasmatically, into the wooden O, a substitute for those casques may be introjected – given the imaginative cooperation of the audience.[7] In place of those 'million[s]', the 'very casques', we have 'crooked figure[s]', 'ciphers'. Rather than literally cramming the past into the present, we are to 'Suppose' that such a filling of the O has been accomplished. In the face of the absence of the historical object, we are to endorse and underwrite its metaphorical substitution in the O, in a bid to guarantee, as the muse apparently would have, its successful mourning. History is to be sublated, acknowledged dead 'save in me', loved as a living part of the present.

---

[7] Although this is a responsibility accorded the audience, there are numerous instances in which the chorus relieves the audience of this particular onus, taking the task over itself. Hence, for example, the conclusion to the prologue: 'for the which supply, / Admit me Chorus to this history.'

II

we'll di[s]gest / The abuse of distance

The work of mourning that the play announces as its explicit project is not, however, without its difficulties. If the mimetic project is designed to permit the loving, figurative assimilation of the past into the O, that project would seem to be invalidated, given the chorus' repeated insistence on the violence done to the past in representing it, from the start. Just as the author 'Mangl[es]', we are told in the epilogue, the full course of the glory of the age he seeks to commemorate, so the substitution of a figure or a sign for the thing itself – actors for solders, say – disfigures, or as the chorus would have it, 'disgrace[s]', what it is to replace:

> And so our scene must to the battle fly;
> Where – O for pity! – we shall much disgrace
> With four or five most vile and ragged foils
> (Right ill dispos'd in brawl ridiculous)
> The name of Agincourt.
>
> (IV.Cho.48–52)

The attempt figuratively to recuperate history's great account would seem rather to accentuate the loss than to relieve it: history is disgraced not recovered, its loss, in the inability of the theatre to live up to the greatness of its loved object, still more evident.

Though problematized, the introjective project is by no means invalidated by this in fact thoroughly conventional humility topos. If history is disgraced, the chorus's confidence in the capacity of the disgrace to turn into its opposite, to redound to the credit of the disgraced, is evident. For if Agincourt is disgraced, the disgrace is the result of a foil (or four or five), ridiculous in comparison to the thousands of unblunted swords that would have 'graced' the battlefield on 25 October 1415, to be sure, but susceptible to interpretation in the non-military sense, as a figure (a foil) which sets off the quality of that from which it differs in proportion as it differs from that thing. What is necessary, therefore, for the success of the dramatic project, the figurative, loving assimilation of the past, is something like the correct interpretation of a foil, an interpretation which foils the disgrace that cannot fail to inhabit the enterprise. Hence the chorus's request that the audience 'sit and see, / Minding true things by what their mock'ries be' (IV.Cho.52–3).

This is an interpretive 'see[ing]' the chorus relates, specifying the audience's responsibility in the communal endeavour the play represents, to the mode of vision described in *Richard II* as 'perspectiv[al]'. In that play, this mode of seeing is, as Bushy suggests to the grieving queen, who has confided to him that she is feeling the weight of a nameless woe apparently in excess of its specific occasion, a troubling accompaniment to grief, obscuring its provenance. When 'sorrow's eyes' are 'glaz'd with blinding tears', according to Bushy, they are 'Like perspectives', 'divid[ing] one thing entire to many objects', the 'substance of a grief' into illusory 'shadows'.[8] Whereas Bushy anxiously rejects such vision as it causes one 'for things true [to weep] things imaginary', the chorus in *Henry V* embraces it as a necessary and valuable expedient. If justice (as opposed to disgrace) is to be done to history, if 'true things [are to be minded] by what their mock'ries be', then the audience must piece out the imperfections of the theatrical project, according to the chorus, by 'divid[ing]' 'Into a thousand parts ... one man' (Pro. 24), by seeing, that is, through the refracting medium of something like a perspective glass, 'sorrow's eye', one might say in allusion to Bushy's speech. For what the audience views is not the 'substance' of history, but rather its disgraceful imitation and mediation by shadows in a perspectival distortion that precedes the act of viewing. The trick is then a simple one: the audience must not fail to see the foil, to dis-distort or 'retort' (II.i.51) – in a chiasmic procedure whose symmetry is apparently guaranteed – the inevitable disgrace, distortion or mockery effected by the limitations of the medium. Just as the first paradigm of introjection for Abraham and Torok, the filling of the empty mouth with words, can only function with the assistance of the mother (whose constancy is the guarantee of their

[8] Here is Bushy's well-known reply to the queen in its entirety:

> Each substance of a grief hath twenty shadows,
> Which shows like grief itself, but is not so;
> For sorrow's eyes, glazed with blinding tears,
> Divides one thing entire to many objects,
> Like perspectives, which, rightly gazed upon,
> Show nothing but confusion; ey'd awry
> Distinguish form; so your sweet Majesty,
> Looking awry upon your lord's departure,
> Find shapes of grief, more than himself, to wail,
> Which, look'd on as it is, is nought but shadows
> Of what it is not; then, thrice-gracious Queen,
> More than your lord's departure weep not – more is not seen,
> Or if it be, 'tis with false sorrow's eye
> Which for things true weeps things imaginary.
>
> (*Richard II*, II.ii.14–27)

It is often remarked that Bushy plays on (or confuses, as many commentators prefer to put it) two meanings of the word 'perspective'. He seems at first to refer to a perspective or multiplying glass, and then to an anamorphic device or perspective painting. If the chorus in *Henry V* refers implicitly in the passage I am discussing to the former, the King of France will refer explicitly, as we shall see, to the latter.

meaning), so the introjection of the past depends on the constancy of the audience (or the chorus insofar as its preempts the audience's responsibility in this regard). Given that constancy, the metaphorical recuperation of the past would be no more problematic than – to make use of an optical analogy in which an apparent simplicity masks what is a considerable epistemological problem – the reversal by the mind of a (reversed) image on the retina.

Disgestion is the term *Henry V* ultimately generates to designate the work of this particular mourning.[9] It names the general process of introjection and functions, through a complex deploying of the pun legible in its archaic spelling, as a guarantee of the chiasmic reversal of the disgrace or distortion that attends it. I have already noted the play's definition of its enterprise – its disfiguring figuration, which must then be dis-disfigured – as mockery. It is a mock as much as anything else that must be reversed or retorted (this is how we get from 'mock'ries' 'back' to 'true things') by the perspective vision of the audience. But mocks run amok in *Henry V*[10] – a clue that we are to understand the mockery of the mimetic project as a whole, and the retort or inversion of the mock as well, in terms of the play's various allegories of mockery. To unpack the punning complexity of this Shakespearean disgestion, one might note that these allegories of mockery, always involving a certain oral assimilation, are themselves consistently articulated in terms of a putative dialectic of recuperation, the mock always giving rise to a countermock or retort designed to reverse the initial mock, or, in what for *Henry V* is a synonym, the initial jest.[11] The first thematized instance of this mocking of a mock is Henry's declaration of war on France. Answering the claim Henry makes to 'certain dukedoms' (I.ii.247), the Dauphin sends him a tun of tennis balls. Henry responds, as Exeter will put it when he relays Henry's message to the French, by 'return[ing]' the Dauphin's mock 'In second accent' (II.iv.126–7):

> tell the pleasant Prince this mock of his
> Hath turn'd his balls to gun-stones, and his soul
> Shall stand sore charged for the wasteful vengeance
> That shall fly with them; for many a thousand widows

[9] The spelling of the word 'disgestion' and it cognates varies in the play. I am privileging the archaic spelling of its appearance at V.i.26. Some editions, but not the Riverside, modernize the spelling ('disgestion'), although it means departing from the Folio.

[10] A quick glance at a concordance indicates that 'mock' and its cognates appear seventeen times in *Henry V*.

[11] See, in addition to the instance below, this description of Falstaff: 'He was full of jests, and gipes, and knaveries, and mocks' (IV.vii.48–9). The word 'jest' had 'gest' as a variant spelling in this period.

Shall this his mock mock out of their dear husbands;
Mock mothers from their sons, mock castles down.

(I.ii.281–6)

Henry's retort takes the form of, or identifies, a reflexive, second-order
mock that is to be the undoing of the Dauphin's initial mock, a retort in fact,
at least according to Henry, implicit in that initial act of mocking itself.
Resolved, as in the common figurative expression, to make the Dauphin eat
his own words, Henry warns, moreover, that – retorted – the Dauphin's *'jest*
will savor but of shallow wit' (I.ii.295), as the mechanism of this retorting, of
this dis-jesting, is linked to a figurative taking into the mouth. Here then we
have an allegory of the 'Minding [of] true things by what their mock'ries be':
in order not to 'offend one stomach with our play' (II.Cho.39–40), the
chorus promises, in the line which is the epigram to this section of my essay,
to 'digest / Th'abuse of distance' (II.Cho.31–2). As it is the 'abuse of
distance' that constitutes the mockery of the dramatic project, the chorus's
promise is to 'di[s]gest' a mock, to dis-jest a jest.[12]

III

Yes, my lord, you see them perspectively

If the chorus's characteristic self-deprecation seems merely formal, emin-
ently conventional, and not a little disingenuous, the insistent parallels,
linguistic and structural, between the mimetic project as the chorus defines
it and the imperialist war that is the object of its mimesis lend its self-
criticism a certain urgency, collapsing the difference between the discourse
of representation and the discourse of power. If, as we learn in the epilogue,
the play has a '*bending*' author who 'with *rough* and all-unable pen . . . /
Mangl[*es*]' (Epi.1–4) the course of history, the play is about a Henry who
would '*bend* [France] to [his] awe, / Or break it all to pieces' (I.ii.224–5)
with the aid of his 'flesh'd soldier[s], *rough* and hard of heart' (III.iii.91), a
Henry whom the French fear will too closely resemble Edward, Black
Prince of Wales, whose defeat of the French at Crécy '*Mangle* [*d*] the work of
nature, and *deface* [*d*] / The patterns that by God and by French fathers /

---

[12] The chorus's imperative at the beginning of Act V, 'Then brook abridgment, and your
eyes advance, / After your thoughts, straight back again to France' (V.Cho.44–5), identifies
once again the chiastic work of the disgestive project. The brooking of abridgment, in
apposition with the perspective-like 'advanc[ing]' 'back again' of the audience's eyes, is the
punning symmetrical reversal of the bridging of the brook (actually the English Channel, that
'perilous narrow ocean') performed by the chorus. This is, moreover, a brooking that is also a
digesting, as the *OED* confirms.

Had twenty years been made' (II.iv.60–2). And it is about a Pistol who demands of a captive French soldier that he yield up 'brave crowns' on pain of being '*mangled*' (IV.iv.39) by his sword in a threatened act of homosexual rape. If 'bending', 'Mangl[ing]', and being 'rough' are attributes of the play's handling of history in the same way as they define Harry's imperialist war with France, the figurative project of the play would be associated with a violence (a 'defac[ing]', as it is called by the French – though exactly who or what is being defaced is a question we will have to address) which would exceed the bounds of a disgrace or a mockery whose articulation one could chalk up to a conventional humility, and whose recuperation could go, as it were, without saying.

If the play insists on a virtual homology between the theatrical project and Henry's military conquest in the theatre within the theatre, the theatre of operations which is France, its point one assumes is not, however, to assert the violence done to history in representing it. For if the homology between the mimetic and the military would seem, at one level, to call the dramatic project and its elegiac mode into question, it might be argued to function, at another, as a guarantee of their success. The military project is itself, for instance, an imitation: the play becomes, in this light, the imitation of a (successful) imitation. Just as Henry goes into battle having been advised to 'Awake remembrance of these valiant dead [his ancestors], / And with . . . puissant arm [and the help of God to] renew their feats' (I.ii.115–16), so the chorus seeks to renew Henry's feats by attaining – with the help of the audience – to 'imaginary puissance' (Pro. 25). By encouraging a certain identification of the two projects, it becomes possible for the chorus to appropriate the foregone conclusion of Henry's victory as earnest of its own.

And yet the disturbing implications of the strict analogy between the discourse of representation and the discourse of power remain. The chorus's promise to digest its unfortunate but not exactly willful abuse of the past seems like bad faith when, in the military campaign with which the mimetic project is identified, the victims of a premediated abuse must do their own digesting: the English victory at Harfleur is, according to the French, a 'disgrace we have digested' (III.vi.128), a disgrace for which even King Henry kneeling at their feet would be 'but a weak and worthless satisfaction' (line 133). The disfiguration of the historical object, cast by the chorus as a liability to be regretted, is recast in the larger context of the play as a whole as an intentional act of annexing aggression.

If the complicated and overdetermined modalities of this aggression constitute a threatening counterforce to the play's explicitly endorsed recuperative strategy (a matter we must later pursue), the peace treaty that marks the successful end of Henry's French campaign is designed to ward off this force, to restore the plausibility of the introjective project by countering the violence of the imperialist war. The conclusion of the play and Henry's conquest of France consists of Henry's courtship of Katherine and the complete submission of the French King to all of his demands. During the negotiations leading to the peace treaty the relationship between the courtship of Katherine and the conquest (by treaty) of the French cities that were spared Henry's military aggression is aptly defined by the French King. Responding to Henry's rather snide remark that some of the French may thank 'love for my blindness, who cannot see many a fair French city for one fair French maid that stands in my way' (V.ii.317–19), King Charles comments: 'Yes, my lord, you see them *perspectively*: the cities turn'd into a maid; for they are all girdled with maiden walls which war hath [never] ent'red' (V.ii.320–3). The figure used by King Charles, that of a perspective picture or anamorphic device, may remind us of the figure emphasized by the chorus as a key to the success of the metaphorical project being undertaken in the theatre: to see perspectively (as if, in my reading, through a multiplying glass) was to be the guarantee of the mockery-negating retort designed to permit the non-violent, loving assimilation of history. And indeed the courtship scene is presented as a substitute for the war that it ends, capable of redressing in some sense the horrors that war has wrought. Here, rather than being provocative, mocks are 'merci[ful]' (V.ii.201–1).[13] In place of the 'flesh'd soldier, rough and hard of heart' (III.iii.11), who rapes French cities, we are given Henry, who has a 'good heart' (V.ii.162), wooing as best a soldier can, with a tongue that is 'rough' (V.ii.286) but full of praises. As Burgundy suggests, the marriage of Henry and Katherine, the conjoining of the two countries by a treaty founded on love, should allow 'the naked, poor and *mangled* Peace' once again to 'put up her lovely visage' (V.ii.34–7) in a de-defacing or restoration of a face. Read as an analogue of the determinate negation of abuse it is the responsibility of the audience (or chorus) to perform, the courtship scene would be taken as an allegorical guarantee of the mimetic-cum-military jest's disgestion.

IV

[B]ecause, look you, you do not love it, nor ... your disgestions doo's not agree with it, I would desire you to eat it.

The digestion or introjection of the past is governed by an oral metaphor which, if the work of mourning is to be a success, it is crucial not to take

[13] At V.ii.102 Katherine expresses her concern that Henry will 'mock' her, and at line 201 Henry asks her to 'mock [him] mercifully'.

literally. The punning fracture whereby disgestion becomes the dis-jesting of a jest, while emphasizing the patient working through of loss (digesting the past as opposed to swallowing it whole), underwrites at the same time the figurative status of this filling of the O, making possible the assimilation of the oral (digestion) to the visual (perspective vision). Yet the chorus seems at times to take its own figure rather more *à la lettre* than mimetic propriety would allow. If it promises to 'digest / Th'abuse of distance', it glosses this digestion as a curiously literal force-feeding: 'we'll digest / Th'abuse of distance, force a play'. As Dover Wilson pointed out in his New Cambridge edition of the play (1947), this forcing is a farcing, a stuffing or, to extend Wilson's punning philologico-culinary point somewhat, a fantasmatic cramming of the lost object into the O which sounds very much like the impossible cramming introduced and renounced by the chorus in the prologue. I would like to pursue this matter by returning to the quasi-pun linking the play's definition of its project as mockery to the series of thematized mocks which provide the context for its understanding. For a careful reading of this series destabilizes the relation of the jest/dis-jest and, given the increasingly literal orality of its various moments, reveals that the introjective project is haunted by the incorporation that would be its undoing.[14] Though consistently dissimulated under the guise of the propriety of the introjective jest/dis-jest, this incorporation is identified, finally, in a complicated, punning reversal, as the very mechanism of the mock.

I suggested earlier, extrapolating from Henry's declaration of war on France, that the play's various allegories of mockery are articulated in terms of a dialectic of recuperation, the jest calling forth, and countered by, a dis-jest figured as a metaphorical taking into the mouth. Henry's response to the Dauphin's 'mock' or 'jest' identifies, it will be recalled, a second order mock, a consequence of the initial act of mocking itself, which 'will savour but of shallow wit'. The determined difference between mock and retort, between an original jest and its disgestion, is, however, it is clear from this example, an English construction. The French jest is itself a response, after all, to Henry's dynastic presumption, his claim to those certain dukedoms, a claim the French would, no doubt, have considered a mock in its own right.

---

[14] One could pursue this question via the implied equivalence between the mimetic project and the treason of Scroop, Cambridge and Grey. The promise to 'digest / Th'abuse of distance, force a play' is immediately followed by the announcement that 'The sum is paid, the traitors are agreed' (II.Cho.33), an apposition underscored by the fact that the dramatic project is a 'great accompt' (Pro. 17). The 'capital crimes' of the traitors (like the 'capital demand' (V.ii.96) that Katherine comprises?) have, more pertinently, been 'chew'd, swallow'd, and digested' (II.ii.56).

To speak here of a dialectic of recuperation, and not of, say, the repetition of mocks in a cycle of increasing violence, one needs to side with the English.

The second thematization of mockery in the play occurs in the next scene – though the word 'mock' does not appear there, its invocation has a certain formal sanction[15] – when Pistol assumes that he is being mocked by Nim. Things commence with what seems like a fairly innocent greeting:

> (*Nim*) How now, mine host Pistol?
>
> *Pistol* Base tick, call'st thou me host?
> Now by [Gadslugs] I swear I scorn the term.
>   (II.i.28–30)

A few moments later, the initial outburst having been stilled by Bardolph's intervention, Nim offers a second mock or insult, or at least one that is so understood:

> *Nim* Will you shog off? I would have you solus.
>
> *Pistol* 'Solus', egregious dog? O viper vile!
> The 'solus' in thy most mervailous face,
> The 'solus' in thy teeth, and in thy throat,
> And in thy hateful lungs, yea in thy maw, perdy;
> And which is worse, within thy nasty mouth!
> I do retort the 'solus' in thy bowels,
> For I can take, and Pistol's cock is up,
> And flashing fire will follow.
>   (II.i.45–53)

Like the Dauphin's self-reflexive mock, Nim's jest (which, as the note to the Oxford edition suggests, may only be a mock in Pistol's reception) is something he will come, if Pistol has his way, to regret. For in refusing meekly to brook Nim's putative abuse, Pistol speaks of cramming it into Nim's mouth and down his throat, in a rhetorically violent force-feeding. If this 'retort' repeats the figure used by Henry in his response to the Dauphin ('His jest will savour but of shallow wit'), it also introduces a certain literalization: Pistol's retort would constrain Nim literally to eat his words, or rather word, the very word 'solus'.

Perhaps the most remarkable example of an allegory of mockery in the play is, however, Pistol's encounter with Fluellen in the first scene of Act V.

---

[15] The scene fits into the pattern in the play typified by the relation of Act III.ii to Act III.i in which Henry's 'serious' breaching enterprise is counterpoised by a comic foil, this scene being then the foil to Henry's encounter in the previous scene with the Dauphin (via the mediation of the ambassadors). The 'mock[s]' of that scene are repeated here in a comic register.

Before the scene opens, Pistol has mocked – the word *is* a conspicuous feature of this episode – Fluellen's fidelity to a Welsh custom, according to which a leek is worn in the cap on St David's day. Fluellen's response is a still further literalization of the play's characteristic retort: Pistol is not only made to eat his words, he is made to eat the leek as well:

I peseech you heartily, scurvy, lousy knave, at my desires, and my requests, and my petitions, to eat, look you, this leek; because, look you, you do not love it, nor your affections, and your appetites, and your disgestions doo's not agree with it, I would desire you to eat it (V.i.22–9).

As Fluellen later remarks, 'If you can mock a leek you can eat a leek' (lines 37–8).

If these allegories of mockery are thematic analogues of the work of disgestion that underwrites the mimetic project, representations of the jest/dis-jest structure on which the figuration of history depends, they also problematize that structure, calling the recuperative dialectic of the mock-retort into question and raising the specter of the literal incorporation that threatens to destroy the oral metaphor. Where in the first example of a thematized mock one cannot speak of a definitive origin without aligning oneself with the English cause, in the second the mock, never explicitly identified as such, only seems to come into existence with the retort – 'I would have you solus' becoming thus a figure for a mock that may or may not be one. Whereas the rejoinder in the posited mock-retort relation is initially figured as a metaphorical taking into the mouth, it is subsequently cast, moreover, as an increasingly literal, retributive and enforced swallowing implicit in, though still distinct from, the mock it is to retort. If the Dauphin is to find that his jest, when dis-jested, will 'savour but of shallow wit', Nim is made to swallow the letter and Pistol the very object of his abuse. Concomitant with the implied indetermination of the play's mockery is therefore a disgestion itself rendered more and more literal, until to 'digest / Th'abuse of distance' becomes, literally, to 'force a play', a fantasmatic stuffing of the mouth indistinguishable from the cramming of the O renounced at the start by the chorus.

It is on the way this happens in the last of these examples that I would like to concentrate. For if the literalization of the oral metaphor has to this point been associated only with the dis-jest, in Pistol's mocking of Fluellen it is identified as the mechanism of the mock itself. Speaking to Pistol after his humiliation, Gower upbraids him for his 'mock[ing] at an ancient tradition' (V.i.70) and affirms that he has been a witness to that mocking: 'I have seen you gleeking and galling at this gentleman twice or thrice' (73–5). If the play generates the representation of 'mock'ries' at a thematic level in which two distinct phases – mock and retort – are apparent, here it performs the conflation of those phases, allowing us to glimpse, across the propriety of the jest/dis-jest, the incorporative forcing which the thematics of mockery is designed to ward off. For in the specific word which designates Pistol's abusive jesting ('gleeking'), the ultimate dis-jesting of the mock(ed) – the leek – is already incorporated.[16] To mock a leek, we might say, in a revision of Fluellen's dictum, *is* to eat a leek – which is to mock oneself, as Pistol, his mouth full of leek, has been made to acknowledge. My claim would be that we can read in this symptomatic conflation the secret mechanism of the 'mock'ries' we have been investigating. In a word, the play suggests that to mock the past *is* to eat the past. History is the leek the play gleeks. As the verb to gleek also means, according to the *OED*, to look askew or awry at something, the perspective vision required of the audience and designed to guarantee the dis-jesting of the jest is itself, moreover, a gleeking. If the jest/dis-jest pun deployed to guarantee the oral metaphor permitted the assimilation of disgestion to the visual, here the pun which turns the jest into a fantasmatic gleeking assimilates vision to itself.[17] The jest and dis-jest of the introjective project cannot be thought, it would seem, without the particularly violent gleek of the incorporative moment.

V

Behold ... / With fatal mouths gaping

If the allegories of mockery in the play call the dialectical structure of the jest/dis-jest into question, and reveal, concomitant with the collapse of this

---

[16] The word 'gleek' is, in this context, an obsolete verb meaning to mock or make a jest (at a person). It also existed as a noun. I will refer to alternative meanings when appropriate. The other word used by Gower would seem to have similar implications, though it is not quite so fine. '[G]alling' (irritating or scoffing) may, if one hears the noun 'gall' in the verb, evoke the *Ekel* Pistol feels on eating the leek (he is 'qualmish at the smell' (V.i.19)). All definitions come from the *OED*.

[17] This discussion suggests that the chorus's imperative, 'Then brook abridgment, and your eyes advance, / ... back again' (V.Cho.44–5), would not imply the assimilation of the oral to the visual, as I argued earlier (see note 13), but the reverse. The imperative 'brook' is to be identified finally not with disgestion but with gleeking, a literal bearing undigested in the stomach. The argument I will go on to make would suggest, moreover, that the relation between brooking and the eyes that advance back again is specular: brooking (construed as a literal swallowing) produces this perspectival difference, the difference between the brook and the bridge in my first reading of this passage, just as 'forc[ing]' will be seen to produce the difference between 'digest[ion]' and the 'abuse of distance' (an abridgment), the jest and the dis-jest.

structure, a peculiarly literal incorporation, an abuse of the object which becomes, in the shadowy reversal typical of melancholia, an abuse of the self, we need to return to the homology between the mimetic and military projects in order to reexamine the disgestive function ascribed earlier to Henry's courtship of Katherine. For the recurrent discourse, in the military enterprise, of a particular rape (involving the 'forcing' or 'enforcing' of 'circles' by 'spirits') conflates the jest and the dis-jest, while marking, in the context of the mimetic project, the turning round on the self of the violence directed at the lost object. Breaching the propriety of the recuperative dialectic of the mock-retort structure, the discourse of this rape modulates, moreover, into a literal swallowing defined as the regressive mode of a certain seeing.

Henry's perspective vision, his view of Katherine as a suitable substitute for the continued assault on the French cities, was portrayed, it will be recalled, as the determinate negation of the abuse wrought by the war whose end it marks, becoming thus an allegorical guarantee of the reversal of the disgrace, defacing or mangling which attends the figuration of history. But a peace treaty that is really an unconditional surrender does not seem much of an about-face. For, Burgundy not-withstanding, the relation between jest and dis-jest here is one, not so much of negation, as of tautology. If Harfleur is a city 'girdled with maiden walls' (V.ii.322) (assuming it to have been like the other French cities Henry will gain later by treaty) and made to bear the 'forcing violation' (III.iii.21) of the English 'spirit[s]' (III.i.16) whose blood has been 'con-jure[d] up' (III.i.7), Katherine is a 'cit[y] turn'd into a maid', Harfleur becoming Harry's 'flower-de-luce' (V.ii.210), a maid in whose 'circle' he would 'conjure up' the 'enforc[ing]' 'spirit of love' (V.ii.293, 288, 301, 289). As Henry himself puts it, France's 'maiden cities' 'wait on' (V.ii.326, 327) Katherine, their conquest to be consummated at the same time as the marriage: 'so the maid that stood in the way for my wish shall show me the way to my will' (V.ii.327–8). Rather than undoing the violence that preceded it, Henry's courtship of Katherine consolidates it, repeating it, at best, in a different register.

Collapsing the difference in the military enterprise between the jest and the dis-jest, the discourse of this (en)forcing violation comes to designate, insofar as it also defines the terms of the mimetic project, the turning round on the self of this object-related aggression. Harfleur, 'girdled with [its] maiden walls', is a city of which the stage, that 'wooden O', is itself a version: the audience, we remember, is to 'Suppose within the girdle of these walls / ... confin'd two mighty monarchies' in the 'forc[ing of] a play' by 'flat unraised spirits' (given the perspectival dilation which would bend them, like the English 'spirit[s]' at Harfleur, 'up ... / To [their] full height'

(III.i.16–17).[18] Where Henry and his troops are firmly differentiated from the feminine objects of their mimetic desire, the relation between the 'flat unraised spirits' and the O of the stage involves a more rudimentary differentiation. If the flaccid spirits of the dramatic project are to expand to fill the stage's 'wooden O', as Henry's troops are exhorted to '[conjure] up the blood' (III.i.7) in preparation for the rape of Harfleur, they are themselves 'ciphers' (Pro. 17) and, therefore, in a crucial sense, the objects of their own violence.[19] In place of the firm triangulation and obvious gender differentiation of the terms of the military project (Henry–France–Edward, Henry–Harfleur/Katherine–King of France), we have the far more tenuous triadic relation of the mimetic project, a relation consisting of a cipher, an O (from which it is imperfectly differentiated), and a third term, an object of identification or imitation, itself constituted by a difference, the difference between those 'two mighty monarchies' or between the jest amd the dis-jest.[20] The imitation of history, an imitation which operates in and through the economy of the deployed difference between mock and retort, becomes thereby the abuse of the theatre's O, a rape by and of the cipher.

This rape or mangling is portrayed, moreover, in terms we would need to associate with incorporation. The chorus, urging on the audience as Henry will his soldiers, turns the phallic cannon, agent of the cities' forcing penetration, into a voracious maw bent on oral abuse: 'Behold the ordinance on their carriages, / With fatal mouths gaping on girded Harfleur' (III.Cho.26–7). This recalls the image of war's ravaging first used by Exeter in his appeal to the French to submit without a fight:

> [Henry] bids you, in the bowels of the Lord,
> Deliver up the crown, and take mercy
> On the poor souls for whom this hungry war
> Opens his vasty jaws; and on your head
> Turns he the widows' tears, the orphans' cries,
> The dead men's blood, the pining maiden's groans,
> For husbands, fathers, and betrothed lovers
> That shall be swallowed in this controversy
>
> (II.iv.102–9)

[18] In a play noted at certain moments for unerring fidelity to its sources, the decision to figure the English 'ghosts' (IV.Cho.28) at Agincourt as surrounded, or 'enrounded' (IV.Cho.36), when they in fact weren't, foregrounds the analogy between the English troops and the players or shadows encompassed by the circle of the stage.

[19] The line 'Where – O for pity! – we shall much disgrace / . . . / The name of Agincourt' (IV.Cho. 49–52) performs this reversal, if one hears, ignoring the strict parenthesis of the River-side punctuation, which many editions do, the grammatical possibility of the O as direct object.

[20] This triadic relation could be called a gleek: 'a set of three court cards of the same rank'. It is a bizarre fact that a set of four such cards (with all the attendant possibilities of symmetrical arrangement) was called a 'mournival'.

Here the 'forcing violation' of the English, defined as a 'swallow[ing]', links up explicitly with the 'forc[ing]' the chorus says it will do of the play, a 'forc[ing]' which is itself, as we have seen, a farcing or literal cramming. When the 'cockpit' or 'wooden O' is aligned with the 'vasty jaws' of a 'hungry war', the 'vasty fields of France' no longer seem like such a mouthful. And, like the rape by/of the cipher, this too is an act of violence directed against an object *and* the self, the 'gaping' of the 'fatal mouths' itself indicating a vulnerability, as if – as was played out in the scenes of mockery we have examined – 'to swallow up' implies 'to be forced to swallow'. If, finally, the 'Behold[ing]' the chorus exhorts the audience to do is part of the 'work' (III.Cho.25) of the disgestive project, an 'eke[ing] out' of the play's 'performance with your mind' (III.Cho.35) similar to the 'Minding [of] true things by what their mock'ries be', and a type of perspective vision, it is also a seeing associated in an odd way with the mouth. For if those 'fatal mouths gaping' belong most obviously to the cannon, they may also be taken to refer to the subject, even to the mode, of that beholding: 'Behold . . . / With fatal mouths gaping.' Across the dis-jestive 'eke[ing] out [of a] performance' we can detect once again, therefore, the performance of a fantasmatic gleeking.

VI

we'll digest
Th'abuse of distance, force a play

The chorus's promise to 'digest / Th'abuse of distance' is, therefore, duplicitous. On the one hand, we have the jest/dis-jest which constitutes the work of mourning, the chorus promising to dis-abuse the loved object of the abuse done in representing it, an abuse which was associated, however, not merely with the contingencies of theatrical representation, but with an act of annexing aggression. On the other hand, we have the apposition of this promise with the 'forc[ing]' or literal stuffing which is simultaneously an abuse of the past, its violent incorporation, and an abuse of the self, as the continued identification of the subject with its ego-ideal turns the self into the object of its own violence. In this latter respect, to 'digest / Th'abuse of distance, force a play' becomes to digest the abuse of distance forcibly, the digestion referring, not to a metaphorical taking into the mouth, but to a fantasmatic cramming, and the abuse of distance, to an abuse of uncertain agency, like Nim's 'I would have you solus', a mock that may or may not be one. I would like to conclude with a necessarily brief discussion of the multiple and conflicting modalities of these 'abuse[s] of distance', in an effort further to define the relation mourning has in *Henry V* to the melancholia which is its dysfunctional substitute.

The strict triangulation of the introjective project as it is portrayed in *Henry V*, involving as it does a relation between men (Henry and Edward, Henry and the French King) mediated by the feminine (France, Harfleur/ Katherine), may suggest, though this is not a point I want to labor, that the 'abuse of distance', the jest that must be disgested, is inscribed in a scene of a sort of Oedipal rivalry. From this perspective, the virile superfluity of the 'vasty fields' the 'cockpit' can't hold would be the object of an imitation by 'flat unraised spirits' which is also a mangling, or displaced castration fantasy.[21] The identification of such a threat, however, the possibility of figuring the relation of past and present in terms of a familiar, if highly charged, sexual rivalry, would itself be reassuring; for what it posits above all is the fact of relation, a continuity susceptible of delimitation or definition, its constant a certain abuse – call it the threat of castration emanating from the father and, reversed, in this scenario, into a fantasized mangling of the father by the son. If the abuse of distance (subjective genitive) becomes in this way the abuse of distance (objective genitive), that abuse is figured, moreover, through the work of mourning or disgestion, as recuperable. As in the Oedipal analysis of *Moses and Monotheism*, for instance, in which the conspiring sons of the primeval horde kill the father and then, guilt-ridden, end up restoring paternal authority, the mangling jest of the mimetic project is to be dis-jested, sacrifice dialectically converted into the sacred, history introjected in the form of a paternal superego.

But, as we have seen, the mimetic project is governed by a less fully articulated ternary structure, a relation which is not dialectical, the determinate negation of the jest by the dis-jest, but specular, involving the attentuated production of the difference between the jest and the dis-jest and the setting of this relation in relation to the (in)difference between a cipher and an O. This is to locate within and across the Oedipal a specifically pre-Oedipal formation, that of primary narcissism, and to associate the mangling or forcing of the mimetic project with what Julia Kristeva calls abjection.[22]

---

[21] The sexual rivalry implicit in the relation of the mimetic project to the historical object is underscored in the military allegory. The superfluity of history is to be imitated/mangled by a band of 'vile and ragged' (IV.Cho.50) actors, just as the 'confident and overlusty French' (IV.Cho.18) – whose 'superflu[ity]' (IV.ii.11) is the subject of much braggadocio in their ranks at Agincourt – are made to feel their impotence ('Our mettle is bred out' (III.v.29)) by Henry's 'ruined band' (IV.Cho.29), though some 'be ne'er so vile' (IV.iii.62).

[22] This understanding of the specular, and of abjection, is indebted to the work of Neil Hertz and Cynthia Chase. See especially Hertz's 'Afterword: The End of the Line' in *The End of*

According to Kristeva's reading of Freud in *Histories d'amour*, primary
narcissism is a tenuously articulated triadic structure composed when 'a
new psychic action' comes to supplement the auto-erotism of the mother-
infant dyad.[23] This new action, which Freud describes as 'an immediate
identification' with or transference onto the instance he calls 'the father of
personal pre-history', occurs, in Kristeva's account, when the indeterminably significative gestures of maternal care are read by the infant as
signifying the mother's desire for something beyond responding to its needs.
The transference onto the other that is the mother's desire produces the gap
constitutive of 'the beginnings of the symbolic function' (p. 35), or the
difference between signifier and signified – a permanently unstable
differential function set in relation to, and a screen for, the archaic and
rudimentary differentiation of infant and mother. Concomitant with the
production of this gap is the 'abjection' or casting out of the irreducible
uncertainty of those marks of maternal care, which, to the extent that they do
not *signify*, point only to themselves as the immediate fulfillment of the need
that fuses infant and mother. This exclusion is at once a function of the
transference onto the gap and its necessary condition, sustaining the
determined difference which has come to screen the (in)difference between
the meaningful and the non-meaningful, preventing the 'confusion', as
Kristeva puts it, 'of the limits of bodies, of words, of the real and the
symbolic' (p. 35). If this double gesture inaugurates the possibility of
meaning and of any subject position, it also reveals, however, their
permanent instability. Insofar as the maintenance of the gap or narcissistic
void is a function of the continued 'combat' (p. 57) with the maternal abject,
the differentiated unity of the sign depends on the non-absence of the very
thing whose presence threatens the stability of its fixed difference. The
determined organization of difference which comes to define the symbolic
order is lined by the indeterminate negativity of a pre-Oedipal modality,
oriented toward indifferentiation, which disrupts the dialectical mediation
it makes possible.

The specular structure of the play's mimetic project repeats this
inaugural narcissistic configuration. Within and across the dialectical and
stable Oedipal triangulation of the military enterprise, we have the
necessarily tenuous production of the difference between the jest and the
dis-jest, between each of the 'high, upreared, and abutting fronts / The
perilous narrow ocean parts asunder' (Pro. 21–2), or between the 'forcing' of

---

the Line: Essays on Psychoanalysis and the Sublime (New York, 1985), pp. 217–39 and Chase's 'The
Witty Butcher's Wife: Freud, Lacan, and the Conversion of Resistance to Theory' *MLN*
(Winter, 1987).

[23] Julia Kristeva, *Histoires d'amour* (Paris, 1983), p. 33.

Harfleur and the 'enforc[ing]' of Harry's 'flower'. The identification with or transference onto the minimal organization of difference represented by this instance permits the rudimentary differentiation of the cipher and the O, and is a function of the casting out of the uncertainty of a mock that may or may not be one, the rejecting of the 'caves and womby vaultages' (II.iv.124) that interrupt and complicate the dialectical structure of the mock and its return in 'second accent'[24] – the abjection in short, through an act of reading, of the indeterminably significative status of the historical sign. If Kristeva figures this semiological reduction as a casting out or abjection, *Henry V* defines it, more precisely, as a casting in or ingestion. The violent and disfiguring incorporation, 'forcing' or 'gleeking' which haunts the introjective project produces and is repeated to maintain the difference between the 'abuse of distance' and its disgestion, the mock and its retort, the difference which is to put a good, if arbitrary, face on the permanently fragile distinction between an O and a cipher.[25] To digest the abuse of distance, *Henry V* (and Monmouth) tell us, speaking freely, no doubt, with full mouth, one *must* force a play, in an incorporation which destroys the oral metaphor by taking it literally, even as it inaugurates the possibility of the dialectical economy on which that metaphor depends.

[24] Exeter's speech is considerably more complicated than I intimated in my first reference to it:

> if your father's Highness
> Do not, in grant of all demands at large,
> Sweeten the bitter mock you sent his Majesty,
> He'll call you to so hot an answer of it
> That caves and womby vaultages of France
> Shall chide your trespass and return your mock
> In second accent of his ordinance.
>
> (II.iv.120–6)

One has to ignore the uncertain agency of those 'caves and womby vaultages', as I did earlier, if one is to derive the symmetrical structure of the mock-retort from these lines.

[25] The relation between primary narcissism and incorporation is broached by André Green. See 'La mère morte' in *Narcissisme de vie, narcissisme de mort* (Paris, 1983), pp. 222–53, esp p. 248. Although Green is not discussing abjection specifically in this context, the complex he calls 'la mère morte' is structurally analogous. Cynthia Chase relates incorporation to abjection in 'The Work of Melancholy', MLA, December 1985. What is at stake here is not (or not only), it is worth insisting, a developmental narrative leading from the pre-Oedipal to its transcendence in the Oedipal. I am interested in the permanent structural co-implication of these modalities. Thus, the association of introjection with the Oedipal and incorporation with the pre-Oedipal does not narrativize the metapsychological theory of loss; it complicates the strict teleology of a developmental narrative of states. On the relation of state and structure in psychoanalytic theory as it pertains to primary narcissism, see A. Green, 'Le narcissisme primaire: structure ou état', in *Narcissisme de vie*, pp. 80–132.

5

Rhyme Puns

Debra Fried

Rhyme and pun are twins. They both 'join words that have no association by sense but only by sound'.[1] Yet rhyme's sins – to be mannered, quaint, contrived, to recruit or reshuffle words just for the rhyme – are like pun's virtues – extravagance, surprise, excess, a big build-up to a little explosion. Where rhyme seems to reflect grand harmonies, pun indicates grand confusions.[2] As John Hollander notes, rhyme may 'do some of the work of metaphor by associating words through their sounds alone, and by thus juxtaposing them with some of the same strength as an actual image'.[3] But pun, especially in its favored precinct of riddle, transforms and unshapes (staining a newspaper red all over, turning a door into a jar); it does not so much juxtapose as jumble. What happens when these mismatched twins meet in a poem? I wish to investigate how pun qualifies certain functions and fictions of rhyme: that rhyme is not contrived but inevitable, that rhyme's effects depend on temporal sequence, and that rhyme marks line endings, and hence highlights the fact that the units in which a poem arrays itself – lines of equal length, for instance – do not match the units of the words or sense. I will be concerned less, then, with the opalescent shimmer of those single words that, as Derrida says, have good luck, than with how their settings hold certain facets up to the light. How may rhymes invite, temper, annotate or anticipate puns, and how may puns gloss, amplify, tame or invigorate rhymes?

Before looking at how instances of local friction between rhyme and pun

[1] Arden Reed, 'The Mariner Rhymed' in *Romanticism and Language*, ed. Arden Reed (Ithaca, 1984), p. 178. For a survey of views on the links between metaphor and pun, and rhyme and pun, see Walter Redfern, *Puns* (Oxford, 1984), pp. 97–102.

[2] For pun as a figure of confusion, *Paradise Lost* is perhaps the *locus classicus* in English poetry. R. A. Shoaf, *Milton: Poet of Duality* (New Haven, 1985), is the most recent in a tradition of commentators who see pun as a result of disruptions consequent to the fall, as a 'fusion [that] can all too easily become *con*fusion' (p. 63).

[3] John Hollander, *Vision and Resonance: Two Senses of Poetic Form* (New York, 1975), p. 157.

lead to reconsiderations of both twins, we need to ask a related question. When rhyme is dismissed as a lucky deal of the linguistic deck, how may pun remind us that the cards are marked? Michael Riffaterre notes that overdetermination lends to literary discourse 'the authority of multiple motivations for each word used',[4] and in this sense rhyme is one of the most efficient agents of overdetermination. Any rhyme word has at least two reasons for being the word used: because it makes sense, and because it rhymes. We have inherited from the eighteenth century the notion that the second reason is unimportant, or should be. The ear is to receive its pleasures as an incidental byproduct of the mind's satisfactions. Rhyme is designed to make nothing happen, but simply to follow in the wake of the semantic events that matter, a secondary 'echo to the sense'. The Augustan heroic couplet works to promote the illusion that rhyme is servant and never master. Hugh Kenner puts this ambition plainly when he notes of Pope's couplets that Pope 'means to us to be visited by no suspicion that the first rhyme of a pair has suggested the second, or even vice versa: to judge rather that the rhyme validates a structure of meaning that other orders of cogency have produced'.[5] In a well-designed couplet the second rhyme that closes the couplet and completes the syntactic unit would seem to be simply the one right word answering to the demands of meaning. But we may suspect that the well-crafted couplet, even as it fosters the fiction of rhyme as echo to the sense, runs the risk of awakening echoes of all the lurking phonetic cousins of the rhyming word designed to seem the only possible fitting choice.

Shakespeare's Portia uses this capacity of a rhyming series to conjure up the missing elements in the series in the song that she orders to be played while Bassanio puzzles over his selection of the three caskets: 'Tell me where is Fancy bred, / Or in the heart or in the head? / How begot, how nourished?' Get the message? – choose the lead. And so he does. As we generally understand the term, we cannot say that the song makes a pun on the word *bred* or *head* or *lead*. In instances such as these, Hollander notes, 'a word not itself specified may be echoed by other ones' (p. 156). This description fits certain puns as well. Take the classic riddle: Q: Why don't you starve in the desert? A: Because of all the sand which is there. *Sandwiches* is a word we hear that it is not itself specified; it is echoed by the other ones ('sand which is'), and the echo in this case happens to be very exact. Thus if Portia had made Bassanio's riddle even easier, her song might have begun 'Tell me how is Fancy led'. In this case the word not specified – the metal 'lead' – is echoed by the specified 'led', but again the echo is so

    [4] Michael Riffaterre, *Semiotics of Poetry* (Bloomington, 1978), p. 21.
    [5] Hugh Kenner, 'Pope's Reasonable Rhymes', *ELH* 41 (1974), pp. 77–8.

close – it sounds, in fact, just like the specified word – that it seems dishonest to call it an echo or a rhyme. Unlike *bred*, *led* does not simply rhyme with *lead* and hence nudge the hearer to the correct choice; it actually names the correct choice, 'lead'. *Lead* and *led* are too alike to be rhymes – aside from *rime riche* or homonymic rhyme, in English rhymes must be a bit different as well as alike. Thus revised, Portia's musical cheat sheet is governed by a logic like that of Geoffrey Hartman's persuasive double definition of the pun as 'two meanings competing for the same phonemic space or as one sound bringing forth semantic twins'.[6] Or sometimes quintuplets: Jonathan Culler describes the pun as fertile in its 'network of interlingual connections and mimetic relays of signifiers'.[7] Hollander speaks of the 'ad hoc semantic field' of possible rhymes that any rhyme has the potential to invoke (p. 120). Many rhyming paradigms include members that bear a semantic family resemblance (*bright–light–sight–night*), members that bear only a phonetic resemblance (*blight–fright–knight*; not to mention *kite–write–rite*), and others that bear a homonymic or punning resemblance (*sight–site*, *night–knight*). The tidy Augustan couplet attempts to pair rhymes so compatibly that they do not bring to mind other rhymes that might work. But as soon as more than two rhymes are introduced, the range of choices becomes more evident.[8]

In a complex stanza form with a rhyme scheme requiring three or more matches for each end-rhyme, a good number of candidates for possible rhymes may be pressed into service. The results, as in Byron's ottava rima, can be flip and funny, calling for the sort of outlandish rhymes most easily identified as comic or punning (the handy 'pukes in-Euxine' of *Don Juan*) or as in the *Faerie Queene* stanza, they can be broodingly encyclopedic and etymologizing. This stanza from the end of Book I is anomalous in that it has two rhymes instead of the usual three, but it is otherwise illustrative of rhyming effects throughout the poem:

---

[6] Geoffrey Hartman, 'The Voice of the Shuttle: Language from the Point of View of Literature', *Beyond Formalism* (New Haven, 1970), p. 347. Cf. James Brown, 'Eight Types of Puns', *PMLA* 71 (1956), p. 26: 'The pun seems to be organically related to other sound-sense phenomena of literature; in it, for example, one may find perfect and total rhyme compressed into a single symbol of occurrence'.

[7] Jonathan Culler, *On Deconstruction* (Ithaca, 1982), p. 191. See also Roland Barthes, *Elements of Semiology*, trans. Annette Lavers and Colin Smith (New York, 1967), p. 87: 'rhyming produces an associative sphere at the level of sound, that is to say, of the signifiers: there are paradigms of rhymes.'

[8] It would be interesting to examine in this context the Augustan habit of permitting occasional rhyming triplets in poems predominantly in couplets, as in Dryden's 'To the Memory of Mr Oldham'.

> Great ioy was made that day of young and old,
>> And solemne feast proclaimd throughout the land,
>> That their exceeding merth may not be told:
>> Suffice it heare by signes to vnderstand
>> The vsuall ioyes at knitting of loues band.
> Thrise happy man the knight himselfe did hold,
>> Possessed of his Ladies hart and hand,
>> And euer, when his eye did her behold,
> His heart did seeme to melt in pleasures manifold.
>
> (I.xii.40)[9]

The stanza provides a rhyming dictionary; it progresses as though the word *old* were reproducing itself, attaching its single syllable to others in order to introduce rhyming cousins that are ever farther removed: *old—told—hold—behold—manifold*. By the end of the stanza we feel that part of the richness of the word *manifold* is that it has folded into it the sound of *old* and of all the succeeding rhymes on it.[10] Breaking longer words down into shorter ones is a device of comic rhyming and punning. When W. S. Gilbert's modern major general boasts that he is 'teeming with a lot o' news / And many cheerful facts about the square of the hypotenuse', his rhymes draw on the same equations, in which short words add up to long ones, that the waspish Blake calculates on for his punning etymologies, as when he labels 'connoisseurs' as 'cunning sures' or defines equally vindictive 'amateurs' as those who just want to 'aim at yours'.[11] In Blake's hands, cold etymology and lexicography become fiery satire; pun thrives on such sandwiches in the desert.

Generally exiled to light verse or satire, such puns are nonetheless models in miniature of prosody. Poetic form itself has a punning logic or illogic because it constantly sets up equivalences that depend on difference. Poetry is structured on a principle that Wimsatt's groundbreaking essay, 'One Relation of Rhyme to Reason', calls counterlogical diagramming.[12] The principle is simple but its implications are not. Poetry is written in lines of

---

[9] *The Faerie Queene*, ed. Thomas P. Roche, Jr (Harmondsworth, 1978). This is identical to the Yale English Poets edition.

[10] The 'old-manifold' pattern thus has its own cumulative design, in contrast to the stanza's other rhyming paradigm, with its random trisyllable interrupting a run of monosyllabic words (*land—understand—band—hand*). Yet both paradigms use a simple trick that frees rhyme from the appearance of contrivance: the word that initiates the first rhyming paradigm is introduced as simply the necessary second term in the expression 'young and old', just as 'understand' and 'band' seem less a matter of contrivance because they take in stride the idiom 'heart and hand'.

[11] Nelson Hilton, *Literal Imagination: Blake's Vision of Words* (Berkeley, 1983), p. 7.

[12] W. K. Wimsatt, *The Verbal Icon* (Lexington, Ky, 1954), pp. 154–5. The companion pioneer essay is Roman Jakobson, 'Concluding Statement: Linguistics and Poetics', in *Style in Language*, ed. Thomas A. Sebeok (Cambridge, Mass., 1960), pp. 350–77.

equal length but the lines will never do equal work or equal play – arguably not even in verse structured entirely on a rigid parallelism. The same specious equivalence is found within lines, as Wimsatt explains: 'The smallest equalities, the feet, so many syllables, or so many time units, are superimposed upon the linear succession of ideas most often without any regard for the equalities of logic. Two successive iambs may be two words, or one word, or parts of two words, and so on' (p. 154).[13] There is something inherently punning, we might say, in the very principle of versification in lines: like the contingencies of like sounds in a homonymic pun, the matching of equal units of measure in a series of poetic lines promises similarity but delivers dissimiliarity. And rhyme is the most common reminder of this punning principle.

When I speak of rhyme here I will refer almost exclusively to end-rhyme, still one of the most tantalizing and neglected features of poetic form. Rhyme of any kind brings attention to sound patterns and hence, as Donald Wesling puts it, 'every line or two, [rhyme] remind[s] the reader that poetry is a verbal art'.[14] End-rhyme reminds the reader more pointedly that poetry is a verbal art that arrays itself in lines; reminds him, that is, of its structure of specious equivalences. The recurrence of rhyme allows us to measure how much of the poem's semantic chores or how much of an unfolding sentence's syntactic labor each individual line has carried out in the time allotted to it. When written in a single meter, the poem's lines all punch the same time clock, but each does a different job. Rhyme is arguably the most pervasive means whereby English poetry demarcates the line as the unit of phonetic and rhythmic measure, while denying the line as 'unit of logical measure', in Wimsatt's phrase. This is a principle so little assimilated in current teaching about poetry that Paul Fussell's still standard handbook *Poetic Meter and Poetic Form* trumpets forth just the opposite precept that in poetry 'units of equal size and shape imply a degree of equality or even parallelism in the materials they embody'.[15] They imply it, but they don't do it. It is because Fussell's law of equal lines – equal play is usually broken in poetry that puns and rhymes can be funny: it is because the meanings of 'lot

[13] For instance, in lines 4–5 of the Spenser stanza above, the final foot of line 4 is the last two syllables of a three-syllable word (–*derstand*), while the corresponding foot in line 5 is two monosyllabic words (*loues band*). In this last foot line 4 breaks from its pattern of tucking words inside iambs with no spillover, while line 5 picks up this coordination of word and foot only in its final iamb; each of its first four feet includes one word plus the first or last syllable of another word:

Suffice | it heare | by signes | to vn|derstand
The vs|uall ioyes| at knit|ting of | loues band.

[14] Donald Wesling, *The Chances of Rhyme: Device and Modernity* (Berkeley, 1980), p. 23.
[15] Paul Fussell, *Poetic Meter and Poetic Form*, rev. edn (New York, 1979), p. 161.

o' news' and 'hypotenuse' belie their rhythmic similarity so thoroughly that their coupling can joke about the halfbreed nature of English. In Gilbert's outrageous rhyme three words are put in a position of equivalence with one long word; a group of solidly Saxon monosyllables measure up to a single Greek polysyllabic word. Such moments of specious equation are the rule rather than the exception in most poetry. Rhyme can often alert us to what Westling calls 'the intermittent shock when we discover a discourse, which seems natural, is in fact overdetermined by a line of devices of equivalence' (p. 72). For students of poetry since Jakobson this information is hardly a lot of news, but thinking about the pun may provide a new way of making sense of it.

Rhyme, then, necessarily admits that poetry's equivalences are all devices. The equation of lines of matching length and words of matching sound works deliberately against the grain of the unequal units of sense of the lines and the unlike meanings of their end-rhymes. In this way rhyme opens the door to pun. But how does rhyme's receptivity to pun work on the level of local effect in a poem? Two possibilities seem equally plausible. Does rhyme make more audible other contingencies of sound? Does the chime of rhyme train the ear to pick up possible surrounding puns, perhaps by amplifying the general circumambient din of phonemes? Or does rhyme tend to focus the ear's attention on line endings, thus cordoning off the rest of the line as transparent discourse? According to this second suggestion, end-rhyme gives a private concert whose strains do not invade other regions of the poem. The chiming words that end up closing the lines are admitted to be collocations of arbitrary sounds that haphazardly, thanks to the luck of the language's philological lottery, sound like other collocations of arbitrary sounds. But what is fit in between the rhymes, or what leads up to or finds its supposedly natural close in the rhymes, comes from art, not chance. Slippage, excess, and play – or at least a rationed harkening to the call of the phoneme – is permitted at line endings, but not in the intervening words.

In *Poetry as Discourse*, Antony Easthope argues that Augustan poetics reins in the dangerous materiality of words by not only permitting rhyme at line endings but demanding it, so that rhyme is consistently written off to convention, a grudging concession to the materiality of language, but one so scrupulously licensed that it cannot infect its neighbors which are, of course, equally a jostling of like and unlike sounds.[16] The Augustan formula invites the question of the authority with which rhyme in any era may put the infectious, babbling echolalia of the phoneme into quarantine. Can rhyme limit attention to sounds purely to the like sounds that mark line

---

[16] Antony Easthope, *Poetry as Discourse* (London, 1983), pp. 110–21.

endings, and hence inoculate the other words from the dangers of the punning or rhyming chains they might conjure up? Or is the chanciness of end-rhyme always potentially contaminating? What is to prevent the inevitable answer of the second rhyme from turning into any one of a series of wrong numbers: 'True wit is nature to advantage dressed, / What oft was thought – oh heck, you know the rest'? Another of the most famous and truly witty of Pope's couplets, because of the yawning gap between the two rhyming words – a gap in meaning, etymology, and even in language – invokes a still greater slice of the rhyming paradigm: 'Here files of pins extend their shining rows / Puffs, powders, patches, Bibles, Billet-doux'. That *billet-doux* could hardly be bettered; it fits to the letter; as Pope's couplet-closing rhymes often make us feel, for that slot in the line and in the couplet and in the poem, it's just the ticket. But especially in a line structured so carefully on chance affinities of sounds, we cannot entirely block out other words it also sounds like, other rhymes that would have been possible, and that hover over our reading of this one as the word *lead* informs the rhymes of Portia's song. The second line's initial 'puffs' and 'powders' might seem to promise that the line should end with a glance of Belinda's 'nose', to which she might apply them, while the line's alliterative consonants invite both 'pose' and 'bows', and coming as it does at the end of the inventory of Belinda's dressing table, the line both hints and represses consideration of how much she 'owes' for all these spoils. Even in Pope's perfect, canonical couplets, files of rhymes, if not quite files of puns, extend their shining rows.

Discussions of the couplet tend to formulate the relation between two lines as a little story with a happy ending: we say that the second line of the couplet echoes or chimes with or closes or completes the first. But the disruptive slippage of pun threatens to mock the obedient response of rhyme. In some cases we may wish to say that the answering rhyme line is rather a distorted memory of the first; 'drest', filtered through the intervening baffles of the second line, comes out 'expressed'. The earphones of pun enable us to hear the second line of a couplet as the first misheard, refiltered, rechanneled, muffled, translated or mistook, as in the cumulative word-of-mouth distortions in the game of telephone. The first line may be less completed in the second than corrected, amplified, or revised. Or the first line may be the inadequate formulation only found in its pure form in the second. Rhyme counters the transience of orality. A spoken word is an event that can never be exactly repeated, not a cherishable mark, nothing you can look up. Each line of a rhymed poem evaporates as soon as it is uttered, with its receding into the already-said marked by its end-rhyme. But with the advent of the next line, the one just spoken into the abyss of fleeting time reappears as a similar sound. We rightly think of rhyme as essential to verse as spoken and heard, but it is also a memory device like writing.[17]

Turning to some illustrations, I will largely ignore the visual character of rhyme and pun, and consider audible effects. In two brief Shakespearean passages, from *Macbeth* and from the sonnets, the same pun is made audible by rhyming effects. Informed that his son died with his 'hurts before', Siward eulogizes him with a gentle quibble:

> Had I as many sons as I have hairs,
> I would not wish them to a fairer death.
> (V.viii.48–9)[18]

The pun on *hairs* and *heirs* is reinforced by the repetition of the sound of *hairs* in *fairer* in the next line. The pun would be less vivid to the ear if the line read, for example, 'I would not wish them to a braver death'. Because the sound of *hairs* resonates in *fairer*, *hairs* can resonate with its homonymn *heirs*. Another way to formulate the effect of rhyme and pun in this pair of lines would be to note how the echo of the first end-word with the penultimate word of the second line suggests a near-miss of a rhyming couplet; the pair could so easily become a couplet, or almost one: 'Had I as many sons as I have hairs / I would not wish them to a death more fair.' The terminal word *hairs* already has its rhyme, we might say, in its punning twin *heirs*, and hence it would be redundant to make the teleuton of the succeeding line a rhyme with *hairs*. Mere empty air, pun begets its own heir.

This exchange takes place in the final one hundred lines of the play, so we would expect rhyme to begin to sound, even on the battlefield, signalling reconciliation and closure. Placing this pair of lines in its context, we can see the interplay of rhyme and pun.

> *Siward*   Had I as many sons as I have hairs,
>   I would not wish them to a fairer death.
>   And so, his knell is knoll'd.
>
> *Malcolm*   He's worth more sorrow,
>   And that I'll spend for him.

---

[17] Pun and rhyme, figured as slips of the tongue or chance substitutions, are both curiously related to the slip of the keys in typographical errors. A rhyming word may not echo its partner, but rather flub or slur it, in a misalliance of sounds as suggestive as the fruitful typos that Barthes discusses in 'Writers, Intellectuals, Teachers': not those mistakes that result from hitting the wrong key that just happens to spell out another word in the language (*port* for *poet*), but typos that spell no word in the language, the kind of mistake that 'opens up for me the *right of association*' (*peot* for *poet*) and in turn corresponds, for Barthes, to the brand of interpretation that favors the 'efflorescence of the signifier' (*Tel Quel* 47 (1971), p. 13).

[18] *The Complete Works of Shakespeare*, ed. David Bevington (Glenview, Ill., 1980).

Siward   He's worth no more.
They say he parted well, and paid his score,
And so, God be with him!

(V.viii.49–53)

Siward's blunt avoidance of rhyme through pun in lines 48–9 is reinforced
by 'his knell is knoll'd', a consonance that lends a tone of finality to the
father's refusal to mourn; the conjugation of the verb chimes the death bell:
ding-dong, knell-knolled. But he finishes with a couplet that continues the
scene's dominant economic metaphor: 'He's worth no more. / They say he
parted well, and paid his score' (V.viii.51–2). This couplet in turn recalls a
pun initiated a bit earlier in the scene, when Ross brings him the news with,
'Your son, my lord, has paid a soldier's debt' (V.viii.39). The familiar pun on
debt and *death* consoles the mourner with its phonetic assurance that death
is as inevitable as paying a debt, a righting of the balance, a totting up, rather
than a loss or gap in the accounts.

It is difficult to be certain to what degree such puns and rhymes are
motivated in a narrative or dramatic context. Clearly Siward and Ross do
not pun strictly in character as Hamlet does. But it may be instructive to
examine how the relay of pun and rhyme in this exchange works toward
coming to terms with a young man's early death, and an accounting of what
has been lost in exchange for what has survived at the end of *Macbeth*.
Malcolm's announcement that 'Macduff is missing, and your noble son'
(V.viii.38), which figures death as something missing ('I would the friends we
miss were safe arriv'd' in his entrance line in the scene) is replaced by
Siward's monetary language, as he sees the returning army but before he
hears the news of his son's death: 'Some must go off, and yet, by these I
see, / So great a day as this is cheaply bought' (V.viii.36–7). Ross in turn
echoes these figures when he tells the father, 'Your son, my lord, has paid a
soldier's debt', which may not turn the victory into a bargain, as Siward at
first supposes, but changes death from something missing to the replace-
ment of something owed or missing. Before Siward turns Ross's pun (*[paid a
soldier's] debt/death*) into a rhyme (*[worth no] more-[paid his] score*), he
counters with his own pun (*hairs/heirs*). The metaphor implied in the
consoler's pun (death is a debt) sees death as a restoration of tidiness or the
righting of an imbalance, the debtor's account reduced to a tidy zero. The
figurative connection implied in the mourner's pun, while not properly a
metaphor (heirs are not hairs, but are like heirs in number only), suggests
plenty, unreckonable multitude, a countless progency sprouting up; it is
almost a benign Hydra myth encapsulated in a pun. In his pun, Siward
figuratively multiplies his losses, as though testing Ross's caution against
extravagance of grief that 'Your cause of sorrow / Must not be measur'd by

his worth, for then / It hath no end' (V.viii.44–6). As the dead soldier paid his debt with his life, so the mourners must not squander their grief; Malcolm's insistence that the mourners have not yet paid their debt to the deceased ('He's worth more sorrow, / And that I'll spend for him') Siward counters with rhyme ('He's worth no more. / They say he parted well, and paid his score'). Ross's and Siward's puns help to bolster logically opposed but consoling metaphors. Puns themselves emblematize the swift economies of death as debt-paying, and embody the stoicism of Scots curtness; the bringer of bad puns is welcome.

Rhyme can even enable us to hear a pun when the punning words are not there at all. Stephen Booth annotates the sonnets with a particularly keen eye to how connotations of Shakespeare's words are often fueled by the illogic of rhyme and pun. Booth writes,

In the sonnets Shakespeare uses more of the ideational potential in words than the logic of their exposition needs or can admit. He often uses words that have a common pertinence to a context other than the one in which he uses them. . . . Shakespeare uses syntactically and logically pertinent ideas, ideas latent in words because of their habitual uses in other contexts, in rather the way he uses rhythmn and rhyme . . . he 'rhymes' ideas and 'rhymes' ideas with sounds. . . . Shakespeare plays to the mental faculties that under cruder conditions cause us to make and understand puns.[19]

We have seen how rhyme amplifies a pun in *Macbeth*, but rhyme can also make audible what Booth calls a 'potential pun'. He notes of the opening of Sonnet 68 that 'the particulars of the lines are summed up in a potential pun on "heir" and "hair" – words that do not appear in the poem' (p. 489):

Thus is his cheek the map of days outworn,
When beauty lived and died as flow'rs do now,
Before these bastard signs of fair were borne,
Or durst inhabit on a living brow –
Before the golden tresses of the dead,
The right of sepulchers, were shorn away,
To live a second life on second head –
Ere beauty's dead fleece made another gay.
                                        (Sonnet 68. 1–8)

As Booth suggests, the sonnet's contrast of the aging man's face with fashionable false cosmetics and stolen ornaments (chiefly 'tresses') suggests the *hair—heir* pun, but the pun is insinuated chiefly by a relay of like sounds, idiomatic expressions just slightly off-key or mispronounced, and elided

[19] Stephen Booth, ed. *Shakespeare's Sonnets* (New Haven, 1977), p. 371. All citations from the sonnets are from this edition.

words. The effect centres in the third line. While the first quatrain refers chiefly to the aging lover's refusal of cosmetics, as 'cheek' and 'brow' suggest, the second quatrain's focus on false 'tresses' allows the phrase 'signs of hair' to bristle through the 'signs of fair' in line 3. That line begins with 'Before', as does line 5, and (in an elided variation, 'ere'), line 8. *Heir* and *ere* are homonymic puns, so that if we recast line 3 as '[Ere] these bastard signs of fair were born', we do hear *heir* and *hair* after all. *Heir* emerges by a second chain of semantic and phonetic associations as well. In the context of this poem's treatment of questions of lineage – arguably in any context in English – the phrase *bastard signs* invokes the familiar idiom *bastard sons* (with a hint of a teasing paradox in *bastard sons and heirs* that bastard sons cannot rightly be heirs). Hence 'bastard signs of fair' contains both 'signs of hair' and a hint of the idiomatic 'son and heir', especially since the line ends with perhaps the most expected verb for such a subject, 'born', itself of course a pun; hairs are borne, and heirs are born. But if we allow the sense of 'hair' to dominate over 'heir', we might guess that line 3 should answer the 'outworn' of line 1 not with 'born' but with 'shorn', which does indeed terminate line 6. The unspecified pun on *hair—heir* then teases out some puns on words that are specified. The *sign—son—heir* matrix in turn lends to the phrase 'the right of sepulchers' an almost legalistic feel of questions of lineage, with perhaps a hint at the 'rite of se-pulchres' that are profaned by the shearing of hair from the beautiful dead.

The pun in the next example is more immediately audible, but the amplification it receives from rhyme is more complicated.

> Now with the drops of this most balmy time
> My love looks fresh, and death to me subscribes,
> Since spite of him I'll live in this poor rhyme,
> While he insults o'er dull and speechless tribes.
>
> (Sonnet 107.9–12)

Booth sees in line 11 what he calls a 'potential but unexploited play on *him* ["hymn"] and *rhyme* ["hymn"]' (p. 347). The pun 'spite of him/hymn, I'll live in this poor rhyme' suggests that the contest between death and rhyme, or death and the poet, is a war of genres. One of the ways death is made to 'subscribe' to the poet is by being turned into a name for another poetic mode: to drown out death's hymn – perhaps a triumphant song of 'insult' over 'dull and speechless tribes' – the poet incants his countersong of 'rhyme'. The poet's rhyme is poor but louder than death's muted hymn, which we can hear but faintly in the muted pun on 'him' (faint in part because, with the exception of the *eye/I* pun, we rarely expect to find puns on pronouns). Through this pun we hear the poet make death 'subscribe' to him, attributing to death a lower, less audible music than the poet's own.

The pun depends on reading the line as an independent unit. Only if we balance the first clause's qualification ('spite of him') against the main clause's declaration ('I'll live in this poor rhyme), can 'him' be prominent enough, audibly and syntactically, to be weighed against its sound-alike 'rhyme'. An important fine tuning mechanism that helps to make that pun audible is the integrity of the line. And the line is a unit staked out by end-rhyme. The pause at 'him' is heightened by matching the caesura in the preceding line, as the parallelism of 'him' and 'rhyme' is emphasized because of the closure as 'rhyme' echoes 'time'.

When such quibbles are not buttressed by a structure of equivalences charted by rhyme, they must be spelled out, diffused, or distributed at greater length in order to be heard. We hardly think of Whitman as succumbing to the lures of such fatal Cleopatras, but of course the title *Leaves of Grass* is a pun, and the very plentitude of his cataloguing rhetoric leaves plenty of room for a jovial cameraderie of sounds wedged in shoulder-to-shoulder, as it were, to engage in some curious couplings. 'Vocalism' inventories the trials and qualifications of the orator, 'full-lung'd and limber-lipp'd' (line 2).[20] I must quote a long passage to arrive at the pun, but the need to do so is part of what I wish to investigate in this example:

> For only at last after many years, after chastity, friendship, procreation,
>   prudence, and nakedness,
> After treading ground and breasting river and lake,
> After a loosen'd throat, after absorbing eras, temperaments, races, after
>   knowledge, freedom, crimes,
> After complete faith, after clarifyings, elevations, and removing obstructions,
> After these and more, it is just possible there comes to a man, a woman, the
>   divine power to speak words. (lines 5–9)

In a poem composed largely of a list, it may seem that pun has little chance to grab a foothold. Each word stands out so much as a flag of the category it names in each line's parade of nouns that it would seem to shirk the possibility that it might find itself shadowed by some other word that elbows into the procession on the basis of a specious phonetic cousinship. The accumulation of words seems a simple reflection of the accumulation of traits and experiences required of the orator. Yet this processional order of substantives makes slips in parallelism particularly vulnerable to the incursion of pun. What would compel or resist our reading 'eras' (line 7) as an anagrammatic pun on 'ears'? On the basis of structures of parallelism already established, we might well expect after the line's opening phrase 'after a loosen'd throat' that the next item in the inventory should be 'after

---

[20] Walt Whitman, *Leaves of Grass*, eds Sculley Bradley and Harold W. Blodgett (New York, 1973). 'Vocalism' appeared in its final form in 1881 in *Autumn Rivulets*.

absorbing *ears*', thus unifying the line as a catalogue of the organs that need
to be opened or exposed in order to gain 'the divine power to speak words'.
But 'absorbing' turns out to apply not to the organ one does the absorbing
with, but to what is absorbed. In 'eras, temperaments, races', the phoneme
'ears' is dilated or extended, or as Hartman would say decondensed or
decollapsed or 'distribut[ed] in linear fashion by transfer or contamination'
(p. 343). Other curious punning effects in this passage seem to me to be
independent of the question of rhyme. The pun in 'after absorbing *eras*' may
be in some degree prepared for by 'after many *years*' (line 4), where again a
label for a large measurement of time has the sound of *ears* in it. If we attend
to orthography and not to our ears, we can note time twice in '*temp-era-
ments*'. Without the cordons of rhyme and of meter marked by rhyme, the
local resonance of a single word is amplified by more of the poem. This
effect is not just a function of Whitman's noun-rich style; it is also a function
of the lack of rhyme-marked line endings, and the lack of equivalent line
lengths. Such puns are surely not what Whitman has in mind in the closing
prophesy that the voice of 'the develop'd soul' (line 17) will have 'the quality
to bring forth what lies slumbering forever ready in all words' (line 21), yet
the very itemizing style that makes his words seem to stand at attention *as
words* also provides room for puns to loaf at ease.

Puns amplified by rhymes are not the exclusive domain of embroidered
courtier poetry, or the tongue-twisting extravaganzas of a Hopkins or Dylan
Thomas. I will close with a foray into territory we might imagine untouched
by flip quips and the allures of wordplay, the chaste tidy stanzas of
Housman. I trust the pun in *A Shropshire Lad* XI will announce itself with no
italics from me:

> On moonlit heath and lonesome bank
>   The sheep beside me graze;
> And yon the gallows used to clank
>   Fast by the four cross ways.
>
> A careless shepherd once would keep   5
>   The flocks by moonlight there,
> And high amongst the glimmering sheep
>   The dead man stood on air.
>
> They hang us now in Shrewsbury jail:
>   The whistles blow forlorn,   10
> And trains all night groan on the rail
>   To men that die at morn.
>
> There sleeps in Shrewsbury jail to-night,
>   Or wakes, as may betide,

A better lad, if things went right,   15
Than most that sleep outside.

And naked to the hangman's noose
The morning clocks will ring
A neck God made for other use
Than strangling in a string.   20

And sharp the link of life will snap,
And dead on air will stand
Heels that held up as straight a chap
As treads upon the land.

So here I'll watch the night and wait   25
To see the morning shine,
When he will hear the stroke of eight
And not the stroke of nine;

And wish my friend as sound a sleep
As lads I did not know,   30
That shepherded the moonlit sheep
A hundred years ago.[21]

In 'ring' (line 8) we have a perfect conjunction of our two topics: a rhyme that is a pun. It might seem that the quibble on *ring* and *wring* is a euphemism for a gruesome means of death (as *hanging* is a softened name for *strangling*). The pun substitutes the signal for the execution to take place (ring) for the true agent of execution (wring).[22] This poem about the deathly force of perfect timing illustrates the simultaneity of pun and the sequentiality of rhyme. We hear *ring* at the same time that we hear *wring*, while in its rhyming partner, *string*, which both chimes with *ring* and contains it, we hear (or at least see) *ring* again, but as a delayed echo. The return of the sound of *ring* in *string* not only keeps us remembering the pun but also corresponds, after a lapse of two lines, to the instantly doubled meaning of *ring* as *wring* in the pun. This poem might be said to figure rhyme as a pun that takes longer, or a delayed pun. Hartman suggests that the intermediate material that separates two rhyming words wedges apart the composite creature of pun and keeps the

---

[21] All citations are to *The Collected Poems of A. E. Housman* (New York, 1965).
[22] A similar substitution governs Housman's familiar 'Eight O'Clock', where the clock strikes the hour and the deathblow at once:

> Strapped, noosed, nighing his hour,
> He stood, and counted them, and cursed his luck;
> And then the clock collected in the tower
> Its strength, and struck.

The pun on *ring* and *wring* encapsulates the figurative logic of this stanza; like the *hair/heir* pun in Shakespeare's Sonnet 68, it is there without being there.

rhymes from recollapsing on top of each other, back to their originary unity: 'When a pun or portmanteau word sorts itself out, and similar sounds are put in end-line positions, we get rhyme' (p. 347).[23] Often the only way to explain a pun to someone who misses it is to repeat it, slowly; a rhyme does its own repeating. Pun's instantaneous doubling meets rhyme's sequential echoing in the penultimate stanza:

> So here I'll watch the night and wait
> To see the morning shine,
> When he will hear the stroke of eight
> And not the stroke of nine.

Just before Housman's noose tightens we hear in this stanza the punning 'stroke of fate', by the same elision that enabled us in to hear in Sonnet 68 'hair' in 'signs of fair'. The prisoner does not live to realize that what he hears as the momentous 'stroke of fate' is merely the prosaic, hourly 'stroke of eight', to be followed by the unstartling, insignificant 'stroke of nine', merely punctual and not prophetic. The poet provides a footnote, after line 6, that explains the idiom behind the poem's odd conjunction of shepherding and hanging, 'Hanging in chains was called keeping sheep by moonlight'; the first two stanzas show where the idiom came from. But now that hangings are civic and not rural, the old idiom yields to the new pun. For the rustic 'clank' of hanging in chains, we have the ruthless, public 'ring' of death; the mythic, conveniently Oedipal 'four cross ways' as the site of execution is replaced by the urban jail (with perhaps the trains' whistles and groans replacing the baaing of the sheep). At the pastoral crossroads, the blow of the gallows may indeed seem like the stroke of fate, but in the jail or urban square the consolations of such mythologizing are mocked by pun. Fate's stroke is now punctual, public, merely what happens daily between the stroke of seven and the stroke of nine.

Yet in this stanza the rhyme is arguably more punning than the pun. The word that completes this *abab* scheme could not conceivably be any more fitting than it is. *Nine* is clearly the one, the inevitably right word; clocks cannot strike backwards, or strike any way but one hour after the next. The rightness, the inescapable aptness of that final rhyme on *nine* has a

---

[23] If rhyme is a divided and delayed pun, then of what is pun a divided or inadequate approximation? Shoaf argues that for Milton pun is a debased and fictive eternity, and hence eating the apple gives Adam and Eve an appropriately bogus simulacrum of God's instantaneous process of knowing: 'the simultaneity (of meanings) in a pun is time's version of eternity's instantaneity of knowing. . . . In a pun or metaphor, the simultaneity of meaning gives us a feeling of the access of power (the overcoming of time): we feel we know more, faster, than we feel we do in ordinary discourse' (*Milton*, p. 62). For a 'temporal perspective' on the heroic couplet, see Fredric V. Bogel, 'Dulness Unbound: Rhetoric and Pope's *Dunciad*', *PMLA* 97 (1982), p. 845.

surprising yet inevitable punch-line effect like a good pun. It fulfills at one stroke two orders of cogency, completes at once two simultaneous sequences: *nine* is the second term in the sequences *shine—nine* and *eight— nine*. It thereby makes rhyme rather like a mere counting or ticking off of the next, and the only possible item in a sequence or series.

Rhymes on the cardinal numbers account for and yet explode the fiction that rhyme is an inevitable confirmation of the sense. *Eight—nine* can be thought of as a sequence in time, for the clock always strikes eight before it strikes nine, and it thus lends to rhyme and rhyme scheme the aura of orderly sequence. But as a series of integers *eight—nine* is arguably sequential but not temporal: like the alphabet, the integers are simply defined as arrayed in that order. We could use the alphabet, like any *a priori* sequence, as a numbering system, at least up to twenty-six; but A no more essentially comes before B *in time* than eight does before nine, as an agreed-upon sequence of words. In the light of this double connection of the integers to iron-clad order and arbitrary listing, we can see why Housman's figures for fate are often numerical, as in the last stanza of 'When first my way to fair I took' (*Last Poems* XXXV):

> – To think that two and two are four
> And neither five nor three
> The heart of man has long been sore
> And long 'tis like to be.[24]

Or, more familiarly, as in the little subtraction problem he solves in 'Loveliest of Trees' (*A Shropshire Lad* II):

> Now, of my threescore years and ten,
> Twenty will not come again,
> And take from seventy springs a score,
> It only leaves me fifty more.

The surety of mortal mathematics is figured in the inescapable rightness – a rightness derived from the correctness of the calculation – of the rhymes, particularly 'score' and 'fifty more'. When the Biblical life-span is worked into the calculation of seventy minus twenty, with a result not of a scripturally resonant 'twoscore and ten' but a humble 'fifty', it releases *score* for a bitter Housmanian pun: a score is a debt (*Macbeth*'s 'paid his score'), but also a count or tally – a cut or nick to mark a point – it can be both an amount earned and an amount due; 'score' is time's tally, the debt we rack

---

[24] This stanza would seem more flip and punning if lines 3–4 were switched with lines 1–2; here the descending numerical sequence 'four-three' governs the sequence 'sore-be' in such a way that we are less likely to notice that it would be possible, and conceivably more logical, if line 2 read 'And neither three nor five'.

up to death even as we pay out each year of life.[25] For Housman, to write poetry is to reckon up that score, and it is scarring work: 'Out of a stem that scored the hand / I wrung it in a weary land' (Terence, this is stupid stuff' (*A Shropshire Lad* LXII)). Its function in a rhyming sequence reveals in 'score', the innocent round number with its Biblical echoes, a punning connection to the painful incisions of time-markers: a score can score as a ring can wring. Housman's puns of fate suggest the fate of puns: mere signifiers, servants of meaning (a clock's chime, a slashed line on a score sheet) become masters, so that the very signals that mark the passing of time – the clangs, nicks, ding-dongs, tic-tocs, jots – themselves do time's slaying work. Housman's Time needs to carry only its hour-glass, which will do the work of its sickle.[26]

Having elevated pun to a mythopoeic force in Housman, I wish to close with a caution. It is dangerous to assume that the local tics of puns in lyric poems must serve a coherent reading of the poem, and that puns that do not mean anything in this sense are simply not there.[27] Like the Augustan poetic of sound as echo to sense, this tendency toward making puns serve meaning robs them of some of their wildness and shimmering contingency. Like someone who responds to coincidental encounters by denying the sheerly accidental ('It's a small world'), such readings can seem defenses against the weird accidents, amazing flukes and lucky hits that the one-armed bandit of language dishes up. Yet one can heft even the lightest pun to test its weight against contextual pressures without insisting that whatever puns, puns right. By testing how puns fit or fight other poetic orders of equivalence, correlation, and cogency, we may keep the door ajar to renewed attention to poetic form in the light of current theoretical concerns with overdetermination, indeterminacy and phonemic play.

[25] If we make the numbers less rounded off in order to shuffle more names for numbers into line-end position, we end up not with Housman, but with something that sounds like an Ogden Nash send-up of actuarial tables:

> Now of my threescore and fourteen
> Twenty won't again be seen,
> And take from seventy-four a score
> It only leaves me fifty-four.

[26] Housman's punningly striking clocks join a line of familiar puns about time that turn its markers into its physical agents, such as the riddling inscription for a sundial, 'They all injure, the last kills' (cf. Thoreau's quip in *Walden* ("Economy") that you cannot 'kill time without injuring eternity'), and even the man who threw his clock out of the window because he wanted to see time fly.

[27] See Booth, p. 370:

Most people who talk about poetry will not admit secondary senses or overtones or invasions of logically impertinent contexts unless the presence of such ideational static is capable of promotion to the distinction of full-fledged, syntactically admissable ambiguity and therefore capable of interpretation.

6

'The Pas de Calais': Freud, the Transference and the Sense of Woman's Humor

Joel Fineman

If your four negatives make your two affirmatives, why then the worse for my friends and the better for my foes.

(Twelfth Night V.i.21–3)

For Freud and for Lacan both, transference is a theoretical idea initially developed to account for specific practical failures.[1] Freud thought out his first thoughts on transference in relation to the irresolute conclusion of the Dora case, the failure of which Freud attributed to his inadequate and belated appreciation of the nature and force of Dora's transference to his own person. Lacan developed his ideas about the transference in the course of a polemical attack on the analytic practice of ego psychology, where the stress on an interpersonal relation between two potentially autonomous egos, along with an accompanying concern for a neat – Lacan thought an inane – symmetry or complementarity between the patient's transference and the analyst's countertransference, provokes and secures, according to Lacan, an imaginary identification between patient and analyst that, of necessity, orients the direction of the treatment towards an exercise of power.[2] For Lacan, such a regime of power is the inevitable result of an inability to sustain a *praxis*, specifically an analytic practice, 'in an authentic manner', and it is possible, of course, to see evidence of Lacan's claim – i.e., an instance of a psychoanalytic rush to power that derives its motivation

---

[1] This chapter was originally delivered, in somewhat different form, to a conference on 'Lacan and the Transference' at The University of Massachusetts at Amherst, 14–16 June 1985.

[2] 'I hope to show how the inability to sustain a *praxis* in an authentic manner results, as is usually the case with mankind, in the exercise of power.' Jacques Lacan, 'The Direction of the Treatment and the Principles of its Power', *Ecrits*, trans. Alan Sheridan (New York, 1977), p. 226.

from an inauthentic psychoanalytic practice – in Freud's treatment of Dora. At any rate, Freud's manhandling of Dora's transference has often been criticized on just these grounds.

Apart from the connection to the question of therapy, however, there is nothing at all theoretically new about the idea of transference. That affectively charged events in the present recapitulate, that they repeat, the psychic reality of infantile experience goes, so to speak, without saying in any psychoanalytic discourse, and it is only because this repetition can be put to use in therapy, when subjected to what both Freud and Lacan call 'interpretation', that the phenomenon of transference deserves and receives any special theoretical attention.

As a phenomenon of repetition, however, the logic of the transference seems, at least at first glance, at odds with the logic of a therapy. It is assumed by psychoanalysis that the patient is compelled to repeat, Freud sometimes says 'to act out', in his analysis precisely that which brings him to analysis, the patient thereby living out the nosographic past in the therapeutic present. This repetition is the essence of transference, its most urgent and insistent motivation, and this is irreducibly the case, since Freud characteristically gives an absolute quality to transferential repetition, as in the discussion of the repetition compulsion in *Beyond the Pleasure Principle*, the primary evidence for which Freud draws from the phonemonon of transference. But if transference in analysis is an enjoined, necessary repetition in the present of the past, how is it possible that any therapeutic innovation can ever be achieved? According to the theory of transference, every moment of analysis, from beginning to interminable end, is assimilated to, is fed into, a machinery of recapitulation such that the interventions of the treatment, the surprises of analysis – indeed, the very cure that analyst and patient together are embarked on – are nothing more than symptomatic repetitions of the illness they address. Hence the theoretical problem, a problem of recursive, replicating repetition, that the transference poses to the practice of psychoanalysts. Written out as transference, the therapeutic present necessarily becomes another chapter in the same old story, a story that already includes, and thereby renders secondary, the interpretative novelty that sees the way in which the story it interprets and partakes in is a repetition of the past.

This is why, for Freud and Lacan both, the *interpretation* of the transference becomes so central an issue. For there to be any consequence whatsoever of any analytic treatment, there must be a way in which the repetition of the transference becomes a repetition with a difference, one that makes a difference to or in a patient who would otherwise stay the same. For Freud this difference comes when the analyst, interpreting the therapeutic present, 'obliges [the patient] to transform his repetition into a memory'. 'By that means,' says Freud, 'the transference, which, whether affectionate or hostile, seemed in every case to constitute the greatest threat to the treatment, becomes its best tool, by whose help the most secret compartments of mental life can be opened.'[3] For Lacan, who conceives the process Freud called 'Repeating, Remembering, and Working Through' in a somewhat different way, therapeutic innovation also derives from the interpretation of the transference, for, as Lacan puts it, 'In order to decipher the diachrony of unconscious repetitions, interpretation must introduce into the synchrony of the signifiers that compose it something that suddenly makes translation possible – precisely what is made possible by the function of the Other in the concealment of the code, it being in relation to that Other that the missing element appears.'[4] This is how Lacan explains the fact that the analyst, frustrating the patient's infinite demand, resisting the patient's seduction, opens up a way, through the interpretation of the transference, for the patient to speak the signifier of an unconscious desire. But again, for Lacan as for Freud, it is only through the translation opened up by the interpretation of the transference that the therapeutic process can come up with something novel: 'My doctrine of the signifier is first of all a discipline in which those I train have to familiarize themselves with the different ways in which the signifier effects the advent of the signified, which is the only conceivable way that interpretation can produce anything new.'[5]

How is it, though, that the interpretation of the transference, an active construction on the part of the analyst – whether understood as Freud's translation of unconscious material into conscious material, or as Lacan's account of the emergence, through 'the different ways in which the signifier effects the advent of the signified', of an hitherto unspeakable signifier of desire – can escape the vicious hermeneutic circle traced out by the logic of transferential repetition? The question must be asked, for the very possibility of therapeutic practice hinges on its answer. Without an account of the way in which a psychoanalytic interpretation can be something other than a repetition of the same, the analytic patient will be thoroughly determined by the past that he perpetually and, in fact, in principle, *ab ovo* reenacts.[6] And this is a political as well as a clinical question, for the possibility of any psychoanalytic *political* practice – the possibility of any psychoanalytic intervention making any difference whatsoever – also hinges

[3] Sigmund Freud, *The Complete Introductory Lectures on Psychoanalysis*, trans. J. Strachey (New York, 1966), Lecture 27, p. 444.

[4] Lacan, 'Direction of the Treatment', p. 233.

[5] Ibid.

[6] *Ab ovo*, given the principle of deferred action, whereby a traumatic first time only becomes such retroactively, after the fact of itself, when activated by a second time that makes the first time primal.

on a way of understanding how a psychoanalytic interpretation of the transference can be something other than a repetition of the same.

I put this point in this way in order to address the practical question of the relation in psychoanalysis of interpretation to transference. This is Lacan's question when he asks in 'The Direction of the treatment' 'What is the place of interpretation?'[7] As answer, I want to suggest that the 'place' of psychoanalytic interpretation, i.e., the *topos* of psychoanalytic interpretation – somewhat more strongly, the commonplace of psychoanalytic interpretation – is more strictly circumscribed by the structure of the transference than is usually recognized and that, for this reason, the effect of any psychoanalytic interpretation, regardless of its content, will always be the same, even when, and just because, it introduces something novel. I take as an exemplary example a dream Freud took from his analysis of what he called 'a skeptical woman patient'. Freud first reports this dream in *The Introductory Lectures*, but he was quite struck by the example, so much so that he added it to the 1919 edition of *The Interpretation of Dreams*, as a footnote at the beginning of chapter 7, where it is supposed to serve as confirmation of Freud's claim in the text that 'one can reconstruct from a single fragment not, it is true, the dream – which is in any case a matter of no importance – but all the dream-thoughts.'[8] Freud reports the dream as follows:

A skeptical woman patient had a longish dream in the course of which some people told her about my book on jokes and praised it highly. Something came in then about a *'channel'*, *perhaps it was another book that mentioned a channel, or something else about a channel . . . she didn't know . . . it was all so indistinct.*

As it stands, the dream presents a mystery, a mystery compacted in the vague amorphous 'channel' which is all the woman patient carries with her as the residue of her dream. Following out his standard practice, however, Freud then asks the woman for her associations to this single fragment she remembers, and though, at first, registering resistance, nothing occurs to the woman in the context of 'channel', the next day she comes up with a joke to the following effect. An Englishman and a Frenchman are on the ferry between Dover and Calais. For some reason or another, the Englishman, speaking French, announces: '*Du sublime au ridicule il n'y a qu'un pas.*' 'Yes,' says the Frenchman, who is also a well-known author, '*le Pas de Calais*', meaning, Freud takes the trouble to point out, that the Frenchman thinks France sublime and England ridiculous. As far as Freud is concerned, this joke resolves the mystery of the fuzzy 'channel' of the dream. Freud explains:

[7] 'Direction of Treatment', p. 232.
[8] Freud, *Introductory Lectures*, Lecture 7, p. 118; Freud, *The Interpretation of Dreams*, trans. J. Strachey (New York, 1965), p. 556.

The *Pas de Calais* is a channel – the English channel. You will ask whether I think this had anything to do with the dream. Certainly I think so; and it provides the solution of the puzzling element of the dream. Can you doubt that this joke was already present before the dream occurred, as the unconscious thought behind the element 'channel'? Can you suppose that it was introduced as a subsequent invention? The association betrayed the skepticism which lay concealed behind the patient's ostensible admiration; and her resistance against revealing this was no doubt the common cause both of her delay in producing the association and of the indistinctness of the dream element concerned. Consider the relation of the dream-element to its unconscious background: it was, as it were, a fragment of that background, an allusion to it, but it was made quite incomprehensible by being isolated.[9]

Quite apart from the fact that this little story provides an excellent allegory of the relations between French and English psychoanalysis, there are many things to say about the way Freud takes this joke about his joke-book as corroborating confirmation of the fact that from a single fragment 'one can reconstruct all the dream thoughts'. To begin with, Freud's reconstructing story, his interpretation of the lady's transference, demonstrates the way in which Freud characteristically commits himself to a posture of hermeneutic authority and interpretative totality in the face of, or in response to, what is essentially enigmatic, constitutively shrouded, foundationally opaque – e.g., the 'navel' of every dream that Freud refers to in *The Interpretation of Dreams*, which is where the dream 'reaches down into the unknown', and which corresponds here to the lady's 'indistinct channel'.[10] Thus, equally characteristically, on the basis of his recon-struction, Freud can see the lady's resistance to psychoanalysis, objectified in the indistinctness of her 'channel', as the proof of the psychoanalytic pudding, so that the lady's skepticism with regard to psychoanalysis

[9] Ibid., pp. 556–7.

[10] Ibid., p. 564. For Freud, skeptical jokes such as the lady's raise fundamental epistemo-logical questions, *as* jokes, about the truth of the transference. The famous example is the joke about the two Jews in a railway carriage. ' "Where are you going?" asked one. "To Cracow", was the answer. "What a liar you are!" broke out the other. "If you say you're going to Cracow, you want me to believe you're going to Lemberg. But I know you're going to Cracow. So why are you lying to me?" ' Freud says of this joke: 'The more serious substance of the joke is the problem of what determines the truth. The joke, once again, is pointing to a problem and is making use of the uncertainty of one of our commonest concepts. Is it the truth if we describe things as they are without troubling to consider how our hearer will understand what we say? Or is this only jesuitical truth, and does not genuine truth consist in taking the hearer into account and giving him a faithful picture of our own knowledge? I think that jokes of this kind are sufficiently different from the rest to be given a special position. What they are attacking is not a person or an institution but the certainty of our knowledge itself, one of our speculative possessions. The appropriate name for them would therefore be "skeptical" jokes.' *Jokes and their Relation to the Unconscious*, trans. J. Strachey (New York, 1960), p. 115.

becomes for Freud the symptomatic witness of psychoanalytic truth. We can recall that Freud does exactly the same in his analysis of Dora, another example of a skeptical woman patient whose resistance Freud's interpretations energetically resist, and another case in which Freud's interpretations work to transform ridicule of psychoanalysis into admiration.

At the same time, however, Freud's story about the story of the *Pas de Calais* does more than enable him, through interpretation, to get the last laugh out of and on the lady's skeptical derision. For the little joke about the *Pas de Calais* not only thematizes but also acts out both Freud's and Lacan's understanding of the psychoanalytic transference, to the extent, at any rate, that the skeptical lady's story about the crossing of the channel is the story, precisely, *of* the transference, the *Übertragung*, the *transferre*, the crossing over, back and forth, between patient and analyst that Freud's interpretation of the story says the story is about. It is necessary to understand this point quite literally, for it is not only at the level of the plot that the Frenchman's English Channel is something to be crossed. More concretely, the '*pas*' of the '*Pas de Calais*' functions, at the level of the letter, as the signifier that occasions and sustains the desire of the narrative in which it plays a part, and it does so precisely as Lacan says it should when he speaks about the way in which 'interpretation must introduce into the synchrony of the signifiers that compose it something that makes translation [*la traduction*] possible'. In a merely etymological sense, 'transference' and 'translation' here translate each other; they are the same word, meaning 'to carry over', 'to carry across', both of these being translations of the same idea in Greek, where such crossing over is called 'metaphor', *metaphorein*.[11] The coherence and consistency of this metaphoric constellation allows us to say, speaking thematically, that the crossing of the *Pas de Calais* – from France to England, from the sublime to the ridiculous – is the metaphor of the Freudian transference, and this because such crossing amounts to the metaphor of metaphor itself. Accordingly, we can also say – but, again, only on the basis of this etymological derivation – that Freud's interpretation (his account of the skeptical deep meaning of the *Pas de Calais* joke) of the lady's indistinct 'channel' makes 'translation possible' by directly introducing metaphor into transference.

Grounded only in etymology, however, such an interpretation remains a merely thematic intervention, one that cannot carry any psychoanalytic weight, since the unconscious, for Freud as well as for Lacan, is concerned with signifiers not with signifieds. But with *pas*, as we hear it doubly articulated in the joke about the way the *pas* which is not but a step is not the

---

[11] Freud especially liked 'translation' jokes, e.g., '*Traduttore — Traditore*'. *Jokes*, pp. 34 and 121.

same as the *pas* of the *Pas de Calais*, we have a situation in which, as Lacan puts it, 'the signifier effects the advent of the signified, which is the only conceivable way that interpretation can produce anything new'. Specifically, we have an instance of the consequential operation of metaphor as Lacan has formally defined it, as the substitution of one signifier by another signifier such that the signified of the first signifier is assimilated to the second signifier at the cost of the remarked exclusion of the initial signifier, whatever it might be, from the entirety of the signifying chain.[12] Lacan's well-known algorithms for the reciprocally constitutive interrelationship obtaining between the linguistic axes Roman Jakobson called metaphoric (paradigmatic selection) and metonymic (syntagmatic combination) formalize this point with only slightly comic over-precision. On the one hand, according to Lacan,

$$f\left(\frac{S'}{S}\right)S \cong S(+)s$$

expresses 'the metaphoric structure, indicating that it is in the substitution of signifier for signifier that an effect of signification is produced that is creative or poetic, in other words, which is the advent of the signification in question. The sign $+$ between () represents here the crossing of the bar $-$ and the constitutive value of this crossing for the emergence of signification.'[13] On the other hand, according to Lacan,

$$f(S \ldots S')S \cong S(-)s$$

expresses 'the metonymic structure, indicating that it is the connection between signifier and signifier that permits the elision ... [of the original signifier, and where] the sign $-$ placed between () represents here the maintenance of the bar $-$ which, in the original algorithm [$\frac{S}{s}$, or signifier over signified; this is how Lacan represents Saussure's understanding of the sign] marked the irreducibility in which, in the relations between signifier and signified, the resistance of signification is constituted.'[14] Taken

---

[12] The chronology involved here – first and second signifiers – is, of course, merely heuristic, the subject's sense of successivity, which justifies affective terms such as 'loss', being a function of structural retrospection.

[13] Jacques Lacan, 'The Agency of the Letter in the Unconscious or Reason since Freud', *Ecrits*, p. 164.

[14] Ibid. For Lacan, the occultation of the original signifier is what makes this signifier the constitutive cause of the subject's desire for what this signifier signifies, structurally occasioned, by the operation of metaphor, as something lacking, and registered as such by metonymic resistance. For this reason, in the full explication of the formula for metonymy, which I have abbreviated above for the sake of clarity, Lacan explains the occultation of the

together, the formulae explain why, as Lacan says – here speaking against a naively nominalist account of metaphor – 'The creative spark of the metaphor does not spring from the presentation of two images, that is, of two signifiers equally actualized.' Rather, 'It flashes between two signifiers one of which has taken the place of the other in the signifying chain, the occulted signifier remaining present through its (metonymic) connection with the rest of the chain.'[15] In this way, through the association of the signified of one signifier with an altogether different signifier, we can understand, on the one hand, how it is that a metaphor manages to signify anything whatsoever, at the same time as we understand, on the other, through a metaphor's necessary metonymic evocation of an absent or occulted signifier, what it is about a metaphoric signification that will strike us as peculiar, i.e., what Lacan here calls its 'creative spark'.

For Lacan, this metaphoric–metonymic correlation describes the generalized and normative operation by means of which 'the signifier effects the advent of the signified', but the most explicit demonstration of this normative occurrence can be seen in that which makes a joke a joke. Thus, explaining his understanding of metaphor as a function of the substitution of one signifier for another, Lacan observes, 'We see, then, that metaphor occurs at the precise point at which sense emerges out of non-sense, that is, at the frontier which, as Freud discovered, when crossed the other way produces the word that in French is *the* word *par excellence*, the word that is simply the signifier "*esprit*".'[16] And it is in this inspired or spiritual comic sense that, we can say, the thematics etymologically embedded in the lady's jokes about the crossing of the English Channel are immanent to Freud's very registration of the transferential meaning of the joke. For the novelty produced by Freud's interpretation of the joke about the *Pas de Calais* and of

---

original signifier in subjective terms. Metaphorization, through which the subject accedes to language, accounts for the production of the subject as a desiring subject; thus: 'the metonymic structure, indicating that it is the connection between signifier and signifier that permits the elision in which the signifier installs the lack-of-being in the object relation, using the value of "reference back" possessed by signification in order to invest it with the desire aimed at the very lack it supports. The sign – placed between () represents here the maintenance of the bar – which, in the original algorithm, marked the irreducibility in which, in the relations between signifier and signified, the resistance of signification is constituted' (p. 164).

[15] Ibid., p. 157.

[16] In a passage on the problematics of translation, Lacan footnotes this point so as to make the connection to Freud's joke-book explicit:' "*Esprit*" is certainly the equivalent of the German *Witz* with which Freud marked the approach of his third fundamental work on the unconscious. The much greater difficulty of finding this equivalent in English is instructive: "wit" burdened with all the discussion of which it was the object from Davenant and Hobbes to Pope and Addison, abandoned its essential virtues to "humour", which is something else. There only remains the "pun", but this word is too narrow in its connotation' (ibid., p. 177).

the joke's relation to the skeptical lady's report of her dream consists in the way the metaphoric slippage it discloses between two *pas*'s – again, the *pas* which is not but a step and the *pas* of the *Pas de Calais* – is shown to correspond to the way the lady betrays 'the skepticism which lay concealed behind her ostensible admiration'. This is the translation *of* metaphor which is precisely that which the interpretation of the transference is supposed to bring about. Between the one and the other, between skepticism and belief, *il n'y a qu'un pas*, but for this very reason, as Freud interprets the joke, one moves, in one directed direction, *from* one *to* the other, i.e., from skepticism to belief because something missing is revealed. As skeptical dreamer, the lady dreams of a boat that travels derisively from France to England, from the sublime to the ridiculous, but because Freud gets the *point* of her joke, he can thereby reverse the lady's skeptical direction: to France and the sublime from England and the ridiculous. Passing from one *pas* to another, therefore, Freud's interpretation, which puts the lady in her transferential place, translating her ridicule into admiration, exemplifies at least one of 'the different ways in which the signifier effects the advent of the signified, which is the only conceivable way that interpretation can produce anything new'.

The point that seems important to stress is that the scope of this interpretative novelty is very strictly determined, whether understood performatively or thematically. Coming from *pasus*, *pas* is a simultaneously spatial and temporal figure of passage as such, passage in a double sense, first, as the movement across a distance, a passage or a passing, second, at the same time, passage as the very distance, space, breadth, opening – again, the passage – that passage passes over. *Pas* is thus, at once, not only the place but also the movement of the transference, its own *double entendre* making a place, within itself, for the movement of the transference or, the other way around, motivating a movement that traces out a transferential place. Given the etymology of *pas*, this is obviously the case thematically, but the point to emphasize is that, when metaphoricity is understood as substitution, this is also the case performatively, for the moment there are two '*pas*'s – and that there are two '*pas*'s is the point of the joke (not to mention the fact that it takes two feet to take one step) – then there is metaphor, and where there is metaphor there is necessarily one *pas* missing that metaphor, as metaphor, will metonymically evoke. We arrive, therefore, at a rule or regulation: if there are two '*pas*'s – *pas-pas* – then there is always one *pas* missing, a principle of *pas-pas* → ~~*pas*~~*-pas* that Lacan characterizes as 'the function of the other in the concealment of the code, it being in relation to that other that the missing element appears'. This is why Lacan also says that the structure of metaphor determines for the subject the structure of desire, a desire, precisely, for the signifier whose loss presents the pace, footstep, track, the *pas*, of *translatio* itself.[17] According to Lacan, this lost signifier, present only in the echo that remarks its absence, both constitutes and sustains the desire of a subject who, entering language through metaphor, subjected to and by metaphor, thereafter comes continually upon this missing signifying link whose loss reverberates throughout the signifying chain. Lacan makes this point directly when he glosses the metonymy formula, in a passage that I earlier elided, namely: 'It is the connection between signifier and signifier that permits the elision in which the signifier installs the lack-of-being in the object relation, using the value of "reference back" possessed by signification in order to invest it with the desire aimed at the very lack it supports.'[18]

In the terms presented by the skeptical lady's dream, we can say that *pas*, because it metaphorically traverses itself, necessarily surpasses itself, thereby motivating, in itself, its own crossing over upon or through itself, so as to leave over, as testamentary ruin of itself, as mark of its own internal diversion, the indistinct fragment of the 'channel' from which, Freud says, 'it is possible to reconstruct all the dream thoughts', i.e., from which it is possible – according to Freud's fundamental definition of what it means to interpret a dream – to identify the wish or desire that motivates the dreaming of the dream in the first place.[19] Correspondingly, this is also how 'interpretation', for Lacan, 'in order to decipher the diachrony of unconscious repetitions', 'must introduce into the synchrony of the signifiers that compose it something that suddenly makes translation possible'. Again, the 'something' that makes translation possible, suddenly, is the substitutive structure of metaphor – *pas* for *pas*, one for the other, *pas de deux* – that precipitates the *pas du tout* or even the *pas tout* – the one which is not altogether one – whose noticed absence motivates the metonymic temporality of erotic yearning. It is not surprising, therefore, that psychoanalytic interpretation, introducing metaphor into transference, will find in every indistinct channel the double and divergent articulation of *pas* – a *pas de chat* – as it here emerges in what Freud says is the point of the lady's joke: a two-step *pas-pas* that always serves to initiate a single step in the right psychoanalytic direction, a direction we can identify, moreover, using the title of Lacan's essay on the transference, as 'The Direction of the Treatment and the Principles of its Power'. *Pas*, as the passage over passage, carves out within itself, as the point of *any* joke, a signifying gap or opening across which and within which desire will always find its motive and also

[17] Related to this is the implicit foot fetishism informing Freud's account of Jensen's *Gradiva* – '*gradus*': 'step', 'walk', 'gait'.

[18] Ibid., p. 164. See note 14 above.

[19] This is why the interpretation of the dream is complete when we arrive at its 'navel', where it 'reaches down into the unknown'.

find its path. The structure of metaphor, in this way generating a novel signifier – a signifier not only of another signifier's signified but also of that other signifier's loss – thus necessarily, inexorably, provides the Freudian and Lacanian sense of the lady's humor.

It is important to notice the straightforward way in which the double *pas* of the *Pas de Calais* joke, as the smallest minimal unit of psychoanalytic wit, an 'equivoceme', thus recapitulates and calls out for the central thematics of psychoanalytic therapeutics: the arrival of the symbolic name of the father – *PaPa* – whose 'No' – *pas* – is also for Lacan 'the function of the other in the concealment of the code, it being in relation to that other that the missing element appears'. The predetermined appearance of this missing element, its predetermined appearance *as* missing – in the dream the indistinctness of the 'channel', in the interpretation of the dream what Freud reveals as the lady's 'resistance against revealing' – is what guarantees or warrants the Heideggerean erotics that makes the psycho-analytic truth into a fetish. Thus, the doubt of Woman – Freud's skeptical lady – functions as both frustrating object and animating impulse of Freud's hermeneutic want, something that keeps the analysis moving to and towards its interminable end. In either case, thinking of Truth or of Woman, the interpretation of the transference yields familiar topoi – the Truth of Woman or the Woman as Truth – in accord with the scenario of translation sketched out by the passage of *pas* through the detour of its round-trip passage through itself (that these topoi are typically marked with question-marks – 'What is Truth?' 'What does Woman want?' – follows from the way the punctuating structure of metaphor puts its own signification into question).[20] As his practice in the Dora case makes clear, Freud is true to

---

[20] Consider Freud's 'specimen dream' of Irma's injection, where the question of Irma's desire elicits from Freud the uncanny image of the printed formula for 'Trimethylamin', which Freud would have understood to formulate literally the chemistry of female sexuality (*Interpretation of Dreams*, p. 140). See also the question-mark whose punctuation interrupts normal syntax in Dora's dream of a letter she received from Frau K: 'if you would like? you can come'. Freud, *Dora: An Analysis of a Case of Hysteria*, trans. J. Strachey (New York, 1963), p. 114. The same question-mark governs Lacan's understanding of the relation of analyst to patient in the transference: 'man's desire is the *désir de l'Autre*. . . . That is why the question *of* the Other, which comes back to the subject from the place from which he expects an oracular reply in some such form as "*Che vuoi?*" "What do you want?", is the one that best leads him to the path of his own desire – providing he sets out, with the help of the skills of a partner known as a psychoanalyst, to reformulate it, even without knowing it, as "What does he want from me?" It is this superimposed level of the structure that will bring my graph (cf. *Graph III*) to completion, first by introducing into it as the drawing of a question-mark placed in the circle of the capital O of the Other, symbolizing by a confusing homography the question it signifies.' Lacan, 'The Subversion of the Subject and the Dialectic of Desire in the Freudian Unconscious', *Ecrits*, p. 312.

this truth when he verifies psychoanalysis by reference to that which he insists escapes psychoanalysis, Dora's lesbian relation to Frau K., which 'ex-ists' as the excess to the phallocratic that the phallocratic presupposes.[21] But so too is Lacan true to this truth when in 'Intervention on Transference', his commentary on the Dora case, Lacan puts his faith in the way the psychoanalyst, simply through his presence, brings dialogue to therapeutic discourse. 'A subject,' says Lacan, 'is strictly speaking, constituted through a discourse. Whatever irresponsibility, or even incoherence, the ruling conventions might impose on the principle of this discourse, it is clear that these are merely strategies of navigation intended to insure the crossing of certain barriers, and that this discourse must proceed according to the laws of a gravitation peculiar to it, which is called truth.'[22]

This is the regulating, orientating truth of the psychoanalytic interpretation of the transference, the truth that guides the captain of the psychoanalytic loveboat as he ferries back and forth between the sublime and the ridiculous, and a truth that is measured by the force of its titanic effect. What we see here, however, in the story of the *Pas de Calais* story, if this story is in fact exemplary, is that the effect of the interpretation of the transference, its truth or the effect of its truth, is the specific clinical sympton of transference itself. And if it is the case that the very indeterminacy of the transference is what determines the truth of its interpretation as something determinate, as a question which, *as* question, is an answer one can always count on, then it becomes reasonable to wonder, after Freud, whether the repetition with a difference produced by the metaphoricity of *pas* is not, as such, a repetition of the same, a difference now that makes no difference precisely because it tells the same old story of difference itself. If so, this would explain why even the authentic practice of psychoanalysis is itself 'inauthentic', which in turn would explain what seems to be a characteristically psychoanalytic rush to power. To put the point yet more bluntly and summarily, we can say that the *Pas de Calais* story is a narrative of

---

[21] 'The longer the interval of time that separates me from the end of this analysis, the more probable it seems to me that the fault of my technique lay in this omission: I failed to discover in time and to inform the patient that her homosexual (gynaecophilic) love for Frau K. was the strongest unconscious current in her mental life. . . . Before I had learnt the importance of the homosexual current of feeling in psychoneurotics, I was often brought to a standstill in the treatment of my cases or found myself in complete perplexity' (*Dora*, p. 142). As Suzanne Gearhart observes, Freud eventually at least sometimes, promotes this failure into a theoretical necessity, to a point where it precludes the possibility of a positive transference between a male analyst and a female homosexual, as in Freud's 'Psychogenesis of a case of Homosexuality in a Woman'. See S. Gearhart, 'The Scene of Psychoanalysis: The Unanswered Questions of Dora', *In Dora's Case: Freud — Hysteria — Feminism*, eds C. Bernheimer, C. Kahane (New York, 1985), p. 117.

[22] Jacques Lacan, 'Intervention on Transference', trans. J. Rose, *In Dora's Case*, p. 93.

metaphor that recounts the master narrative that specifically literary
language always tells about its own figurality. To the extent that Lacan and
Freud's theories of the transference recapitulate this story, we can say that
psychoanalysis interprets and partakes in a very traditional literariness –
and saying this tells us something important, for it helps to account, at least
in part, for psychoanalytic power. For the same reason, however, we can also
say that, in doing so, the novelty of psychoanalysis by no means introduces
something new.

But, we must add, it is not only psychoanalysis that is thus constrained;
so too is the skeptical lady, at least in so far as she is caught up in her
reading of the psychoanalysis she wants to put down, as in the lady's
dream, where 'some people told her about my book on jokes and praised it
highly'. I have been arguing that the structure of metaphor that governs the
transference also governs the interpretation of the transference, and that
this accounts for the topical complicity that obtains between the transference and its interpretation. For the same reason, however, it can also be
assumed that an engaged resistance to psychoanalysis will be equally
subjected to the rule of metaphor. I say this bearing in mind Derrida's
well-known 'post-structuralist' criticisms of the 'structuralism' of Lacanian
psychoanalysis.[23] As I have meant to imply throughout, Lacan's account of
the reciprocally constitutive correlation of spatializing metaphor (selection
from a code of signifiers that are structured as a code by binary differentiation) and temporalizing metonymy (combination over time of metaphorically selected signifiers) formulates, using the now somewhat dated
vocabulary of structuralist linguistics, the same logic of displaced spacing
and deferred timing that Derrida attempts to give a name to with his
neologism '*différance*'.[24] That such a theoretical homology joins Derrida to
Lacan, and through him to a determined Freud, no doubt requires far more
rigorous demonstration than can be presented here, but at the level of topoi
it is relatively easy to adduce what seem to be instructive repetitions of the
same. Leaving commonplaces such as Truth and Woman to the side, we
can take '*pas*' as a convenient example, since this is the title Derrida gave to
his reading of Blanchot. Commenting on a sentence of Blanchot –

[23] As in 'The Purveyor of Truth', *Yale French Studies* 52 (1975) (expanded on in *La Carte postale
de Socrate à Freud et au-delà* (Paris, 1980)), *Positions*, trans. A. Bass (Chicago, 1981), *Spurs:
Nietzsche's Styles*, trans. B. Harlow (Chicago, 1979).

[24] Arguing that every structuralist metaphor establishes the temporal metonymy of its own
origin, and taking as example the way Roman Jakobson understands /pa/ to be the first
phoneme of all speech, I have elsewhere discussed the way the 'post' of Derridean 'post-
structuralism' is predicated by a specifically structuralist understanding of rhetorical figurality,
in 'The Structure of Allegorical Desire', *Allegory and Representation: Selected Papers from the English
Institute, 1979–80*, ed. S. Greenblatt (Baltimore, 1981), pp. 26–60.

'*L'éloignement est ici au coeur de la chose*' ('Distancing here is at the heart of things') from '*Les deux versions de l'imaginaire*', in *L'Espace littéraire* – Derrida remarks:

La proximité du proche n'est pas proche, ni propre donc, et tu vois s'annoncer, de proche en proche, toutes les ruptures de sécurité. Quand je dirai éloignement, *désormais, quand je le lirai dans l'un de ses textes, entends toujours le trait invisible qui tient ce mot ouvert sur lui-même, de lui-même é-loigné: d'un pas qui éloigne le lointain de lui-même. Pas est la Chose.*[25]

The proximity of the near is not near; nor, then, is it proper to itself, and you see revealed, nearer and nearer, all ruptures of security. When, henceforth, I say *distancing*, when I read it in his texts, you should always hear the invisible stroke that holds this word open upon itself, distanced from itself by a step which distances the distant from itself. Step and stop is the thing.

If this '*Pas*', which '*est la Chose*' – '*cet étrange "pas" d'éloignement*' (p. 124) – is not what Lacan called '*La chose freudienne*', it nevertheless emerges as the same kind of intervening and interventive 'interval'.

Cet intervalle a la forme de l'absence qui permet le pas et la pensée, mais il intervient d'abord comme rapport du pas au pas ou de la pensée à la pensée, comme inclusion héterologique de pas à pas, de pensée à pensée, pas sans pas ou 'pensée sans *pensée'. Ce jeu (sans jeu) du sans dans ses textes, tu viens de voir qu'il désarticule toute logique de l'identité ou de la contradiction et qu'il le fait depuis 'le nom de mort' ou la non-identité du double dans le nom.*[26]

This interval has the form of an absence that permits stepping (stopping) and thought, but it first intervenes as the link of step to step, or of thought to thought, as the heterological inclusion of step within step or of thought within thought, step without step or 'thought without thought'. You have just seen how this play (without play) of the 'without' in his texts disarticulates any logic of identity or of contradiction, and how it does so commencing with 'the dead-name' or with the non-identity of the double in the name.

And this is not for Derrida a contingent or an accidental or an anecdotal fact, for, as Derrida goes on to explain:

Il y a toujours deux *pas. L'un dans l'autre mais sans inclusion possible, l'un affectant l'autre immédiatement mais à le franchir en s'éloignant de lui. Toujours deux pas, franchissant jusqu'à leur négation, selon le retour éternel de la transgression passive et de l'affirmation répétée. Les deux pas, le double pas désuni et à lui-même allié pourtant, l'un passant l'autre aussitôt, passant en lui et provoquant dès lors une double prétérition instantanée, mais interminable, voilà qui*

---

[25] Derrida, 'Pas (préambule)', *Gramma*, 3/4 (1978), p. 120.
[26] Ibid., p. 139.

forme une limite singulière entre la garde et la perte, entre le souvenir aussi et l'oubli. Ils ne s'opposent pas plus dans leur différence infinie, que le pas à l'autre pas. Selon ce simulacre de cercle — retour éternel du double pas — celui qui dit 'Viens' n'inaugure qu'à répondre déjà. Il suit celle qu'il paraît appeler et dont lui souvient son appel. 'Faux-pas' du désir, comme il est dit dans Le Pas au-delà, *et franchissement du cercle* (*pas de cercle*). *Pas est l'oubli, pas d'oubli doublement affirmé* (*oui, oui*).[27]

There are *always two* steps. One within the other but without any possible inclusion, one affecting the other immediately but by overstepping it while distancing itself from it. Always two steps, overstepping even their negation, in accordance with the eternal return of passive transgression and repeated affirmation. The two steps, the double step disunited and yet conjoined to itself, one immediately passing the other, passing within it and thereby provoking a double *praeteritio*, instantaneous but interminable: this is what forms the singular limit between keeping and losing, and between memory and forgetting as well. These are no more opposed in their infinite difference than is the one step to the other step. According to this simulacrum of the circle – eternal return of the double step – he who says 'Come' only inaugurates by already replying. He follows her whom he seems to call and of whom the call recalls him. *Faux-pas* of desire, as it is put in *Le Pas au-delà*, and step outside the circle (no circle, circle step). *Pas* is the forgetting, the step and stop of forgetting doubly affirmed (yes, yes).

Again, there is more that must be said here, a lot more; but the quotations allow the suggestion that between the psychoanalytic *pas-pas* and the Derridean '*oui, oui*' *il n'y a qu'un pas*, which in turn would explain why Freud's 'reconstruction' and Derrida's deconstruction both tend to circle (no circle) around the same fragmented point of difference. Men of *La manche*, the theory of the one plays ('*sans jeu*') an old practical joke on the theory of the other.

---

[27] Ibid., pp. 153–4.

7

The Sujet Suppositaire: Freud and Rat Man

Avital Ronell

'Wann haut'n (Van Houten) *die Mutter?* (When do mothers smack?) It was only later that I realized that my pun really contained the key to the whole of his sudden recollection from childhood ... (Displacement from the behind forwards; excrement becomes aliment; the shameful substance which has to be concealed turns into a secret which enriches the world.)

To bring obstinacy into relation with interest in defaecation seems no easy task, but it should be remembered that infants can very early behave with great self-will about parting with their stools, and that painful stimuli to the skin of the buttocks (which is connected with the anal erotogenic zone) are *an instrument* in the education of the child designed to break his self-will and make him submissive.

'Character and Anal Erotism', Sigmund Freud

Back to School

Mr Edward Glover, whose scholarship receives favorable citation from Jacques Lacan, might be held responsible for a peculiarly ironic inflection in the case history of psychoanalysis. In 'The Function and Field of Speech and Language' Lacan acknowledges an essay of Mr Glover whose title eludes mention in the body of his text but which in part runs, 'The Therapeutic Effect of Inexact Interpretation'. While it is not a work meant to pacify those whose major stake in criticism lies in the resistance to theory, it shows that 'not only is every spoken intervention received by the subject in terms of his structure, but the intervention takes on a structuring function in him in proportion to its form. It is precisely the scope of nonanalytic psychotherapy,' argues Lacan, 'and even of the most ordinary medical "prescriptions", to be interventions that could be described as obsessional systems of suggestion, as hysterical suggestions of a phobic order, even as persecutory supports, taking their particular character from the sanction they give to the subject's *méconnaissance* of his own reality.'[1]

The ostensibly 'remarkable' point that Glover appears to be urging concerns a hermeneutics 'where the question of correctness moves into the background'. The locality of a background upon which this question is posed – or rather, to which this question, by force of an *intervention*, owes its displacement – will engage if not command our every move in this chapter. For if the question of correctness retreats into the place of a background, entailing an implicit about-face of traditional interpretive values, then the entire maneuver participates like Rat Man's army in the rhetoric of the Freudian *Umkehrung*, reversing the face value of things to display the preferred 'arse upwards'.[2] As mere reversal, this in turn would maintain the 'intervention' of which Lacan speaks in its classic column, however, still following the marching orders and route traced out by the commanding symbolicity of male homosexuality whose structures, in place since the time of Plato, continue to assure the paradigm for the transmission of knowledge. Supposing that the production of knowledge, meant or unmeant, depended upon this type of seed implant to guarantee transmission to posterity, and in order to constitute itself as a body of knowledge, this forces an issue that does not properly belong within the confines of scholarly writing but that nonetheless requires some sort of intervention from 'our' side, if only to leave the question open: whether any teaching whatsoever can take place,

---

[1] Jacques Lacan, 'The Function and Field of Speech and Language in Psychoanalysis', in *Écrits*, trans. Alan Sheridan (London, 1977), p. 87. In its entirety, the title of Mr Glover's essay reads 'The Therapeutic Effect of Inexact Interpretation; a Contribution to the Theory of Suggestion' (*IJP* XII:4).

[2] This is Strachey's interpretation of 'reversal' in *The Interpretation of Dreams, Complete Psychological Works* (London, 1953–74), vols 4 & 5. While any reading of the body reflects, at least in part, the organization of a social space and the hierarchical ordering of its representations, anal zones have tended to attract the politics of the pun. As W. Redfern points out in *Puns* (Oxford, 1984), Swift's *Regarding the End* reminds us that eschatology and scatology are close kin, since both concern the final issue of things (Spanish uses the same word for both: *escatológico*): '. . . his love of inversion and reversal, his black outlook are all inspirations for his punning' (p. 54). In regard to the about-face and the militarisms that attend the scenography of the Rat Man case, we might also refer to the example of Alphonse Allais whose poem, 'Xylopages' (the title refers to woodcuts and to wood-boring insects), puns on the militaristic 'Fais ce que dois' as follows:

> Un général anglais, dans une bataille,
> Eut les deux fesses emportées par la mitraille.
> Il en fit faire une autre paire en bois,
> Mais jamais il ne les paya.
> Moralité
> Fesses que doit!

(The moral: Do as you must / He owes for his ass.)

given its genuine and deeply rooted history of phantasm-patterning, in a representational field where sodomy has been legislated out of the constitutional space of a subject's legal bearing. Can a knowing subject constitute itself, or even receive the seed of knowledge, where the effects of juridical shutdown are to reorganize the very conditions of an authentic pedagogy? As empty receptacle, virginal space and originary innocence, the pupil has come to receive the desire of the teacher who fills this subject with the pedagogical deposit whose nature resembles that of a phallic desire.[3] The 'truth' of such a transmission is measured by the test of alterity in the relation to the excretory device or, more properly speaking, to the receptacle through which the teaching subject (who does not know what it knows) attempts to find articulation in the Other.

Given the particularly grim moment of legal history in which we find ourselves, the remake of a question first posed in the great Freudian pedagogics seems to fall on propitious grounds. Freud has made us enquire into the modes according to which the pupil, or analysand, receive the so-called intervention. What constitutes an intervention? While to his credit Lacan does not describe the nature of the intervention in the fallen terms we have chosen to elaborate in this chapter, he narrows the field of 'The Function' to a specifically spoken intervention, stressing that 'speech is in fact a gift of language, and language is not immaterial. It is a subtle body, but body it is' (p. 87). What sort of body shows itself as an intervention made into the subject?

The intervention is not 'simply to be received by the subject as acceptance or rejection' but, argues Lacan, 'really to recognize him or to abolish him as subject. Such is the nature of the analyst's *responsibility* whenever he intervenes by means of speech' (p. 87). It is precisely at this moment, when citing the analyst's responsibility, that Lacan abdicates a place of enduring insight for Mr Glover, permitting the structure of an intervention based on a double grounding of inexactitude to take hold of his text. The moment Lacan openly receives the discourse of Mr Glover, recognizing the other by means of standard reference systems, he also ushers in the question of whether he as speaking subject is about to be recognized or abolished by the intervening text. The analyst's responsibility has him slide into the place of the Other.

If we could agree to let the incursion of Mr Glover function as an intervention within Lacan's text, allegorizing the point he is about to make, then we would begin to perceive what kind of internal rectifications are

---

[3] In this regard see the articles of Jane Gallop ('The Immoral Teachers') and Shoshana Felman ('Psychoanalysis and Education: Teaching Terminable and Interminable') in 'The Pedagogical Imperative: Teaching as a Literary Genre', *Yale French Studies* 63 (1983).

occurring here. To explain the significance of Mr Glover's intervention (though he does not call this citation an intervention), Lacan introduces 'in other words', in words of the other which I, Lacan, have now become by virtue of having recognized Mr Glover: 'In other words, not only is every spoken intervention received by the subject in terms of his structure, but the intervention takes on a structuring function in him in proportion to its form.' Despite the 'remarkable' paper for which Glover is here re-marked, that mark cannot help being somewhat influenced by the obsessional systems of suggestion which it has recommended to itself. At the same time Lacan will have effected a shrewd move by accepting the hysterical suggestion, possibly of a phobic order, which at once assumes responsibility for a mastering interpretation and places on another's work the onus of having named the therapeutic results of an interpretation always falling short of itself. In other words, Mr Glover's intervention might be seen as that which takes on a structuring function in Lacan proportionate to its form, which means further that it at no point touches the sanctity of the Lacan text. The hysterical inclusion of Glover's argument would fill Lacan's essay at a blank moment, making the hysterical text 'pregnant' – and thus we have come down to the point of entry for making men pregnant.

'Speech is in fact a gift of language, and language is not immaterial. It is a subtle body, but body it is. Words are trapped in all corporeal images that captivate the subject; they make the hysteric 'pregnant', be identified with the object of *penis-neid*, represent the flood of urine of urethral ambition or the retained faeces of avaricious *jouissance*' (p. 87). There. We have hit bottom. But in order to open the gateway that will push pun forward, we need momentarily to read a 'decondensation' that begins to flood the field of speech and language.

Illustrating the degree to which language solidifies into a body, Lacan argues its capacity for mutilation, as if dismemberment were to act as sign for its originary body-building: 'What is more [which is less], words themselves can undergo symbolic lesions and accomplish imaginary acts of which the patient is the subject. You will remember the *Wespe* (wasp), castrated of its initial *W* to become the S.P. of the Wolf Man's initials at the moment when he realizes the symbolic punishment whose object he was on the part of Grusha, the wasp' (p. 87). But Lacan's next example comes from the case of Rat Man, the work responsible for establishing a rigorous theory of interpretative acts. Lacan is implicated in, if not acting out, the text that serves as an example, initiating a kind of self-designated metaphilosophy of obsessional suggestive systems, supported only by glycerinic insertions into the subject which thereby receives his structuring. Lacan asks you to unforget the most slippery of signifiers, asking or commanding that 'You will remember also that S that constitutes the residue of the hermetic formula into which the conjuratory invocations of the Rat Man became condensed after Freud had extracted the anagram of the name of his beloved from its cipher, and which, tacked on to the final "amen" of his jaculatory prayer, externally floods the lady's name with the symbolic ejection of his impotent desire.'[4] Where Lacan wants the S or the intervenient Semen condensed, he can be read unconsciously to launch a supository movement in the signifier's temporality of condensation and liquefaction whose disseminative expanse he still holds back. (That is, condensation here produces flooding and appears to occur *after* Freud decondenses the invocation.)

To present our brief succinctly, we shall evoke anality via the exemplarity of the Rat Man case. The anus can be said to mark a locus of privileged transaction between at least two gendered entities. It organizes a space from where rental agreements are negotiated, leases are taken out by one gender to permit the other gender provisionally – depending on the terms of the agreement – to occupy its space. The other of genital sexuality, determinable neither as masculine or strictly speaking as feminine, anality nonetheless constitutes a sexuality, a shared space that is often vaginized. Guided by Freud's theory of obsessional neurosis, I should like to try to read this locality of a feminine trait, which however also permits a man to be 'feminized' when 'used' anally by an other of either sexual determination.

There would be a question regarding the transmission of sexual marks as a condition of knowledge to be posed – but this will have to be elaborated elsewhere – under the name of 'Oedipedagogy', a study that would include what Jane Gallop has recalled as the de Sadian libertines' art of *socratiser* and the institutions of oral and anal examinations. Such a pedagogy, toward which Freud stretches us, would take its point of departure on the etymological span linking the Sphinx to sphincter, bound to one another by a notion of 'binding'. As threshold to all pedagogy, the Sphinx has participated in the acquisition of a feminine trait. Monsterized, as far as pedagogical figurations go, she is interspecial and, like her question, double-meaning. In accordance with some versions of the myth, she submits to corporal punishment, turning disciplinary measures upon herself when it becomes necessary to let the other pass. Sometimes she dissolves by

---

[4] Rat Man produced an abbreviated protective formula, *Glejisamen*. 'It is easy to see,' Freud writes, 'that this word is made of up

GISELA
S   AMEN

and that he had united his *Samen* ("semen") with the body of his beloved – i.e. putting it bluntly, had masturbated with her image.' 'Notes Upon a Case of Obsessional Neurosis', *Complete Psychological Works*, ed. J. Strachey, vol. 10, p. 281.

pulverization, her implacable stoniness collapses. The other, at least in
terms of Oedipedagogy's wish-fulfilment, is the becoming of the *sujet supposé
savoir*. It is to him that sexual markings are transmitted as a condition for
knowledge. The answer he gives is 'man'. He has gained admission to a
newer phase of finitizing activity, having passed the guessing game, the great
enigma or in German usage, the *Rätsel* from which emerges the Rat in our
case. The issue of a pedagogy, particularly one structured by Oedipal
constraints, is not something that vaguely admits itself into a discussion of
the Rat Man's story. 'Extracts from the Case History' forms its first sentence
by constituting a man on the grounds of his education: 'A youngish man of
university education introduced himself to me . . .'.[5] A certain type of
knowledge, say, a body of knowledge, has insinuated itself into the youngish
man who introduces himself to Freud. But the young man has not only
inflated himself with the knowledge gained from a university education. He
has also read Freud. Unlike the hysteric, however, he will not have become a
reading body, for his illness, which belongs only to 'a dialect of the language
of hysteria', does not involve the leap from a mental process to a somatic
innervation – hysterical conversion – 'which can never be fully comprehensible to us' (p. 157). We shall see that the articulation of his symptoms
are bound primarily to the bodily orifices – a point which brings us to the
place of 'differomorphic organs' as they come to light in Lacan's Seminar of
21 January 1975, presented under the American title of *Feminine Sexuality*. Of
the radical abstraction, the figure of writing *a* (the *Objet petit a*), the subject
caused by an object, Lacan writes this:

The *petit a* could be said to take a number of forms, with the qualification that in
itself it has no form, but can only be thought of predominantly orally or shittily. The
common factor of *a* is that of being bound to the orifices of the body. What
repercussion, therefore, does the fact that the eye and the ear are orifices have on the
fact that perception is spheroidal for both of them? Without the *petit a*, something is
missing from any theory having any possible reference or appearance of harmony.
And why? Because the subject is only ever supposed. It is its condition to be only
supposable. If it knows anything, it is only by being itself a subject caused by an
object – which is not what it knows, that is, what it imagines it knows. The object
which causes it is not the other of knowledge (*connaissance*). The object crosses this
object through. The other is thus the Other, which I write with a capital O. The
Other is thus a dual entry matrix. The *petit a* constitutes one of its entries.[6]

    [5] 'Notes Upon a Case of Obsessional Neurosis', known as the case of Rat Man, *Complete
Psychological Works*, vol. 10, p. 18. Henceforth, page numbers will be inserted in the body of the
text.
    [6] The *Objet petit a* is 'Lacan's formula for the lost object which underpins symbolization,
cause of and stand in for desire. What man relates to is this object and the "whole of his
realization in the sexual relation comes down to this fantasy" '. Juliet Mitchell and Jacqueline

I am sure of little so much of this probability: as we release Lacan's discovery of the supposable subject to the energy of interpretive warps and distortions, the master pedagogue, were he to issue a grade or response, would not make it an 'A' of any size but would quote his own passage thus: 'which I write with a capital O'. This, then, will furnish our point of entry, slow in coming but owing its existence to a distortion of the spirit of the letter. One can expect little more from a *petit a* operator who takes off from the condition of a supposable subject. My question asks what the nature of the object causing the subject might indeed be. (As if an obsessional neurotic style were capable of producing a single question.)

'Permit to Remain'

The question might have been raised, I suppose, of the punctilious interval – as to why, at this point in time, we organize a moment of general thinking around the pun. In some circles of truth's closure, pun has remained the name of an indictment, an accusatory identification of that which takes too much pleasure, disarranging academic languages, promoting a rhetoric of looseness within a comprehensive recreational linguistics, valuelessly succumbing to the most indefensible copulations of meaning, related, as will be my subject, to the temporal succession of shame over pleasure, incriminating the grammar of some strict order of things, and so forth. It may not yet be necessary to compute the defensive expenditures that go into protecting the usages of puns in parapoetical texts nor even to enter the place where such disputes tend to be articulated. This suggests one reason for holding back a reading of thinking and drinking – a confluence of spirits in fact too sober for this interpretive occasion, though dealing with the issue of disinhibition and the mechanisms of pleasure in rapport to communicability. One could focus the pun within a history of intoxication – a step that Heidegger, in an anti-Aristotelian move, tries to stop up in his treatment or more accurately still in his suppressive evocation of Nietzsche and Kant's *Rausch* ('intoxication'). Heidegger's intervention detoxifies Kant and Nietzsche by means of a pun-insert that returns the *Rausch*-motif to a kind of founding physio-logic, namely, by arguing: 'wir leben indem wir leiben' (we live in that we 'body').[7] So while Kant and Nietzsche are getting high, Heidegger brings them down with a controlling pun-sequence, as if the pun were the most pious, recollective usage of language – the Old Testament

Rose, eds, *Feminine Sexuality: Jacques Lacan and the 'Ecole freudienne'* (New York, 1982), p. 48 (quoting Lacan's *Écrits*, p. 157). The quotation in the text appears on p. 164.

[7] Martin Heidegger, *Nietzsche* (Pfüllingen, 1961), vol. 1, p. 64.

and the Talmud pun incessantly – allowing therefore for some degree of
retention or at least a necessity of restoring an original meaning. Like the
great rituals of religious ceremonials which recall by means of recon-
structive energies and incantation, a prior sense. This precisely is what can
drive one away from drinking and thinking, a kind of drinking prohibition
legislated by the pun, which postulates a pitch-giving meaning on which a
subject can jam polysemically, without breaking harmony, the paradoxical
reunion of the linguistic accident with some sort of anterior substantiality.

In regard to the pun, however, the problem of *hoarding* seems more
compellingly chronic than that of drinking, although according to Freud's
interpretation both activities – hoarding and drinking – are closely allied in
the symptomatology of obsessional neurosis. Both open up, we may add, the
question of sexual difference. Thus the Rat Man will have 'first noticed the
difference between the sexes when he saw his . . . sister (five years his senior)
sitting on the pot' – a gaze that can be seen as originating the rat phantasm
which will consist in turning around the pot, finding the sex to create a
funnel for the rats.

Let us then start with this clue of the other's sitting on the pot, which
empirically may not have shown what Rat Man claimed to have seen or not
to see, remembering that the right posture for a psychoanalytic session is in
fact a *Sitzung*. Our first step will be to construct a kind of suppositorium
whose translucent covering would permit us to observe the movement of the
pun in relation to a case history whose solution purportedly rests on a
spontaneous generation of puns. However, if this opening for the possibility
of thinking the suppository, as a logic and a discourse, as a partial erection of
a subject – if this should appear detached from a structure of deeply
sustained meaning or motive, or if the movement of thought should appear
halting, showing a rather inactive reliance upon vague and general
foundations, this is due in part to the smooth insertability of my suppository
discourse into that of a 'complete obsessional neurosis', as Freud puts it.
For the tone and definition which Freud accords to obsessional neurosis get
translated into a type of mimetic command which he dictaphones into this
interpretation. Regardless of the degree to which the argument continues to
participate in what it tells, producing noticeable ellipses and omissions,
retaining points that ought to have been made – that is, retaining them at
will as intrinsic ideality or dropping them as extrinsic excrement, it
nonetheless constitutes itself in the relatively serious attempt at positing or,
more seriously, at suppositing a link between the status of paronomasia,
sexual difference and the task that psychoanalysis sets for itself. In order to
prepare the rectoscopy that will guide our investigation further, it seems
appropriate first to cite what Freud's Rat Man calls 'the beginning of my
illness': 'I used to have a morbid idea that my parents knew my thoughts; I

explained this to myself by supposing that I had spoken them out loud, without having heard myself do it. I look on this as the beginning of my illness' (p. 162). The beginning of my illness, then, consists in suppositing: I had the idea that they knew my thoughts; 'I explained this to myself in supposing'.

Before beginning the reading proper, in order to introduce and induce it, we ought to refer to an important text which elucidates the subtle shift of interpretive paradigms that the case study promotes. It has to do with a mistaken association, but one that is prescribed by law. When the writer joins the hermeneutic police force, provisionally dropping out of the detective's bureau of intelligence, his thinking is no longer in the service of truth, and has abandoned the desire to arrive, for instance, at a strictly truthful resolution. This explains why, in order to find the truth, a policeman sometimes is represented as having to leave the force, because police work consists in performatively apprehending a figure of suspicion, placing it under arrest. Freud writes of the opportunity he took of giving the analysand 'a first glance at the underlying principles of psychoanalytic therapy' (p. 175). Proceeding from the inference that the patient has a criminal profile, he explains, producing himself as a citation:

Where there is a *mésalliance* between an affect and an ideational content, a layman will say that ... the inference that the patient is a criminal ... is false. On the contrary, the physician says: 'No. The affect is justified. The sense of guilt cannot in itself be further criticized. But it belongs to another content, which is unknown (*unconscious*), and which requires to be looked for. The known ideational content has only got into its actual position owing to a mistaken association. We are not used to feeling strong affects without their having any ideational content, and therefore, if the content is missing, we seize as a substitute upon another content which is in some way or other suitable, much as our police when they cannot catch the right murderer, arrest a wrong one instead.' (p. 175)

Whence a means of maintaining a strict order of functional meaning or apprehension: a police officer cannot provide you with a reason or a discourse that would explain why he is doing what he does; he himself operates according to a law that exceeds his grasp, whereas detective work in principle seeks only to grasp, often in ways indifferent to the performative telos of an arrest. What if psychoanalysis, whose moves are determined by an activity of substitution, also at times exchanged the investigatory badge for a policing instrument, the invisible extension of the arm of the law, 'and, therefore, if the content is missing, we seize as a substitute upon another content which is in some way or other suitable, much as our police,' etc.? But this would be the more naive of the options made available by Freud's understanding of a police license issued by the unconscious to its supervisor. A detective does not always have to work in the name of the law, whereas the police only work in this name, as its representatives. The subtle but immeasurable shift from detective to police work in the sense discovered by Freud suggests on the one hand the degree to which the subject has the right to remain silent as a condition of its correct apprehension. On the other hand, about to be linked to the first, psychoanalysis, working for the good of the whole subject in which a criminalized symptom is on the loose, may have to crack down arbitrarily, to appease a certain law which exercises control over its procedures. Such a show of police force, often amounting to brutality, may be brought down only on the ghetto zone where the dialect of obsessional neurosis is spoken, a zone which knows no amnesia. For this reason, police intervention into a zone so circumscribed also implies a risk for the representative of the law, who may be caught in the heat of a countertransference. In hopes of avoiding such a confrontation, we shall stick to finding clues.

The Rat Man came to see Freud after having leafed through the *Psychopathology of Everyday Life*, claiming to know something 'about my theories'. 'Actually, however, he had read none of my writings, except that a short time before he had been turning over the pages of one of my books and had come across the explanation of some curious verbal associations' (pp. 158–9). His attention was caught, perhaps even trapped, by the verbal associations and wordplays that were turned over with the pages; we could say that he arrived at Freud's door in search of a commanding pun. Back to the suppositorium. Exhibit A involves two containers of live suppositories, manufactured on the East Coast. Citing the directions, we ask that they be received in the preferred manner of Rat Man, who spontaneously converted a given statement into a command. Item 1 reads as follows, 'Directions: Insert one suppository into the rectum. Permit to remain. Bowel action will usually result within a few minutes.' Item 2: 'Insert one suppository high into the rectum and retain fifteen minutes.'[8] Copyright Princeton, NJ. Both

---

[8] The degree to which words are loaded is suggested by the brand name of this container: *Squibb* means not only a filler in journals but also a little pipe or hollow cylinder of paper, filled with powder, or combustible matter. Examples stressing the explosive character of the pun are legion: 'Never point a pun at a friend. It might be loaded.' To emphasize the specificity of the suppository logic for the case of pun, we refer to two French sources, beginning with Corvin's *Petite Folie collective*: 'The pun is a stretched tautology, shimmering with meaning, an explosive incantation which plays upon repetition all the better to destroy it, and drags the mind along the slope of the Same the better to leave room for the break-in of the Other' (Redfern, p. 32). Jacob's *Naming-Day in Eden* offers the following gelastic formulation:

> The Janus word makes of human speech a *slippery instrument*. It is, however, the reflection of the double nature of man himself, of the contradiction that lies at the very heart of humanity. In Eden man knew no ambiguity, but when he fell, he became Janus-faced, a *parvus mundus* of opposites, perilously poised at the juncture of nature and spirit, the riddle of the crossroads, the glory and the jest of the world. (p. 150)

rectal evacuants stress retention, though according to different nuances of command utterances: Permit to remain/retain fifteen minutes. (In this context one might consider the halt after which all of Rat Man's symptoms advance. During a halt in army maneuvers he loses his pince nez and must send for a new pair, whose arrival occasions an obsessional vow. One might also compare these instructions with Jones's definition of obsessional neurosis, anchored as it is in a concept of retention, 'the retention of the complex in consciousness', or with a subject's reception of neurosis as a kind of torpedoed suppository aimed at the ego that receives it as something alien, retaining it with an urge to evacuate.)

The two sets of directions differ in their interpretation of the degree of insertion: the first container indicates 'into the rectum' whereas the one from Princeton says 'high into the rectum', characteristically stressing that which is elevated above the others. What *is* a rectum? The answer to this question leads directly to the solution of the rat problem; and to an understanding of the Western phantasm of evacuating, purging, and cleansing, in other words, to a certain birth of tragedy, if we bear in mind that as concerns birth and men, the latter, according to Rat Man, are believed to bring forth children anally. *Rectum*: the lowest segment of the large intestine extending from the sigmoid flexure to the anus. *Sigmoid*; curved like the letter S; *sigmoidally*, in the manner of a double curve. The destination of the suppository, therefore, would be indicated as the sigmoid valve, the end station of the S, whether or not *barré*, whether or not standing for the signified with which the suppository will never absolutely coincide, but toward which it aspires. Freud himself reproduces the sigmoidal structure which he calls the principle of the Adige at Verona: the river makes a loop, creating nearly identical points of entry and exit (p. 265).

While these compulsive definitions may appear funny, scholarly or unworthy of serious thought – which, if so judged, would have them remain a citation of obsessional neurosis, where high thought is mimed, allowing an irregular, unworthy object to be hermeneutized to death; while the suppositorial injection may seem somewhat debased in its literal application, it can be made to function as a reliable wedge for understanding the precise movements of the Rat Man text and indeed of obsessional neurosis as such, which Freud stresses is hermeneutically more difficult than hysteria, precisely owing to the issue of retention. Consider this, if you will, also in light of the generation of pleasure, where 'psychical damming up' is avoided, or as the relief of anxiety which occurs within an energetics of discharge and deblocking. Indeed, the entire Rat Man project belongs to a sustained temporality of retention, for this is the only one of Freud's case studies to have retained the notes and records which Freud normally let go.

The Editor's Note to the Standard Edition (p. 253, emphasis added) reads accordingly:

It was Freud's practice throughout his life, after one of his works had appeared in print, to destroy all the material on which the publication was based. It is accordingly true that extremely few of the original manuscripts of his works have survived, still less the preliminary notes and records from which they were derived. The present record provides an *unexplained exception to this rule*, having been found among Freud's papers in London after his death. . . . These notes . . . have not yet (1954) appeared in German.

Yet while he himself retained what usually turned into the excremental deposits of a text, detachable and forgettable, one of the dilemmas that Freud faced with the Rat Man case is that the treatment quickly led to the removal of the subject's inhibitions. It is as if the cure had come too fast, as Freud's comments in the Notes make explicit. The cure appears to have precipitated a kind of *Trauerarbeit*; the patient departed so soon. This departure, doubled by the announcement of his death at the end of the text, suggests the memorialization taking place in the Rat Man case whose prepartory stages survive in the form of encapsulation. Yet, in terms of the internal rectifications of the work, we still don't know what it means to be cured *too fast* – say, within the phantasmal space of fifteen minutes. We can assume that the preparatory stages of this reading are completed now.

Permit to remain.

Requiring it of Them

I shall not in the present chapter attempt any discussion of the psychological significance of obsessional thinking. Such a discussion would be of extraordinary value in its results, and would do more to clarify our ideas upon the nature of the conscious and the unconscious than any study of hysteria or the phenomenona of hypnosis. It would be a most desirable thing if philosophers and psychologists who develop brilliant theoretical views on the unconscious upon a basis of hearsay knowledge or from their own conventional definitions would first submit to the convincing impressions which may be gained from a first-hand study of the phenomena of obsessional thinking. We might almost go to the length of requiring it of them, if the task were not so far more laborious than the methods of work to which they are accustomed. I will only add here that in obsessional neuroses the unconscious mental processes occasionally break through into consciousness in their pure and undistorted form, that such incursions may take place at every possible stage of the unconscious process of thought, and that at the moment of incursion the obsessional ideas can, for the most part, be recognized.

We might almost go to the length of requiring it of them, if the task were not so far more laborious than the methods of work to which they are accustomed.[9]

One may well have sensed it: the preliminary stages of my discussion are multiply suppository in the most immediate sense that a piece of Freud has been inserted and retained, if momentarily, so that he could help us out. A kind of double suppository effect emerges here, in so far as Freud wishes psychoanalysis or more precisely, the first-hand study of the phenomena of obsessional thinking (not 'neurosis' but *thinking*) to be forcibly inserted into those who develop 'brilliant theoretical views' or into what sometimes receives the name of philosophy. This kind of Hamletian admonition, 'there is more here than your philosophies have dreamt of', inserts this case history into the site of necessary playing within a play, retaining the other, a procedure for which the fantomal shape of the melting suppository ('dissolved into a dew') will serve as a sign. (Others have noted the similarities obtaining between the Hamlet and Rat Man texts. Lacoste in particular has pointed to the father complexes shared by both heroes, to the fact that Hamlet, when he kills Polonious, rather convulsively screams 'a rat, a rat', to the famous acknowledgement of the doctor in Vienna to whom Hamlet futurally appeals, and Lacan has suggested that the case study unfolds with the dignity of high tragedy's inaugural reticence.[10] Both dramas end with the arrival of arms; Fortinbras, leaving a surviving Horatio to 'report [Hamlet's] cause aright'.)

Now, to narrow the focus and fix the point of entry, I hope merely to wonder aloud to what extent punning belongs to a suppository logic whose point of departure appears to be based on what Freud exposes as the 'obessional neurotic style'. As readers of the case may recall, a major component of obsessional neurosis is indecision – a doubting mania particularly manifest, as Freud puts it, in a subject's vacillation between the male and female. Indeed, Rat Man and Freud will construct a suffering split subject founded on successive insertions of puns that function like a 'Stattsorgan', providing temporary gender assignments. In the Notes, Rat Man is shown to be absorbed by an aspect of the *Stattsorgan*, the organ of state for which he prepares his exams. This can be read or apprehended in the form of its substitutive prothetic application, that is, as something replacing the organ – *statt-Organ*, being detachable, excretable but not fully castratable. In any case, we seek out the meeting place of psychoanalysis and

[9] This is taken verbatim from Part II of the case study, entitled 'Theoretical: Some General Characteristics of Obsessional Formations', p. 228.

[10] Patrick Lacoste, *Il Ecrit* (Paris, 1981); *Écrits*, p. 237.

certain points along the intestinal tract – in sixteenth-century French *rencontrer* had both the sense of 'to meet' and the transitive sense of 'to joke or make puns'. A certain epistemophilia, resembling that of Rat Man, leads us back to the meeting place, therefore, of anal and oral retention systems and this by way of the pun. Some of the suppository definitions of pun, documented by Walter Redfern, trace back to 'a funnel-shaped vessel' or a 'slow, inactive person'.[11] This background material is placed at the service of a suppository discourse which in Freud's case involves inserting the 'ersatz' (as substitutive act or masculinizing positing) at a crucial juncture of reversal; in other words, we are dealing with a type of embolophrasia, which originally meant 'something thrown in, inserted' and which the *Dictionary of Speech Pathology and Therapy* has asserted to be a container, in Leiris' sense of language, of punning speech itself. Under punning speech one finds: 'A form of embolophrasia characterized by pathological play on words of the same sound but of different meaning. Sometimes manifest in the manic phase of manic-depressive psychoses.' I might add here, as a free-floating intervention, that according to the *Leçons sur les maladies mentales* (1890), neologisms are much commoner in persecution-mania patients than in others. Again, we might rightly refer to the couple Hamlet and Rat Man, persecuted and telecommanded by phantom-insertions or *Stattsorgane* which often carry a juridical authority.

The first phase of suppositorical maneuvering embraces the neurotic ersatz which emerges in a passage of Rat Man leading to the anus. This is where Freud dictates his intervention whose transcription reads, '– Into his anus, I helped him out'. In order to locate and name the subject's suffering, Freud supplies the phrasing. We shall take a closer look at the semantics of intervention in a moment.

The second suppositorical phase of treatment concerns the glycerinic signifier that cleanses Rat Man's impacted symptomatology, thereby simultaneously deblocking and curing the patient, rather too quickly. Put that, too, on momentary hold. The case in its entirety bases the possibility of a cure upon successive detonations of puns touched off in one cluster by the word '*Rat*', in another by the copulation of *Amen* and *Samen* ('amen' & 'semen') in the supersititous religiosity of the subject. The seminal fluidity of the dramatically sliding signifiers is to be linked in our discussion with the glycerinic effect of language. However, at this juncture we can merely suggest how very neatly the case of Rat Man inserts itself into the idiom of the Derridean text (*La Carte postale*) concerned with the technology of the courrier. To recover one such moment decongesting and moving the entire

[11] Walter Redfern, *Puns*, p. 21. Citing M. West's study of Thoreau's scatology, Redfern documents Thoreau's 'excremental wordplay', p. 67.

scenography of the subject's phantasms, maneuvering the semantic fields of the case like the army maneuvers through which Rat Man enters a critical phase of narration, we note the centrality of the post office, if only in honor of the context or *Inhalt* (the internally inflected holding, *Inhalt* is another key word of the case). Of the many lessons on which 'The Notes Upon a Case of Obsessional Neurosis' prides itself, one is dispatched as follows: 'After his friend had brought him to his senses he had dispatched the small sum of money in question [the C.O.D payment for the new pince-nez] neither to Lieutenant A. nor to Lieutenant B., but direct to the post office. He must therefore have known that he owed the amount of the charges upon the packet *to no one but the official at the post office*, and he must have known this before he started on his journey' (p. 172).

Lacan reads his neurosis as a notice of non-payment for the father's debt and the case in terms of a forced subjectification of the Rat Man.[12] We might also view the restitutional tactics in light of partial parcelling out of the subject, the robotization and militarization of a self deflated by a tight financial regime whereby it gets to play itself on a kind of psychically projected video screen of self-elimination. The patient lays emphasis on acts of 'sending in', releasing a kind of initial capital flow; Rat Man suddenly produces up front money whose essential cash flow begins to move, though after a provisional retention of funds, out the back end. The relation of such increments – *Ratten* – to excrement receives abundant documentation throughout the case (particularly given the returns on the merging of faeces and money, both of which are hard to part with). The transactions consisting in sending in a sum of money in order to open an account can be understood in terms of enema, from the Greek 'to send in'. In the text, all of this is organized, if secretly, around the related notions of a *Stattsorgan* and post-office. In this respect, we can recall that Rat Man enters false calculations when he sends money by the post, expecting his lost pince-nez to be replaced by the next day's mail. But these desired substitutions for the missing pince-nez merely point up to the temporal immediacy in the subject's demand as concerns the *Stattsorgan*, a demand for replacements and dispatches that the post office is expected to yield. No need to show how the letter for Rat Man functions as suppository, inserting the mail into the slot, attaining to the *Stattsorgan*, the fantasy of a finite retention of his request, and so forth.

Left to its lot, this genre of mail transaction nonetheless reminds us that administering an enema, arranging a suppositorical procedure for treatment constitutes a rather familiar moment in Freud's contractual decisions. To the Wolfman case Freud gives his word as follows: 'I promised the patient a

[12] Lacan, 'Function and Field', pp. 88–9.

complete recovery of his intestinal activity.'[13] The promise exhausts itself, being delivered only when Freud makes the Wolfman's bowels speak: 'in the course of the work his bowels began, like a hysterically affected organ, to "join the conversation" '. Hence in the best of cases the talking cure implies a modality of double-talk, a double source or end for the locality of speech. Hence suppository is sent to us from *supponere*, that which comes from beneath, situating a place of underness charged with retaining, linkable to the *Unter*bewusstsein, that which retains everything, the entification made to speak. Why would the so-called Rat Man's locality of speech be the rectum? In the first place, the first telephone connection to the patient may have been made by the wire of an enema extending from the nurse's hand to his rectum. She, like the analyst, was behind him. Enema administration and the experience of female penetration ought not to be undermined – almost all of Freud's patients can be assumed to have been subject to the primal treatment of enema that went down as does aspirin for the maladies of nowadays. Rat Man tries to resist the enema in his treatment by Freud, as the original notes illustrate:

Jan. 2 [1908]. – (Undisguised expression) ... Besides this he apparently had only trivialities to report and I was able to say a great deal to him to-day. While he was wishing Constanze the rats he felt a rat gnawing at his own anus and had a visual image of it. I established a connection which throws a fresh light on the rats. After all, he had had worms. What had he been given against them? 'Tablets.' Not enemas as well? He thought he remembered that he had certainly had them too. If so, no doubt he must have objected to them strongly, since a repressed pleasure lay behind them. He agreed to this, too. Before this he must have had a period of itching in his anus. I told him that the story of the herring reminded me very much of the enemas. (p. 308)

Freud refers to the preceding entry:

Connected with this, though it was not clear at what point, there was a transference phantasy. Between two women – my wife and my mother – a herring was stretched, extending from the anus of one to that of the other. A girl cut it in two, upon which the two pieces fell away (as though peeled off). All he could say at first was that he disliked herrings intensely. (pp. 307–8)

There is still another reason for locating the Rat Man's speech in a zone of rectal expressivity. In this case it may be linked to the rat phantasm itself: nothing can be ejected from the rat's mouth; this explains its use in laboratory experiments. The rat does not vomit, does not come out with it orally. Nonetheless the structure of double talk is maintained. Dr L. Shengold's 'More about Rats and Rat People' reminds us, apropros of the disconnection between thoughts accomplished by 'inserting a time interval'

---

[13] Freud, *Three Case Histories* (New York, 1963), p. 265.

between them, of the vertical splits that occur in the mental apparatus of rat people, making possible such phenomena as the Orwellian 'double-think' which is conditioned – again by rat torture – onto the victim-hero of *Nineteen Eighty-Four*.[14] Persecuting and persecuted, rats mark the historical phantasmata of great invasions. Their phallic power is coextensive with cannibalistic penetration, since 'the danger throughout is that of a phallus equipped with flesh-eating power'.[15] A final connection might be Lou Andreas Salomé's 'rental agreements': elsewhere Freud borrows from Lou the following conception in a transaction which he acknowledges: the rectum 'rents' vaginal properties, becoming the symbolic placeholder for the inmixation of male and female traits.[16] Rat Man, it seems, has dreamt of having faecal intercourse with Freud's daughter.

'The Faecal Mass of the Second-Stage that is Clearly "Not-Me"'

From the postal system into which part of this case's phantasms are deposited there emerges a question of address. Honoring the sadistic captain of his narration, Rat Man quickly takes to addressing Freud as 'Captain' as well. If the structure of address has a cognitive value, then there always exists an uncertainty about addressing oneself to the right captain and lieutenant, the right place-holder. Thus the lieu-tenants turn out to be substitutes for other destinations, they function like compulsive dead-letter officers or like dummies in the Lacanian sense. The text launches as well a whole problematics of a specifically *military* post office to which Rat Man owes his father's debt. Now the military post office enables another type of address to gain prominence, and this bears heavily upon the fortune of the pun, meaning the *good* pun or joke. Rat Man's father has left him a number of bad word-plays, a legacy which we could say is of the order of the *militerary* regime. Rat Man has to make good. As Samuel Weber has shown, Freud establishes a stringent economy in order to probe the nature of the joke, creating a balance of expenditures and savings of what I loosely translate into releases and retentions participating in the suppository logic.[17] Always involved in a concept of Thirdness or relation to a third party, the delivery of a good joke poses the question of address: if savings are involved, the Rat Man appears to suggest, then the crucial element resides

[14] L. Shengold, 'More About Rats and Rat People', *Journal of the American Psychological Association* 36 (1982), p. 462.

[15] Ibid., p. 483.

[16] Lou Andreas-Salomé, 'Anal und Sexuell', *Imago* 4:5 (1916), p. 259. See the case of Wolf Man.

[17] Samuel Weber, *The Legend of Freud* (Minneapolis, 1982).

in the possibility of saving up a good pun or a good joke, saving it for someone who is not present to its emergence, someone not entirely there, who is elicited only in the mode of his departure. Hence, for 'a long time he had not realized the fact of his father's death. It had constantly happened that, when he heard a good joke, he would say to himself: "I must tell Father that" ' (p. 174). This coincides with the moment Rat Man develops his neurotic machine of obsessional understanding, changing vowels, persistently hearing puns and generally indulging in grammatical aberrancy. While tightly held to a singular context in a spirit of pure origination, the good pun appears always to be oriented toward the future of its repetition, being addressed and breaking through to an absent receiver – one who can no longer receive you but whom you nonetheless continue to receive. Like Hamlet, the other melancholic punster and obsessional neurotic, Rat Man still waits for his father between the two sides of morn, waiting to address his father's apparition with the fantomal, double speech of the pun, in order to give him in exchange his word, his parole: 'often, when there was a knock at the door, he would think, "Here comes Father", and when he walked into a room he would expect to find his father in it. And although he had never forgotten that his father was dead, the prospect of seeing a ghostly apparition of this kind held no terrors for him; on the contrary, he had greatly desired it' (pp. 174–5).

Always bordering on auditory psychosis, Rat Man's invaginated organ of reception translates utterances by transforming them, through an internal converter, into perlocutionary speech acts. Plain assertions of the sheerly constative sort, when deposited into Rat Man, spontaneously acquire the authority of commands. So the morning a conductor vaguely asks whether he might be waiting for the ten o'clock train, Rat Man receives the message as a command and despite having projected an entirely different agenda for the day, he finds himself under orders to take the ten o'clock train, just as he later finds himself under doctor's orders, taking in Freud's capsulated train of thought anally. To get a precise sense of where we're heading, follow this line to the end station in Freud's description of the train episode:

The whole process then passed into the obsessional patient's consciousness accompanied by the most violent affect and *in a reverse order* – the punitive command coming first, and the mention of the guilty outburst afterwards. I cannot think that this attempt at an explanation will seemed forced (p. 188, Freud's italics).

The question of forcing something up or into Rat Man is not an empty one. Remember that Rat Man was the most intensely coached of Freud's patients. A typical session begins with this sort of move: 'I thought it advisable to bring a fresh piece of theory to his notice' (p. 180). Freud introduces this piece to fit in with another theoretical requirement, namely, that 'the unconscious is to be understood as the precise contrary of the conscious – He was much agitated at this'. The structure of insertion followed by agitation typically stimulates a physiological stirring. Or, when Rat Man offers a perfect fit Freud remarks parenthetically, 'I had explained the idea of "resistance" to him at the beginning of the hour'. We conclude that, in the beginning, Freud inserts his logic which in turn activates the thinking of Rat Man.

There can be no doubt in our minds that this procedure repeats Rat Man's original traumatism. The first blow to Rat Man, offers Freud in the section headed 'The Beginning of the Treatment', occurred when a young tutor 'had entered his employ only in order to gain admission into the house. This had been the first great blow of his life' (p. 160). Listen with an oculist's precision to the entries made into Rat Man. In German it is said that the tutor 'sich mit ihm nur eingelassen habe, um Zutritt ins Haus zu gewinnen [*eingelassen*: literally, he let himself into Rat Man]. Es war dies die erste grosse Erschütterung seines Lebens.' At this point I would like to demonstrate how Freud repeats this forced entry in order to get to the bottom of the rat problem, insinuating himself into the subject at the very moment he develops the decisive reading of the obsessional neurotic style. This brings us in yet another turn to the origin of the pun and to the rise of such incontestable punsters as Shakespeare's Bottom.

Before focusing the laser precision with which Freud reproduces the initial blow, I must offer a few remarks regarding the other animal in Freud's life, the other heterogyn stylized by obsessional neurotic traits. I restrict these remarks to the establishment of a suppository discourse, which means they are intended to remain fragmentary by necessity and subordinate to the requirements for cracking the Rat Man case. When Wolfman stepped into Freud's office his first gesture was to offer to have rectal intercourse with the physician and to defecate on his head. We know the complimentary nature of such a gesture, in so far as excrement babies are later divined to be resourceful gifts and linked, as in Rat Man, to the reproduction of children emanating from the anus. In any case, please continue to retain the relationship of faeces to money which should help clarify Rat Man's urgent sense of owing, his terrible irregularity which Freud promises to regulate if not certify. With Wolfman, Freud and his patient experienced a serious blockage in their sessions, doubled by the patient's hysterical constipation. Nothing moves, nothing comes out of Wolfman. In Freud's words, 'nothing changed and there was no way of convincing him' (p. 265). What gets things stirring is Freud's insertion, at this paralyzed moment in the analysis, of the suppository discourse. If Freud will not induce Wolfman to speak, at least he encourages his bowel to come out with it: 'I promised the patient a complete recovery of his intestinal activity, and by means of this promise made his incredulity manifest. I then had the satisfaction of seeing his doubt dwindle away, as in the course of the work his bowel began, like a hysterically affected organ, to "join in the conversation", and in a few weeks time recovered its normal functions.' (p. 265).

The supposition to be inferred permits us to think that if Freud could not induce a talking cure based on the normal, rather normative understanding of intersubjective communicability, then he can deblock the silence by releasing a suppository torpedo whose aim would be to encourage a narration from the bowel. Interestingly, Freud calls this renewed activity a conversation, as if conducted by two equal partners, i.e., Freud and the bowel – what he later describes as the feminine side of Wolfman, the hystericized organ of identificatory pathos with Sergei's mother. In fact he may be treating the mother, the female hysteric, who begins to agitate and to speak through her son's belly, ventrilocating her anguish. And so one should always be on the lookout for a 'small trait of hysteria which is regularly to be found at the root of obsessional neurosis' (p. 265), the 'front bottom' (p. 208), or the mother who is stirred to speech by Freud's suppository manipulations. Indeed, it is with the aim of giving his patients 'visible' pleasure, as in Rat Man, that Freud inserts his little container of promises; in the Wolfman case he similarly speaks of the 'pleasure attached to the function of evacuation' in conjunction with anal jokes, wordplays and exhibitions. A suppository moment of retention inflects the description of Wolfman's *jouissance*: 'And this enjoyment (of joking, etc.) had been retained by him until after the beginning of his later illness' (p. 266). In the joke book, borrowing the notion of *Einfühlung* from a certain Lipps, Freud explains how, by the help of a joke, an internal resistance is overcome and an inhibition lifted, psychical damming up is avoided. The mechanism triggering the generation of pleasure averts a constipatory blockage of the psyche. It seems that either something like a play on words or 'fresh pieces' of psychoanalytic theory have to be inserted in the subject and momentarily retained, before the pleasurable evacuation, including the evacuation of the mother, can take place, can take her place. We return to the lieu-tenants to whom Rat Man feels he owes everything.

To make good a promise, we arrive at the pleasure of Freud's insertion into Rat Man. At the crucial narratological moment, when the fundamental phantasm achieves disclosure (we think), and well before the solution of the Rat idea via the life-giving puns is established, Freud reveals the moment from which this famous case derives its name and entitlement:

Here the patient broke off, got up from the sofa ... (I had explained the idea of 'resistance' to him at the beginning of the hour, when he told me there was much in himself which he would have to overcome if he was to relate this experience of his.) I

went on to say that I would do all I could, nevertheless, to *guess* the full meaning of
any hints he gave me. Was he perhaps thinking of impalement? – 'No, not that . . .' –
he expressed himself so indistinctly that I could not immediately *guess* in what
position – 'a pot was turned upside down on his buttocks . . . some *rats* were put into
it . . . and they . . .' – he had again got up, and was showing every sign of horror and
resistance – '*bored their way in . . .*' – Into his anus, I helped him out. (p. 166)

Freud does not supply his supposition with a confirming report. It's
simply a case of – Into his anus, I helped him out. In German, Freud
actually fills this space out, or fills his anus with 'In den After, durfte ich
ergänzen'. He has just articulated his way of helping his patient overcome
the internal resistance, suppressing the signs of horror's speechlessness: 'Er
gab alle Zeichen des Grausens und Widerstandes von sich – . . . In den
After, durfte ich ergänzen.' 'I took the pleasure of filling.' We should not fail
to note that the rhetoric of insertion remains the same for Rat Man's first
blow as for the rat's rectal entry and Freud's After-words: the rats were
eingelassen; the tutor had 'sich mit ihm nur eingelassen'. A bit later Freud
strains the text to come out with the connector-puns on which the cure of
Rat Man is based. Generated from the start-word *RAT*, they begin to take
on genuinely glycerinic qualities, the gelastic glissement of speech reminiscent of the sliding potentialities of language in Lacan's sense, 'le glissement
progressif des sens'. The sliding glycerine signifier makes us note the tropes
of fluidity and slipperiness that flood all treatments of the pun, breaking into
a concept of language as substance or solidifying agent with a kind of patient
fluency. Modalities of solvency and currency feed directly into what Freud
identifies as the currency of the Rat idea. With a toss of the decisive dice, he
starts the Rat-series rolling with *Spielratte*, referring to Rat Man's father, a
chronic – one is tempted to say, chtonic – gambler. *Spielratte* in turn comes
up with *Rate*, instalments, and another turn of the wrist yields *hei-raten*,
marriage. The stakes are particularly high with *heiraten*, as the primary
conflict arises with a paternal prohibition on Rat Man's plans of marriage.
Given the fervor, not to say acumen with which Freud tracks down the
punogenic structure of Rat Man's disorder, I think it necessary to replay the
earliest appearance of the Rat in his language. The earliest appearance is in
fact a double feature which Freud leaves entirely unacknowledged, double
like the very structure of paronomasia or pun which speaks twice as much by
being split.

In the original notes to the case history the first mention of 'rats' comes in
the context directly following Freud's faecal speculations: 'the thought that I
desired to have him as a son-in-law. He was probably one of those children
who retain their faeces . . . the thought "rats" at once occurred to him'
(p. 287). In the published study the first, which is to say the second, or rather

the last appearance of the rats takes place when the rats in fact do not appear, but when Freud divines their critical significance for the psycho-neurosis of the patient, inserting them into his anus – at this point, remember, Rat Man is standing upright, completing as it were the phylogenic history of man that Freud describes in the same case. We cannot know how close he stands to Freud at the moment of intervention. In any case, he is no longer horizontal, he is up when Freud promises 'voll zu erraten' and then again, back for more: 'er drückte sich so undeutlich aus, daß ich nicht sogleich erraten konnte, in welcher Stellung' ('he expressed himself so indistinctly that I could not immediately guess in what position'). Freud gives his promise fully to guess, *voll zu erraten*, to smell a rat (the whole narration of Rat Man's ills begins with his losing the pince-nez and focuses considerably on his, and civilization's osphresiolagnia). However, in so engaging himself, Freud also reproduces the position of the patient's parents who the child believed could read his thoughts ('he was afraid that his parents had *guessed* his thoughts'), leading to the delusional belief in his 'omnipotence of thought' or what Freud also recognizes as an endopsychic perception of the repressed. In other words, Freud's promise to guess the unspeakable thoughts of Rat Man also extends the promise to participate deep within the offending symptomatology, closing off any guarantee of a cure. Freud may be looking for marriage, but in fact he engages himself on very precarious grounds, compromising the cure – first insofar as the cure will be set henceforth as a symptom of the disease, indeed, in part constituted by it and secondly because Freud, Captain Freud, emphatically becomes the horrifying rat created by the other Captain, inserting himself into the anus (– Into the anus, I helped him out: as analyst, it is Freud's task to help him out). The counter or original transfer could be said to develop between the rat as boring signifier and the physician. Freud assumes the role of fully *er-ratting*, enratting himself in the masculine pronomial form or, guessing again, he names the other by having his speech intervene as an injunction: *er: Ratten!* Given that Rat Man is a translator, he would have obeyed his doctor's orders, making the necessary transfer of accounts.

Still, why would Freud permit the symptom itself if not the cure to rest on such doubtful grounds? Why not deliver a confirming clue, a positive endorsement, a gesture perhaps, or have Rat Man – the other one, the patient – crawl back to the couch, collapsed with relief? The decision not to give a decisive accord fits the requirements of an obsessional neurotic style which proceeds by ellipsis and omission, just as does the articulation of the problem with which Freud helps out. The ellipsis makes room for the insertion of a missing link into (– Into) a resistant hermeneutics of the obsessional neurotic style. In this case the link is shaped by the pun, the ellipses or points, the series of punctae mobilized to fix the moment of intrusion which can even take the form of phonetic alteration 'He declared that the mute "e" of the second syllable gave him no sense of security against the intrusion, which he so much dreaded, of some foreign and contradictory element'.[18] There is nothing to guarantee Rat Man's protection from such an intrusion of a foreign element into the ellipsis of his symptom. Nothing to assure us that Freud did not intervene precisely at a place of dread, inserting a liquefying speech like an inoculating stylus that repeats for the first time the poison in order to evacuate, to draw out the silent agent of disease. The cruelly poisonous point is virtually admitted by Freud himself when he offers, 'I had told him that I myself was not fond of cruelty like Captain M., and that I had no intention of tormenting him unnecessarily' (p. 169).

Be that as it may, we know only that Rat Man has a relation to utterance that turns over certain of these to the custody of compulsive commands, so that Freud's anal insertion would necessarily be received by Rat Man as a master key, an order and ordinance. Be *that* as it may, Freud's insertions become progressively easier: 'I could easily insert the idea which he had so energetically repudiated into a context which would exclude the possibility of any such repudiation' (p. 179). The intervention is well on the road to becoming the object causing the subject, if subject there be.

To base the possibility of reading the Rat Man on a mode of *erratten*, and to generate a string of puns out of a secret matrix doubling for RAT, means to find a bottom line which is not one, that is to say, it is based on fundamental indecision. Freud guesses and gambles, places his bets, thus basing his findings at the heart of the obsessional neurotic style. Wait. The heart is a false organ, we are speaking to or from an opening, perhaps 'the *béance*, impossible to fill, of the symbolic debt', the behind which like the image of Christ is always hidden from view (Does Christ have a behind? Wolfman reportedly asked as Wolfchild. Can he shit?) In other words, does the secret of Christ reside in the possibility that he, suspended by the three points, was never to be approached from behind, neither evacuating nor constipating, just hung, he suggests, like a sacred pun enigmatically filling an ellipsis, with pun ambiguous, pleasing in suspense.

Like the pun, *erraten* occupies a place of no place, the space between two lieutenants, naming the mobile indecision. Freud's predicament forces him to guess, *erratten*, rather than to know. He appears to be positioning himself within an epistemological fault in which one simply cannot decide for one

[18] 'Our patient used to employ as a defensive formula a rapidly pronounced "*aber*" ("but").
. . . He told me on one occasion that this formula had become altered recently; he no longer said "*áber*" but "*abér*". When he was asked to give the reason for this new departure, he declared that the mute e of the second syllable gave him no sense of security against the intrusion, which he so much dreaded, of some foreign and contradictory element, and that he had therefore decided to accent the "*e*" ' (pp. 224–5).

semantic field over the other, thus serving notice of the doubt against which the psychoanalytic compulsion must struggle. The radical doubt thus described and strenuously engaged as it is in the Rat Man case creates a compulsion to pun, on the part of the rat subject, be this Freud or Rat Man. They produce a desire that is to be reconstituted as source and origin, the control tower that monitors indecision in the face of some terror. Such might be the case for the ontologically down and out – I would guess Beckett fits into this ellipsis, and a number of others as well. Such would be the symptomatology of the suppository subject who has to supposit and who, like Freud, knows no echo of a confirmation. If there is something to know in what discloses itself as a sort of abysstemology, it can only be the bottom, the originary split.

Since we have hit bottom, passed that is to what Freud has called the lowest form of the verbal joke, it is time to bring to your attention the poem whose argument unfolds a certain suppository subject in its relatedness to pun. It was published in 1826 by the pseudonymous Bernard Blackmantle, Esq. In the preface, the masked writer embraces the concept of pun by way of the word 'posito'. He, or she, if they are split, honors the salutory agency of pun. We slip away, leaving with the indecision of an uncommented poem, a place from where to co-originate the obsessional neurotic style. Shifting into lower gear still, I might have read the poem's amphibiguity or the evacuation of heaven.

The Origin of Punning:
From Plato's Symposiacks
by Dr Sheridan

ONCE on a time in merry mood,
Jove made a Pun of flesh and blood:
A double two-faced living creature,
Androgynos, of two-fold nature,
For *back to back* with single skin
He bound the male and female in;
So much alike, so near the same,
They stuck as closely as their name.
Whatever words the male exprest,
The female turn'd them to a jest;
Whatever words the female spoke,
The male converted to a joke:
So, in this form of man and wife
They led a merry punning life.
　　The gods from heaven descend to earth,
Drawn down by their alluring mirth;
So well they seem'd to like the sport,

Jove could not get them back to court.
Th' infernal gods ascend as well,
Drawn up by magic puns from hell.
Judges and furies quit their post,
And not a soul to mind a ghost.
'Heyday!' says Jove: says Pluto too,
'I think the Devil's here to do;
Here's hell broke loose, and heaven's quite empty;
We scarce have left one god in twenty.
Pray what has set them all a-running?' –
'Dear brother, nothing else but punning.
Behold that double creature yonder
Delights them with a double *entendre*.'
    'Odds-fish,' says Pluto, 'where's your thunder?
Let's drive, and split this thing asunder!'
'That's right,' quoth Jove; with that he threw
A bolt, and split it into two;
And when the thing was split in twain,
Why then it punn'd as much again.
    ' 'Tis thus the diamonds we refine,
The more we cut, the more they shine;
And ever since your men of wit,
Until they're cut, can't pun a bit.
So take a starling when 'tis young,
And down the middle slit the tongue,
With groat or sixpence, 'tis no matter,
You'll find the bird will doubly chatter.
    'Upon the whole, dear Pluto, you know,
'Tis well I did not slit my Juno!
For, had I done't, whene'er she'd scold me,
She'd make the heavens too hot to hold me.'
    The gods, upon this application,
    Return'd each to his habitation,
    Extremely pleas'd with this new joke;
    The best, they swore, he ever spoke.

8

Unpacking the Portmanteau, or Who's Afraid of *Finnegans Wake?*

Derek Attridge

Samuel Johnson's celebrated quarrel with Shakespeare's puns – 'A quibble, poor and barren as it is, gave him such delight, that he was content to purchase it, by the sacrifice of reason, propriety and truth' – reflects an attitude that the intervening centuries have not entirely expunged.[1] The pun remains an embarrassment to be marginalized or controlled by relegation to the realms of the infantile, the jocular, the literary. It survives, tenaciously, as freak or accident, hindering what is taken to be the function of language: the clean transmission of a pre-existing, self-sufficient, unequivocal meaning. It is a characteristic mode of the dream, the witticism, the slip of the tongue: those irruptions of the disorderly world of childhood pleasures and unconscious desires into the clear and linear processes of practical and rational thought, those challenges to what Johnson very precisely articulates as the domain of 'reason, propriety and truth'.

The pun is seen in this light because it undermines the basis on which our assumptions about the communicative efficacy of language rest: in Saussure's terms, that for each signifier there is an inseparable signified, the two existing in mutual interdependence like two sides of a sheet of paper.[2] To the extent that a language, natural or artificial, fails to match single signifiers to single signifieds, it is held to fail as language; the possibility of the pun is the mark of our fallen condition – our language, like every other aspect of our existence, is touched with imperfection. But the possibility of the pun is not, of course, the pun itself; it is merely the presence of ambiguity in

---

[1] *Johnson on Shakespeare*, ed. Arthur Sherbo, The Yale Edition of the Works of Samuel Johnson, vol. VII (New Haven and London, 1968), p. 74.

[2] Many taxonomies are applicable to the range of effects we call 'the pun'; I am concerned only with the general phenomenon of homonymy in language and its exploitation in literature. See the suggestions by James Brown, in 'Eight Types of Puns', *PMLA* 71 (March 1956), pp. 14–26, and L. G. Heller, 'Toward a General Typology of the Pun', in Marvin K. L. Ching et al., *Linguistic Perspectives on Literature* (London, 1980), pp. 305–18. Both these writers regard the pun as representing a fundamental property of literary language.

language. And linguistic theory has learned to handle ambiguity; indeed, ambiguity plays a crucial part in the argument for a distinction between deep and surface structures which is central to transformational syntactic theory. The same surface structure may have two distinct meanings – 'The shooting of the hunters was terrible', 'Visiting relatives can be tedious' – and it therefore follows that each meaning must be derived from a different 'kernel sentence' or correspond to a different 'deep structure'. Notice, however, that the same valorizing assumptions haunt the linguist's metaphors: it is the single unambiguous meaning that is awarded the complimentary adjectives 'kernel' or 'deep', while ambiguity is associated with the husk, the superficial outside – duplicitous appearance and not monosemous reality.

In spite of its dangerous tendency to polysemy, language works well enough, we are told, because of its appearance in a disambiguating context: we are able to choose one of several meanings for a word or sentence because we are guided by the immediate verbal surroundings, the nature of the speech act in which the words are uttered and perceived, the social and historical setting, and so on. As speakers, we construct our sentences in such a way as to eradicate any possible ambiguities, and as hearers, we assume single meanings in the sentences we interpret. The pun, however, is not just an ambiguity that has crept into an utterance unawares, to embarrass or amuse before being dismissed; it is ambiguity *unashamed of itself*, and this is what makes it a scandal and not just an inconvenience. In place of a context designed to suppress latent ambiguity, the pun is the product of a context deliberately constructed to *enforce* an ambiguity, to render impossible the choice between meanings, to leave the reader or hearer endlessly oscillating in semantic space.

Pope's reference to Cambridge University in the Fourth Book of the *Dunciad* will furnish a well-known example:

> Where Bentley late tempestuous wont to sport
> In troubled waters, but now sleeps in port (lines 201–2).

In most of our encounters with the word *port*, the context in which it occurs (verbal and pragmatic) suppresses large areas of its potential signification; Pope's achievement in this couplet is to leave unsuppressed two apparently incompatible fields of meaning – *port* as 'harbor' and *port* as 'wine' – by inventing a context in which both are simultaneously acceptable. The noble conception of the tempest-tossed bark at last lying peacefully in harbor is radically undercut by the unseemly image of the great scholar reduced to drunken slumber by nightly overindulgence, and the movement between these two is as inescapable as it is perpetual. Bentley's slumber is thus rendered risible by the use of a trope associated with heroic endeavor; yet at the same time something of that heroism rubs off on Bentley's adventures with the bottle.

Pope's lines do not release all the meanings associated with the word *port*, of course; there is little likelihood of a reader bringing into play the idea of 'external deportment, carriage, or bearing' or 'the left-hand side of a ship'. The semantic movement initiated by Pope's couplet, though never-ending, is strictly controlled: the angel of reason dancing on a pun. If we should encounter the word *port* in a severely impoverished context – it appears on a scrap of paper pushed under the door, for instance, or is spoken in a dream – the range of meaning widens, and the pleasure we take in its ambiguity disappears. No longer is language's potential for semantic expansion hinted at but simultaneously kept at bay; it has become threatening and confusing. Remove even more of the context and the expansion accelerates rapidly: imagine the word being encountered by someone who knows no English, or no Indo-European language, or no human language. Eventually its meaning becomes infinite and, at exactly the same moment, disappears.

It is not surprising, therefore, that the pun is marginalized in our most common uses of languages. Outside the licensed domains of literature and jokes, the uncontrollable manifestations of parapraxes and dreams, the possibilities of meaning in a word are stringently limited by its context. The more that context bears down upon the word, the less the word will quiver with signification; until we reach a *fully* determining context, under whose pressure the word will lie inert, pinned down, proffering its single meaning. But at this point something else will have happened to it: it will have become completely redundant. The context will now allow only one meaning to be perceived in the gap which it occupies, and anything – or nothing at all – will be interpreted as providing that meaning. In the terms used by information theory, the more predictable a given item in a message, the less information it carries; the totally predictable word conveys, in itself, absolutely nothing. What we have, then, is a continuum from the totally powerless item, devoid of meaning because already completely specified by its surroundings, to the infinitely powerful item, devoid of meaning because completely *un*specified. Meaning resides between the two. What we call the pun is one stage along the way; what we call 'single meaning' is another. Exclude the pun, and you exclude the process on which all language rests: the process whereby context constrains but does not wholly constrain the possibilities of meaning.

We can approach the pun from another direction, from which we can again see it as a phenomenon which inhabits the normal procedures of language. The semantic fields of *port* in the sense of 'wine' and of *port* in the sense of 'harbor' have no evident synchronic connection. One's understanding of each normally remains uncolored by one's understanding of the other, because of the constraining effect of context already discussed. That is to say, they usually function as two quite different words; and it is an arbitrary quirk of the specific language system of English that associates them at all. Yet what Pope has done is to invent a context in which that arbitrary link comes to seem motivated: taking the language as he finds it, he has succeeded in shifting the world into a pattern in which harbors and wine are superimposed. The material envelope of the sign – its phonemes and graphemes – has been allowed to take the initiative, and has brought about a coalescence of otherwise distinct fields of reference. This, of course, goes against all the rules: phonemes and graphemes should be servants, not masters; the mere coincidence of outward similarity should have no bearing on the meanings within. If this were not the case, language would never get off the ground – we would expect all words beginning with the same letter to be semantically related, for instance, or assume that historical or dialectal changes in pronunciation must entail changes in meaning.

The insubordination displayed by the pun is, of course, a feature of all poetic language: the independence of meaning from its material representation required by the linguistic system is challenged by *every* use in poetry of sound or appearance to make connections or to establish contrasts – every effect of rhyme, rhythm, visual patterning, alliteration or assonance; and the pun is only a particularly extreme case of such articulation at the level of the signifier, relying as it does on *complete* coincidence of sound between two words. And once we generalize the pun in this way, we realize that its mode of operation is not, in the end, peculiar to poetry. For if it were the case that other manifestations of language completely excluded this mode of establishing relationships of meaning, the only linguistic connections and contrasts with any significance would be those already given (but how?) by extralinguistic reality. Meanings would have to relate to meanings by their own nature, and signifiers would be left to form innocent patterns, mere diagrams of froth on the surface of a profound, and unplumbable, sea. Such a theory not only disqualifies the characteristic mode of poetry, of popular wisdom and humor, of any discourse which uses the verbal schemes of rhetoric (and what discourse doesn't?); it also ignores the perfectly normal syntactic and morphemic function of patterning at the level of the signifier. It it not merely by chance that there is a similarity of sound between 'book*s*' and 'cat*s*' or between 'look*ed*' and 'hop*ed*' – and the oppositions single/plural and present/past are not experiential givens that pre-exist the linguistic patterns in which they are manifested. More generally, to the extent that language is held to affect or determine the subject's perception and categorization of the world, patterning in the signifier must have semantic force, since language has no medium in which to operate other than patterns of sonic and visual substance. Clearly, there *is* meaning in the coincidence of the signifier,[3] and an absolute separation between the functions of signifier and signified is impossible. Once again, the pun turns out to be not an aberration of language but a direct reflection of its normal working.

I have suggested two approaches to the pun, both of which reveal it to be a product of language's necessary mode of existence: as one signifier with two possible signifieds, which in a particular context are simultaneously activated; and as two identical signifiers, which in a particular context are made to coalesce. Each of these views of the pun associates it with a feature especially characteristic of literary language. The first of these is polysemy, the second is the semantic use of purely formal similarities; and the pun combines these features in a way which heightens the power of both. But it does so at some cost: the effect has to be created by a carefully constructed linguistic envelope (Pope needs fourteen words to prepare us for a bisemous reading of *port*), and it is limited to exact correspondence of sound. Other kinds of polysemy (a word with secondary associations, for example) and other kinds of assonance (rhyme, alliteration, and so on) are much more readily available, and need no such elaborate scaffolding in order to work. By the same token, however, they are much weaker: the reader can more easily ignore or subdue them, dismissing secondary associations as 'irrelevant' or allowing rhyme words to lie side by side without mutual interference, as if chastely separated by a chivalric sword.

What if there were a way of combining the power of the pun with the ready availability of those weaker effects of polysemy and patterning, of bringing into the foreground those otherwise dismissable associations, and of coupling together in a simultaneous experience those meanings that lie separate in verbal echoes of various kinds, like rhyme and assonance? And what if the operation of this device could be signaled independently of context, and in a completely inescapable way? If this fusion were to be achieved, we may be sure that the processes of exclusion which operate already on the pun would be put into action with redoubled energy, since the new device would expose even more threateningly the myths of a

[3] The operation of popular etymology, which is a significant factor in the diachronic changes in any language, depends on the assumption in the minds of speakers that coincidences of sound are not accidental – an assumption not unreasonably derived from the patterning of morphology and the process of analogical change. Mitsou Ronat usefully relates the portmanteau word to popular etymology in 'L'hypotexticale', *Change* 11 (May 1972), pp. 26–33. I have discussed the importance of popular etymology at greater length in ch. 4 of *Peculiar Language: Literature as Difference from the Renaissance to James Joyce* (Ithaca and London, 1988).

monosemous language and a pre-existing structure of meaning, and put even more strongly in question the belief in language's transparency, stability and rationality. The spirit of Dr Johnson would prove to be still very much alive; and the new device, together with the text and author employing it, would meet with the same hostility as did Shakespeare's use of puns in the eighteenth century. Johnson's denunciation needs very little rewriting to bring it up to date: 'A portmanteau word, poor and barren as it is, gave Joyce such delight that he was content to purchase it by the sacrifice of reason, propriety and truth.'

The portmanteau word challenges two myths on which most assumptions about the efficacy of language rest: like the pun, it denies that single words must have, on any given occasion, single meanings; and like the various devices of assonance and rhyme, it denies that the manifold patterns of similarity that occur at the level of the signifier are innocent of meaning. The portmanteau does this with the pun's simultaneity of operation, but does it more flagrantly and with less warning. There is no escape from its insistence that meaning is an *effect* of language, not a presence within or behind language, and that the effect is unstable and uncontrollable. Notice, too, that whereas the pun can be easily contained by being treated as the index of an imperfect language, allowing ambiguity where it should insist on univocity, it is harder to avoid the realization, at some level, that the portmanteau can be nothing other than a defining feature of language itself, since it derives from the fact that the same segments (letters, phonemes, syllables) can be combined in different ways to produce different meanings. A language in which portmanteau formations were impossible would be a language in which every signified was matched with a unique and unanalyzable signifier – that is, not a language at all.

Not surprisingly, therefore, the portmanteau word has had a history of exclusion even more severe than that of the pun: outside the language of dreams, parapraxes and jokes, it has existed chiefly in the form of malapropism and nonsense-verse – the language of the uneducated, the child, the idiot. (The very term 'portmanteau word' comes from a children's story – *Alice Through the Looking Glass* – and not a work of theory or criticism.[4]) And *Finnegans Wake* has often been relegated to the same border area, a remarkable fact when one considers that it is a work of some 600 intricately wrought pages, written by a deeply committed and highly

---

[4] A text which treats Carroll's portmanteaux with the comic brilliance they deserve – such as Francis Huxley's *The Raven and the Writing Desk* (London, 1976) – is equally likely to be overlooked by the literary establishment.

respected artist, over sixteen painful years, as the culmination of one of the
most brilliant literary careers of the century. We have learned to accept
novels without firm plots or consistent characters, even novels that pun and
rhyme; but sixty years after it first started appearing, the novel that relies on
the portmanteau word is still a disgrace to the institution of literature, an
'aberration' or a 'hoax'.

But how else can the literary institution avoid the claim made by the text:
that the portmanteau word, far from being a sport, an eccentricity, a mistake,
is a revelation of the processes upon which all language relies? How else can
it exclude the possibility that the same relation obtains between *Finnegans
Wake* and the tradition of the novel: that what appears to be a limiting case
or a parody, a parasite on the healthy body of literature, is at the same time
central, and implicated in the way the most 'normal' text operates? It is the
familiar logic of the Derridean '*supplément*' or '*pharmakon*': the 'artifice' to be
excluded from the category of 'natural' literature (with its 'felt life' and 'full
sense of reality') that nevertheless reveals the artificial character of literature
itself.[5] In the *Wake*'s deconstruction of the oppositional structures of the
literary tradition, the portmanteau word proves to be a powerful tool, but its
very power has rendered it ineffective.

To demonstrate the operation of the portmanteau, and to explore the
reasons why, for all their superficial similarity, the portmanteau and the pun
are different kinds of linguistic device, a specific example is needed. The
following passage was chosen randomly; the same points would emerge
from any page of the text.

And stand up tall! Straight. I want to see you looking fine for me. With your
brandnew big green belt and all. Blooming in the very lotust and second to nill,
Budd! When you're in the buckly shuit Rosensharonals near did for you. Fiftyseven
and three, cosh, with the bulge. Proudpurse Alby with his pooraroon Eireen, they'll.
Pride, comfytousness, enevy! You make me think of a wonderdecker I once. Or
somebalt that sailder, the man megallant, with the bangled ears. Or an earl was he, at
Lucan? Or, no, it's the Iren duke's I mean. Or somebrey erse from the Dark
Countries. Come and let us! We always said we'd. And go abroad.[6]

At the risk of seeming to posit the very things I have said the text
undermines – themes, plot, characters, and so on – let me tender a bald and
provisional statement of some of the threads that can be traced through the
passage, in order to establish an initial orientation.[7] The predominant

---

[5] See, for example, Jacques Derrida, '... That Dangerous Supplement ...', in *Of
Grammatology*, trans. Gayatri Spivak (Baltimore, 1976), pp. 141–64, and 'Plato's Pharmacy', in
Dissemination, trans. Barbara Johnson (Chicago, 1981), pp. 61–171.

[6] James Joyce, *Finnegans Wake* (London and New York, 1939), p. 620.

[7] In commenting on this passage I have made use of a number of the standard reference
books on *Finnegans Wake*, and I gratefully acknowledge the labors of their authors.

'voice' in this part of the text – its closing pages – is that which Joyce designated by Δ, the shifting cluster of attributes and energies often associated with the initials ALP and the role of wife and mother. The addressee is primarily the group of characteristics indicated by ⊓, the male counterpart frequently manifested as the letters HCE. Two of the prominent narrative strands involving this couple in the closing pages are a walk around Dublin in the early morning and a sexual act, and both of these are fused with the movement of the river Liffey flowing through Dublin into the sea. Contradictory tones and modes of address are blended; in particular, the eager admiration of a young girl for her active lover, and the disappointment of the aging wife with her now impotent husband. Here, ALP is asking HCE to don his new, expensive clothes and go out with her on a jaunt, but she is also inviting him to demonstrate his naked sexual potency. (At first, the words are also those of a mother to her young son; they echo, too, a letter of Joyce's to Nora on 7 September 1909: 'I want you to look your best for me when I come. Have you any nice clothes now?'[8]) At the same time, what we hear is the river addressing the city of Dublin (reversed in 'nill, Budd'), with its green belt and modern comforts. The relationship is also reminiscent of that between Molly and Leopold Bloom in *Ulysses*: 'Blooming in the very lotust' points to the earlier novel, especially the 'Lotus-eaters' chapter; Sinbad the Sailor ('somebalt that sailder') is associated with Bloom as he goes to bed in 'Ithaca'; and Molly's own closing chapter has something in common with ALP's final monologue. It includes, too, the exploitative relationship of England and Ireland ('Proudpurse Alby with his pooraroon Eireen': Perfidious Albion and poor Eire). The passage enunciates a series of ALP's sexual memories, all of which turn out to be memories of HCE in one or other of his guises: as sailor (Sinbad, Magellan and Vanderdecken, the captain of *The Flying Dutchman*); as military figure (the man with the bandolier, the Duke of Wellington, and the Earl of Lucan – whether the hero of the Williamite wars or the Lord Lucan who fought at Balaclava); and as the stranger (the man with earrings, the man from the Dark Countries) who is also an Irishman (not only Wellington, but Lucan as a village on the Liffey, 'Iren' as Ireland and 'erse' as Irish). That the exploits of these figures are partly sexual (or at least excretory – the two are not kept distinct in the *Wake*) emerges from the 'gallant' of 'megallant', 'erse' understood as 'arse', and another echo of *Ulysses*, this time of Bloom's pamphlet advertising the 'Wonderworker', 'the world's greatest remedy for rectal complaints'.[9] Once phallic suggestions begin to surface, they crop up

---

[8] James Joyce, *Letters*, eds Stuart Gilbert and Richard Ellmann, vol. II (New York, 1966), p. 251.

[9] James Joyce, *Ulysses* (New York, 1961), p. 721; see also pp. 289, 546 and 758 for further references to this invention which 'claims to afford a noiseless inoffensive vent'.

at every turn: a few examples would be 'stand up', 'straight', 'I want to see you', 'second to nill', *bod* (pronounced *bud*) as Gaelic for 'penis', 'cosh' (a thick stick), 'bulge', the 'wonderdecker' again (*decken* in German is to copulate), the stiffness of iron, and the Wellington monument. And the ellipses can easily be read as sexual modesty: 'a wonderdecker I once . . .', 'the Iren Duke's . . .', 'Come and let us . . .', 'We always said we'd . . .'. That will suffice as an initial indication of some of the meanings at work here; other motifs one could follow through the passage would be flowers, sins (several of the seven deadly ones are here), tailoring and sailing (the two often go together in the *Wake*), and battles; and all of these are associated in one way or another with sex.

Let us focus now on one word: 'shuit'. To call it a word is of course misleading, since it is precisely because it is *not* a word of the English language that it functions in the way it does, preventing the immediate move from material signifier to conceptual signified. Unlike the pun, which exists only if the context brings it into being, the portmanteau refuses, by itself, any single meaning; in reading we therefore have to allow it to move towards other signifiers whose meanings might prove appropriate. Let us, first of all, ignore the larger context of the whole book, and concentrate – as we would for a normal pun – on the guidance provided by the immediate context. We seem to be invited to take 'shuit' as an item of clothing, one which can have the adjective 'buckly' – with buckles – applied to it; and three lexical items offer themselves as appropriate: *suit*, *shirt*, *shoes*. The first two would account for the portmanteau without any unexplained residue, but 'buckly' seems to point in particular to *shoes*, partly by way of the nursery rhyme, 'One, two, buckle my shoe'. A writer employing only orthodox devices of patterning at the level of the signifier might construct a sentence in which *suit*, *shirt*, and *shoes* all occur in such a way as to make the reader conscious of the sound-connections between them; but it would be a rather feeble, easily ignored, device. 'Shuit' works more powerfully, because it forces the reader to read productively, because its effects are simultaneous, and because the result is an expansion of meaning even more extensive than that effected by the pun. The pun, as we saw in discussing the example by Pope, carries a powerful charge of satisfaction: the specter of a potentially unruly and ultimately infinite language is raised only to be exorcized; the writer and reader are still firmly in control and the language has been made to seem even *more* orderly and appropriate than we had realized, since an apparent coincidence in its system has been shown to be capable of semantic justification. But 'shuit' and its kind are more disturbing. The portmanteau has the effect of a *failed* pun – the patterns of language have been shown to be partially appropriate, but with a residue of difference where the pun found only happy similarity. And though the context makes it clear that the passage is about clothing, and seems thereby to set limits to the possible meanings, one cannot escape the feeling that the process, once started, may be unstoppable. In the case of Pope's couplet, the dictionary (or our internal lexicon) tells us the accredited meanings of 'port', and we can acknowledge at once that all those besides 'harbor' and 'wine' are excluded by the context. But no reference book exists to tell us all the possible signifiers that are or could be associated in sound with 'shuit', and we have learned no method of interpretation to tell us how to go about finding those signifiers, or deciding at what point the connection becomes too slight to be relevant. There certainly are other signifiers which sound something like 'shuit': and if similarities of sound can have semantic implications, how do we know where to draw the boundary?

The answer to this question may seem straightforward; like the pun, the portmanteau will contain as much as the verbal context permits it to contain. But here we reach a fundamental point about the *Wake*: the context *itself* is made up of puns and portmanteaux. So far I have spoken as if the context is a given, firm structure of meaning which has one neatly defined hole in it, but this is of course a pure interpretative fiction; the text is a web of shifting meanings, and every new interpretation of one item recreates afresh the context for all the other items. For example, having found *suit* in 'shuit', one can reinterpret the previous word to yield the phrase *birthday suit*, as a colloquial expression for 'nakedness' nicely epitomizing the fusion of the states of being clothed and unclothed that the passage implies: one more example of the denial of the logic of opposites that characterizes this text from its title on. Thus a 'contextual circle' is created, whereby plurality of meaning in one item increases the available meanings of other items, which in turn increase the possibilities of meaning in the original item. The longer and denser the text, the more often the circle will revolve, and the greater will be the proliferation of meanings. It is important to note, however, that the network of signification remains *systematic*: the familiar accusation that 'there is no way of denying the relevance ... of any meaning any commentator cares to find', to quote S. L. Goldberg, is without substance.[10] However, it is true that in a text as long and as densely worked as *Finnegans Wake*, the systematic networks of meaning could probably provide contexts for most of the associations that individual words might evoke – though an individual reader could not be expected to grasp them all. This sense of a spiraling increase in potential meaning is one of the grounds on which the *Wake* is feared and dismissed; but is this not the way all texts operate? Every item in a text functions simultaneously as a sign whose meaning is limited – but not wholly limited – by its context, and as a context limiting – but not

---

[10] S. L. Goldberg, *Joyce* (Edinburgh and London, 1962), p. 111.

wholly limiting – the meaning of other signs; there is no escape from this circle, no privileged item that yields its meaning apart from the system in which it is perceived, and which can act as a contextless context to anchor the whole text. The difference between *Finnegans Wake* and other literary works is a difference in degree, not in kind.

The next word, 'Rosensharonals', provides another example of the operation of contexts in the *Wake*. As an individual item it immediately suggests 'Rose of Sharon': a flower (identified with crocus, narcissus and others) to go with bloom, lotus, and bud, and to further enhance the springlike vitality of the male or his sexual organ. It gives us a reference to the Song of Solomon (itself a sexual invitation), reinforcing the text's insistence that apparently 'natural' human emotions are cultural products – love and sexual desire in this passage being caught up not only with the Hebraic tradition, but also with Buddhism (both in the lotus and in 'Budd'), with *Billy Budd* (in many ways a highly relevant story), *Sinbad the Sailor* (as a tale from the *Arabian Nights* or as a pantomine), and with popular songs (*Eileen Aroon*) – 'Eileen my darling' – and phrases from 'I will give you the keys to heaven'). (I suspect that there is also a song called 'The Man with the Bandolier', though I have not been able to trace it: in fact, the text problematizes that very urge to 'verify' what offers itself as an 'allusion'.)[11] The sense of new beginnings is also heightened by a suggestion of Rosh Hashanah, the Jewish New Year. In the context of clothing, however, the name sounds more like that of the Jewish tailor who made the garment in question: 'the buckly shuit Rosensharonals near did for you', and this brings to mind the story of Kersse the tailor and the Norwegian captain from earlier in the book (pp. 311–32), involving as it does a suit with a bulge in it, apparently made necessary by a hunchback. But once we move to the context of the whole work, another story, from the same earlier chapter (pp. 337–55), comes into prominence: the tale of Buckley and the Russian General, which appears in the text at many points and in many guises. Buckley, it will be recalled, is the common Irish soldier in the Crimean War who comes upon a Russian General with his pants down, in the act of defecating, and either does or does not shoot him. The story interweaves with other stories of encounters involving exposure and/or voyeurism, such as the much-discussed event in Phoenix Park involving HCE, two girls, and three soldiers. It has to do with the attack by the younger generation on the older, and the older generation's fall from power before the younger: the

---

[11] Charles Peake has suggested to me a possible reference to a once-famous song entitled 'The Bandolero' (private communication). The word 'bandolier' is also associated with Leopold Bloom: see *Ulysses*, pp. 413, 448. The French word '*bander*' meaning 'to have an erection', is perhaps somewhere in the background.

drunkenness of Noah and the drugging of Finn MacCool by his young bride being other versions. (It's typical of the *Wake*'s method that an indecent anecdote which Joyce heard from his father is accorded the same status as religious myth and epic narrative.) So in the middle of a passage of praise for the virility of HCE comes a reminder of his loss of control, and 'near did for you' becomes a reference not to tailoring but to attempted murder. And our portmanteau *shuit* unpacks itself further, yielding both *shoot* and *shit*.

My aim is not to demonstrate the plurality of meaning in Joyce's portmanteaux; that is easily done. It is to focus on the workings of a typical portmanteau to show both how crucial they are to the method of *Finnegans Wake* and how they help to make it in a sense a central, rather than a peripheral, literary text. The portmanteau shatters any illusion that the systems of difference in language are fixed and sharply drawn, and reminds us that signifiers are perpetually dissolving into one another: in the never-ending diachronic development of language; in the blurred edges between languages, dialects, registers, idiolects; in the interchange between speech and writing; in errors and misunderstandings, unfortunate or fruitful; in riddles, jokes, games and dreams. *Finnegans Wake* insists that the strict boundaries and discrete elements in a linguist's 'grammar of competence' are a neoplatonic illusion.

But the portmanteau problematizes even the most stable signifier by showing how its relations to other signifiers can be productive; we find that we can quite easily relate *suit* to *shirt* just as we do in fact relate *suit* to *suits* or *suited*. Instead of saying that in learning a language we learn to ascribe meaning to a few of the many patterns of sound that we perceive, it may be as true to say that we learn *not* to ascribe meaning to most of those connections (Freud takes this view in *Der Witz*) – until we are allowed to do so again to a certain degree in rhetoric and poetry, and with almost complete abandon in *Finnegans Wake*. The result, of course, is that not only the obvious portmanteau but every word in the *Wake* is tested for its possible associations as we read. The phrase 'bangled ears' does not present itself as a portmanteau, and in most texts it would be read as a somewhat odd, but semantically specific, conjunction of adjective and noun. But in this context, as I have suggested, we are encouraged to hear it as 'bandolier', to combine the attributes of the savage or stranger with those of the soldier. Even the most normal and innocent word will invite such treatment; as Jean-Paul Martin has said, 'The portmanteau word, but also every word, every fragment of a word or of an utterance, marks the interlacing of sinuous and diverse chains of associations which cross codes and languages.'[12] Another theoretical distinction which becomes blurred is that between synchronic

---

[12] Jean-Paul Martin, 'La condensation', *Poétique* 26 (1976), p. 189 (my translation).

and diachronic dimensions, since a pertinent meaning may be retrievable from the history of a word: 'erse', for instance, offers both a Middle English word for 'arse' and an early Scottish word for 'Irish'. Here, too, the *Wake* merely heightens a process that operates in all language, in spite of the Saussurean enterprise of separating with great strictness synchrony and diachrony.[13]

The implications of the portmanteau word, or rather the portmanteau text, go further, however. It undermines the notion of authorial intention, for instance, in a way quite foreign to the traditional pun. The pun heightens the illusion of intention as a presence within the text: part of the satisfaction to be found in Pope's pun on *port* is the feeling of certainty, once the pun is grasped, that it was *intended* by its witty and resourceful author. The careful construction of context to allow both meanings equal force and to exclude all other meanings is not something that happens by accident, we feel; and there is no danger that the coincidence thus exposed will enable language to wrest control from its users. But the portmanteau word, though its initial effect is often similar, has a habit of refusing to rest with that comforting sensation of 'I see what the author meant'. To find *shirt* and *suit* in *shuit*, and nothing else, might yield a satisfying response of that kind: 'Clearly what Joyce is doing is fusing those two words into one', we say to ourselves. But when we note the claims for *shoes*, *shoot*, and *shit* as well, we begin to lose hold on our sense of an embodied intention. If those five are to be found, why not more? The polyglot character of the text, for instance, opens up further prospects: if French ears hear *chute*, one can hardly deny the relevance of the concept of the Fall to the story of Buckley and the Russian General or to the temptation of HCE in the Park.[14] And why should any particular number of associations, in any particular number of languages, correspond to the author's intention? Joyce has set in motion a process over which he has no final control. This is a source of alarm for many readers, conjuring up as it does images of Frankenstein and his monster; Litz, for example, complains, 'In reading it one does not feel that sense of "inevitability" or "rightness" which is the sign of a controlled narrative structure'.[15] Others are more willing to acknowledge the vast scale of what is opened up by the multilingual portmeanteau; Jean Paris observes: 'Once it is established, it must by its own movement extend itself to the totality of living and dead languages. And here indeed is the irony of the portmanteau style: the

---

[13] See my 'Language as History/History as Language', in *Peculiar Language*.

[14] For a discussion of the effects of Joyce's coalescing of languages that focuses on a single (and apparently simple) portmanteau from the *Wake*, see Jacques Derrida, 'Two Words for Joyce', in *Post-structuralist Joyce: Essays from the French*, eds Derek Attridge and Daniel Ferrer (Cambridge, 1984), pp. 145–59.

[15] A. Walton Litz, *The Art of James Joyce* (London, 1961), p. 62.

enthroning of a principle of chance which, prolonging the intentions of the author, in so far as they are perceptible, comes little by little to substitute itself for them, to function like a delirious mechanism, accumulating allusions, parodying analogies, and finally atomizing the Book.'[16] But *every* text, not just this one, is beyond the control of its author, *every* text reveals the systems of meaning of which Derrida speaks in his consideration of the word *pharmakon* in Plato's *Phaedrus*: 'But the system here is not, simply, that of the intentions of an author who goes by the name of Plato. The system is not primarily that of what someone *meant-to-say* [*un vouloir-dire*]. Finely regulated communications are established, through the play of language, among diverse functions of the word and within it, among diverse strata or regions of culture.'[17]

Similarly, the portmanteau word is a powerful weapon in the attack on conventional assumptions about narrative: *récit* cannot be separated from *histoire* when it surfaces in the texture of the words themselves. When, for instance, the story of Buckley and the Russian General is woven, by the portmanteau method, into a statement about new clothing, it is impossible to talk in terms of the narration of a supposedly prior event; rather, there is a process of fusion which enforces the realization that *all* stories are textual effects. Characters, too, are never *behind* the text in *Finnegans Wake*, but *in* it; ALP, HCE, Buckley and the Russian General have their being in the portmanteau word, in acrostics, in shapes on the pages – but this, too, is only a reinforcement of the status of all fictional characters. Finally, consider the traditional analysis of metaphor and allegory as a relation between a 'literal', 'superficial' meaning, and a 'figurative', 'deep', 'true', meaning. The portmanteau word – and *Finnegans Wake* as a whole – refuses to establish such a hierarchical opposition: anything that appears to be a metaphor is capable of reversal, the tenor becoming the vehicle, and vice versa. In the quoted passage, we might be tempted to say that a literal invitation to go for a walk can be metaphorically interpreted as an invitation to sexual activity. At the level of the word, one might say that 'lotust' is read literally as *latest*, a reference to fashion, but that the deeper meaning is *lotus*, with its implication of sensual enjoyment. This is all very well – except that the only reason for saying that the deeper meaning is the sexual one is our own preconception as to what counts as deep and what as superficial. All metaphor, we are made to realize by this text, is potentially unstable, kept in

[16] Jean Paris, 'Finnegans, Wake!', *Tel Quel* 30 (Summer, 1967), pp. 60–1 (my translation). See also the discussion by Jean Paris of the portmanteau word in 'L'agonie du signe', *Change* 11 (May 1972), pp. 133–72.

[17] Derrida, 'Plato's Pharmacy', p. 95.

position by the hierarchies we bring to bear upon it, not by its inner division
into literal and figurative domains.[18]

The fears provoked by *Finnegans Wake*'s portmanteau style are under-
standable and inevitable, because the consequences of accepting it extend to
all our reading. Every word in every text is a portmanteau, a combination of
sounds that echo through the entire language and through every other
language, and back through the history of speech. *Finnegans Wake* makes us
aware that we, as readers, control this explosion, allowing only those
connections to be effected which will give us the kinds of meaning we
recognize – stories, voices, characters, metaphors, images, beginnings,
developments, ends, morals, truths. We do not, of course, control it as a
matter of choice: we are subject to the various grids that make literature, and
language, possible at all – rules, habits, conventions, and all the boundaries
which legitimate and exclude in order to produce meanings and values,
themselves rooted in the ideology of our place and time. Hence our feeling
of security in reading Pope's couplet: we share both the language and the
joke. Nevertheless, to obtain a glimpse of the infinite possibility of meaning
kept at bay by those grids, to gain a sense that the boundaries upon which
our use of language depends are set up under specific historical conditions,
is to be made aware of a universe more open to reinterpretation and change
than the one we are usually conscious of inhabiting. For many of its readers,
Finnegans Wake makes that glimpse an experience of exhilaration and
opportunity, and as a result the book comes to occupy a central place in
their reading; but for many others it can only be a discouraging glimpse of
limitless instability.[19] So the book is treated as a freak, an unaccountable
anomaly which merely travesties the cultural traditions we cherish – and its

[18] I discuss the *Wake*'s effects upon the hierarchic distinction between what is central and
what is digressive in both the novel and the novel tradition in ch. 8 of *Peculiar Language*.

[19] Someone who was able to go further than most in reading a wide range of literature
against the grain of established codes, prefiguring the strategies required by *Finnegans Wake*,
was Saussure; but he took fright at the infinite possibilities he opened up, as Jean Starobinski
documents in *Words upon Words: The Anagrams of Ferdinand de Saussure*, trans. Olivia Emmet
(New Haven, 1979). Starobinski comments: 'If this approach [the theory of hypograms] had
been further developed, it would soon have become a quagmire. Wave upon wave of possible
names would have taken shape beneath his alert and disciplined eye. Is this the vertigo of error?
It is also the discovery of the simple truth that language is an infinite resource, and that behind
each phrase lies hidden the multiple clamor from which it has detached itself to appear before
us in its isolated individuality' (p. 122). The moral which Starobinski draws from Saussure's
abandonment of his project is equally relevant to *Finnegans Wake*: 'Perhaps Saussure's only
mistake was to have posed the alternative so sharply between "chance" and "conscious
deliberation" ' (p. 122).

function as *supplément* and *pharmakon*, supererogatory but necessary, dangerous but remedial, is prolonged.

If, however, the *Wake* is welcomed, it is often by means of a gesture which simultaneously incapacitates it, either by placing it in a sealed-off category (the impenetrable world of the dream), or by subjecting it to the same interpretative mechanisms that are applied to all literary texts, as if it were no different: the elucidation of an 'intention' (aided by draft material and biography), the analysis of 'characters', the tracing of 'narrative', the elaboration of 'themes', the tracking-down of 'allusions', the identification of 'autobiographical references' – the whole panoply of modern professional criticism. The outright repudiation of the Joycean portmanteau, though it may one day seem as quaint an attitude as Johnson's rejection of the Shakespearean quibble, is perhaps preferable to this industrious program of normalization and domestication. Johnson's passionate lament for his flawed idol involves a fuller understanding of the implications of the pun than many an untroubled celebration of textual indeterminacy, and to be afraid of *Finnegans Wake* is at least to acknowledge, even if unconsciously, the force and magnitude of the claims it makes.

9

Eat Your *Dasein*:
Lacan's Self-Consuming Puns

Françoise Meltzer

La sonorité même et l'air de mensonge assumé par la hâte de la facile
affirmation était une cause de tourment.

Mallarmé, 'Le démon de l'analogie'

And now we have reached a point at which the intellect is forced, again, to
struggle against its propensity for analogical inference – against its mono-
maniac grasping at the infinite.

E. A. Poe, 'Eureka: an essay on the material and spiritual universe'

As everyone knows, the pun appears consistently in the writings of Lacan.
Catherine Clément thinks that punning was originally used by Lacan as a
means of relieving the understandably intense atmosphere of his lecture
halls; but that, after a while, the audience came to expect punning, so that
Lacan became a parody of his own discourse, punning whether he needed to
or not.[1] Maria Ruegg, in an article on Metaphor and Metonymy, refers to
the pun on 'non' du père and 'nom' du père, and as if by way of an apology for
Lacan, adds that the rhetorical force of such a figure 'does not lie in the
somewhat heavy-handed and strictly circumscribed polysemics of the pun'.[2]
François Roustang, in a recent address to the Chicago Psychoanalytic
Institute, talked of Lacan's puns as one item on a very long list of seductive
techniques which functioned, in Roustang's view, to mesmerize the
audience into wrongly thinking that something important, not to mention
original, was being said. In all of these readings, the pun in Lacan's
discourse is either apologized for (Ruegg), affectionately tolerated
(Clément), or openly mocked (Roustang). I would argue, on the contrary,
that the pun in Lacan is intimately related to his notion of metonymy and

---

[1] Catherine Clément, *The Lives and Legends of Jacques Lacan* (New York, 1983), pp. 32–4.
[2] Maria Ruegg, 'Metaphor and Metonymy: The Logic of Structuralist Rhetoric', *Glyph* 6
(Baltimore, 1979), p. 155.

metaphor; that, as such, the pun partakes, not only of the rhetorical structures of the Lacanian unconscious, but also of Lacan's mysticism. By 'mysticism', I mean Lacan's attempt to 'rupture' the (male) economy of totality by means of a fantasy of supplementarity – precisely as he argues, in 'The Woman', when describing the woman's *jouissance*. I will propose that we see the pun in Lacan as an attempt to overcome analogy (totality) with supplementarity – an economy of contiguity which will, ultimately, allow for moments of 'grace'.

It is the pun's contiguous, polysemic function which ties it to metonymy and metaphor. The pun, or *calembour*, relies upon similarity of sounds which allow for two or more different meanings. Hence, it is a double hearing – *double entente*, a play upon words – rooted in a homonymic contiguity. It is in this notion of contiguity that the complexity arises.

In classical rhetoric metaphor is a figure of resemblance and analogy *in absentia*. It is a *transferral*, a carrying back (literally) of one thing to another. Fontanier is explicit: 'it consists in presenting one idea under the sign of another more striking or better known idea which, moreover, holds to the first by no link other than that of a certain conformity or analogy.'[3] As such, metaphor is *displacement*. It is also, however, substitution. Here is Quintilian: 'On the whole metaphor is a shorter form of simile, while there is this further difference, that in the latter we compare some object to the thing which we wish to describe, whereas in the former this object is actually *substituted* for the thing.'[4] Transferral, carrying back, resemblance, analogy, implied comparison, substitution – all of these 'metaphors' for metaphor imply a gap between the two functions. If metaphor is anything, it is a non-contiguous economy of doubling.

In classical rhetoric again, we have metonymy as, precisely, a system of contiguity. Metonymy *owes* (as in 'is indebted to') the thing from which it springs. It names after that thing, and is named 'after' it. It is a trope of correspondence, as opposed to metaphor's resemblance. Fontanier: 'metonymy [is a trope] by correspondence, consisting in the designation of one object by the name of another object which forms like it an absolute whole, but to which it owes its existence or manner of being'.[5] Quintilian notes that metonymy is but a short step from synecdoche. Metonymy, he says, 'consists in the *substitution* of one name for another. . . . these devices are employed to indicate an invention by substituting the name of the inventor, or a possession by substituting the name of the possessor'.[6] Metonymy partakes

---

[3] Pierre Fontanier, *Les Figures du discours* (Paris, 1968), p. 99. Fontanier is here discussing tropes in general, which can all be reduced, he says, to a single trope: metaphor.

[4] Quintilian, *Institutio Oratorio*, 8. vi. 8.

[5] Fontanier, *Les Figures du discours*, p. 79.

[6] Quintilian, *Institutio Oratorio*, 8. vi. 23.

of that for which it substitutes; metaphor repeats or doubles that from which it is displaced.

The politics of choosing the masters of classical rhetoric are not for the purpose of falling back on 'canon', but rather for that of demonstrating Lacan's bind – for it is from this canon that he will take his cue. As he himself says, once something is split into two, it can never become one again: 'when one is made into two, there is no going back on it. It can never revert to making one again, not even a new one. The *Aufhebung* is one of those sweet dreams of philosophy'.[7] Or: 'there was not the slightest synthesis – there never is'. And yet this is exactly what Lacan tries to do to metaphor: to take its two terms and fuse them back into one. To put, in other words, metaphor into the same economy of contiguity as metonymy. Before we ask why he does this, let us first look at a few examples of how he does this.

In the first place, Lacan uses (although he alters) Jakobson's bipolar model of metaphor and metonymy. How he alters it has been so thoroughly documented by Maria Ruegg and Anika Lemaire that I will not recapitulate. Let me say only that Jakobson's easy distinction between metaphor as similarity and metonymy as contiguity is problematized, not merely digested, by Lacan, and by Jakobson himself in his later work ('Linguistics and Poetics'). But the distinction follows entirely the axes of metaphor and metonymy traced by our canonical figures, Quintilian and Fontanier. Now, Ruegg argues that this distinction between similarity and metonymy in the two figures is silly, since *both* 'involve some degree of semantic contiguity which provides the necessary link between the two signifiers – the road without which the transfer cannot be made. That the link of contiguity is based, in the first case, on a relationship of part to whole, and in the second, on a comparative relationship of functions or of "common quality" . . . is certainly insufficient grounds for constructing a bipolarization of all language'.[8]

Perhaps so. But let us look at these criticisms more closely. The first is that both figures involve some kind of substitution. Jakobson never says that they do not – though he elides the substitutive nature of metonymy to allow for his polarities. And Quintilian and Fontanier actually say, as we have seen, that both metaphor and metonymy are figures involving substitution. There can be no quarrel here, so let us put this criticism aside. In the second criticism lies the rub: Ruegg says that both figures involve 'some degree of semantic contiguity'. But degrees on which thermometer? Contiguity in metonymy (her example: the part for the whole) is literal and undeniable.

---

[7] Jacques Lacan, 'A Love Letter', in *Feminine Sexuality*, eds J. Mitchell and J. Rose (New York, 1985), p. 156.

[8] Ruegg, 'Metaphor', p. 145.

But what is this contiguity 'based ... on a comparative relationship of functions or of "common quality" '? Comparison and commonality are precisely not systems that touch each other – rather, they duplicate or double each other, and the comprehension stems from the recognition of the first term through its repetition in another. If one wants to call that mental contiguity, fine – there is a *connection* made. But the connection is made by the subject; it is not inherent in the comparison. If I want to call my Volkswagen a 'prancing steed' and say that these are contiguous by virtue of both being modes of transportation, I will have imposed a commonality within the 'whole' of transportation, of which 'Volkswagen' and 'prancing steed' will be parts. I will, in other words, have metonymized metaphor. Which is exactly what Ruegg's reading of the two terms does.

More to the point, however, it is also exactly what Lacan's reading of the term does. Freud's displacement (*Verschiebung*) becomes, with Lacan, metonymy: the word-to-word chain of signifiers, the inability to cross that fatal bar. It is, then, the chain of desire, always displaced, never satisfied. Freud's condensation (*Verdichtung*), on the other hand, becomes with Lacan metaphor: the substitution of one word for another, the sliding of the signifier as if through the bar into signified. It will be noted that both of these systems – the chain and the sliding, condensing, drop into the signified – are systems of contiguity. It will also be noted that the usual, 'classical' adjectives for the figures, substitution and displacement (never mind the limitations of these, which I have just noted) are reversed in Lacan: metaphor becomes substitution, and metonymy displacement. What both of these moves accomplish is to retain the notion of contiguity in metaphor as well as in metonymy (where it was never in any danger of being lost). Within this system, that 'gap' in metaphor, that *in absentia*, is repressed and becomes *in praesentia*. Metaphor must at all costs not be seen as analogy – that noncontiguous figure which insists upon totality.

It is because that metaphor must work, in Lacan, as the access to the unconscious, that it must of necessity be placed within an economy of contiguity. We had no trouble understanding this in metonymy. For Lacan the unconscious breaks through, ruptures conscious discourse, with the two mechanisms of metaphor and metonymy. Dreams, slips of the tongue, symptoms and 'even homonymic convergence' (to which we will return) rupture the text of conscious discourse.[9] In Lacan's words, 'There is a homogeneous structure in symptoms, dreams, parapraxes, and jokes. The same structural laws of condensation and displacement are at work in them: these are the laws of the unconscious. These laws are the same as those which create meaning in language' (*Ecrits*, p. 35). If metaphor, like

[9] Lacan, *Ecrits* (Paris, 1966), p. 265.

metonymy, has structural laws like those of the unconscious, then metaphor must above all not be analogy or *resemblance*: it must allow for contiguity, even as the erased text of the unconscious is blotted out and written over by the consciousness, allowing the former to glimmer through the latter's gaps, allowing both to touch, even as one seeks to cover up the other.

Hence Lacan's attack on analogy:

Analogy is not metaphor, and the use that philosophers of nature have made of it calls for the genius of a Goethe, but even his example is not encouraging. Nothing is more repugnant to the spirit of our discipline, and it was by deliberately keeping away from analogy that Freud opened up the right way to the interpretation of dreams and with it, to the concept of analytic symbolism. Analytic symbolism, I insist, is strictly opposed to analogical thinking, whose dubious tradition results in the fact that some people, even in our own ranks, still consider it to be part and parcel of our method (*Ecrits*, p. 53).

Some people, in other words, still consider analogy to be metonymic (part and parcel) of the analytic method; whereas in fact, analogy is excluded in no uncertain terms – and excluded as well from the idea of metaphor which, as part and parcel, has been metonymized. And this is explicit in Lacan – so much so that even the 'distinction' between metaphor and condensation, on the one hand, and metonymy and displacement, on the other, are collapsed, *both* of them, into condensation: 'Ellipsis and pleonasm, hyperbaton or syllepsis, regression, repetition, apposition – these are the syntactical displacements; metaphor, catachresis, antonomasia, allegory, metonymy, and synecdoche – these are the semantic condensations' (*Ecrits*, p. 58).

So much must metaphor be rendered metonymic, that Lacan even puns it into contiguity. After speaking of history, in the opening section of the 'Rome Discourse', Lacan makes the following remarkable statement: 'At this point it would be too much to say that I was about to *carry these remarks over* into the field of psychoanalysis, *since they are there already*' (*Ecrits*, p. 52; emphasis added). The remarks on history must above all not be read as an analogy to the subject – they are already within him, as a 'historical scar'. The subject must learn to recognize that his unconscious *is* his history. There is then, nothing to be 'carried over' (that is, there is no need for metaphor in precisely its usual, etymological sense), since everything (including the outside) is already a part of the inside.

The refutation of analogy, of metaphor *qua* metaphor, appears, for example, again, in 'God and the Jouissance of The Woman': 'Note that I said *supplementary*', in speaking of woman's jouissance, 'Had I said *complementary*' (that is, comparison, analogy, the railroad tracks which never converge) – 'Had I said *complementary*, where would we be! We'd fall right back into the all!'[10] We would fall back into the male fantasy of the One, of

[10] Lacan, 'God and the Jouissance of the Woman', in *Feminine Sexuality*, p. 144.

the *Tout* – to which the economy of supplement provides an alternative. Unlike the noncontiguous analogy, the supplement can function as condensation (hence, can be less than, as well as more than), rupturing through, rather than carrying back, shaking up (*secouant*) as well as rescuing (*secourant*), a kind of grace out of excess – an excess which must come from within in order to rupture to the outside, be recognized. *Not a complement but a supplement* means not analogy (that neutered untouchable) but supplementarity – that visible tremor which impugns the source even while it exceeds it.

The economy of contiguity is, of course, no surprise in a philosophy which holds, as Lacan's does, that desire is always mediated. Lacan reads Hegel: 'there is no object for man's desire which is constituted without some sort of mediation – which appears in his most primitive needs' (*Ecrits*, p. 181). And this other, again, is already inside for Lacan: the unconscious is the discourse of the other. But the problem of analogy remains, and we have not done with it.

To begin with, despite the refutation of analogy, the Lacanian principal tenet is, in fact, an analogy: the unconscious is structured like a language. Here is Lemaire: 'In the same way, when we hear of people rejecting Lacanian formulae such as "the unconscious is structured like a language", or "the unconscious is a discourse" in the name of a purist adherence to the principles of linguistic science, we can consider them as dismissing, with too hasty a stroke of the pen, the richness of such analogical recourses.'[11] The very system that refutes analogy rests its most basic precepts upon the richness of analogical recourses. Given that the unconscious is structured like a language, the stakes are a lot higher here than a simple quibble of the proper use of rhetorical figures. Enter the politics of rhetoric.

For to insist upon the contiguity of the other is a political stance; and to declare desire to be ever displaced is equally a political statement. These are also, of course, philosophical and, as I have briefly mentioned, theological statements as well. Lacan wants, for instance, to be touched – by the discourse of the other, by the knowledge of his desire, by grace.

The chain of signifiers in Lacan, that tangible metaphor for contiguity, is necessitated in large part by the import he gives to Frege's number theory, and the latter's notion of mathematical sequence. For Frege, as Jacques-Alain Miller has pointed out, identity must be the foundation of truth (an analogue, if ever there was one).[12] But zero has no identity to itself, subsumes itself, and must lead to one. Thus zero equals one (in a limited

---

[11] Anika Lemaire, *Jacques Lacan* (London, 1977), pp. 100–1.

[12] Jacques-Alain Miller, 'Suture (Elements of the Logic of the Signifier)', *Screen* 18:4 (1977–8), pp. 24–34.

sense) and is an identical representing nonidentity. The progress of numbers thereafter is metonymic of zero. I would add to this, however, that the leap from zero to one (which also haunted Pascal) entails leaping over a gap, and that the metonymic sequence that follows is rendered possible by a metaphoric equation – zero equals one – which is, precisely, not founded upon identity. So here we might make our own analogy: the sentence 'the unconscious is structured like a language' may be precisely this metaphoric leap, based upon nonidentity, for Lacan. Zero equals one is, after all, a metaphor, but *not* an analogy, since it is not based on resemblance.

So what, finally, do puns have to do with all of this? Everything. To begin with, the pun is, by Lacan's own admission, contiguous: a homonymic *convergence*. It is, further, based on a nonidentity which is initially mistaken for identity. Bore equals boar only at first phonetic hearing. It is against nonidentity that the pun plays – reverberating, doubling itself deceptively, as a Hermes from the unconscious underworld.

Let us take as an example the syllable 'da'. From Kant, through Fichte, Hegel and Heidegger, we have the notion of 'Da-sein' – one upon which Lacan plays, and plays often. *Da-sein* (as against *Sein*), that which is manifest, there, as against that which is latent. A very convenient psychoanalytic concept. Then in Heidegger, *Da-sein* entails concepts of future and past: 'As authentically futural, *Dasein is* authentically as "having been" (*gewesen*). Anticipation of one's uttermost and ownmost possibility (death) is coming back understandingly to one's ownmost "been".'[13] Hence, Lacan's 'Eat your Da-sein' in the seminar on 'The Purloined Letter'.[14] The Heideggerian notion of Da-sein is the eating of one's own children – one's past, one's future. It is also the recognition of the death instinct, that return to a previous state to which we always move, *forward*. It is all there in the Heidegger quotation. So, too, the Fort: Da! game of Freud's grandson. Repetition compulsion, yes – but also Lacan's *metaphor* for life, of which this game is the condensation. The continual displacement of the object of desire, already formulated in the repetitious gestures of a child. Da – here it is. And there is the conclusion of the Rome discourse: ' "Da," said Prajapati, god of thunder. "Have you understood me?" . . . That, continues the text, is what the divine voice caused to be heard in the thunder: Submission, gift, grace, Da da da.' (*Ecrits*, p. 322). *The Waste Land*, of course, but also three puns within this *reseau* (web) of puns I am pointing to. Submission, gift, grace. 'The mystical,' says Lacan, 'is by no means that which is not political.'[15] Indeed not. Part of the politics of the pun is that its meaning is

---

[13] Martin Heidegger, *Being and Time* (London, 1962), p. 373.

[14] 'The response of the signifier to whoever interrogates it is "Mange ton Dasein",' Lacan, *Ecrits*, p. 40.

[15] Lacan, *Feminine Sexuality*, p. 146.

determined by its circumstances, its position within the economy surrounding it. The pun, that voice of the unconscious, that figure of identity which is not identity, that metaphor then which will allow zero to be one, and metonymy to come into play – the pun in Lacan reverberates repetitiously to its point of origin – grace, the leap of faith. The pun trembles like an orgasm throughout Lacan's writings – a trembling which rescues him, through the very notion of supplementarity, from the sterility of the totalizing 'One', and from the seduction of etymology. Lacan says, 'And why not interpret one face of the Other, the God face, as supported by feminine jouissance' (*Feminine Sexuality*, p. 147) – precisely, the economy of supplementarity. This supplementarity is directly contiguous to the presence of God for Lacan: 'If I am using this S(Φ) to designate nothing other than the jouissance of the woman, it is undoubtedly because I am thereby registering that God has not made his exit' (p. 154).[16] No – God has not exited; he is still there for Lacan (Er ist noch da).

For Lacan, grace and the *in praesentia* of God are tied to supplementarity, which is in turn tied to woman's jouissance, which is in turn tied to experience without knowledge, which is in turn tied to the unconscious. Grace itself, in other words, is part of a metonymic chain which begins with the leap of metaphor and the repression of its analogy after the leap is made. As for the pun, it is able to take on the guise of all of these – *sein*, *da-sein*, *fort-da*, and the *da*, *da*, *da* of the god of thunder. Da, da, da – submission, gift, grace – these are perhaps the important three registers for Lacan which tremble (*secoue*) and rescue (*secour*), like thunder itself, through the reverberations of the pun.

If there is an idealism in Lacan, it is not one of monism. It is rather a Dadaism which, emerging from the literary movement (surrealism) of which Lacan was a part, seeks a politics of breaking out from within. It is the fantasy of contiguity through supplementarity – this 'more than or less than' that can break out of stasis, augment the sequence until it opens out onto the grace of beyond, of consummation. If *Aufhebung* is the 'sweet dream of philosophy', the 'great chain of being' is Lacan's dream – one in which the pun reappears on nearly every link. Aye, there's the rub. Given that, the pun is in no position to be excised – for any purpose – from Lacan's discourse.

[16] The visual pun in Lacan's symbol for the phallus (Φ) has always struck me: not only in its obvious referent to the Greek letter, but also in its visual elision of the number one with zero. The Φ is precisely the concept-zero not identical with itself, as Frege puts it, containing (literally) the possibility of one within itself.

10

The Puncept in Grammatology

Gregory Ulmer

Thomas Kuhn developed the notion of 'paradigm shift' to help account for the fact that sometimes, 'a law that cannot even be demonstrated to one group of scientists may occasionally seem intuitively obvious to another'.[1] Such a law, central to the 'post' paradigm, involves punceptual cognition. One way to determine on which side of the new paradigm one's sensibility lies is to note how one feels about puns, about all manner of homophonic and homonymic formations. If it seems intuitively possible (if not obvious) that puncepts work as well for organizing thought as concepts (sets formed on the basis of similar signifiers rather than similar signifieds), then you are likely to possess a post-modernist sensibility.

At the same time, Walter Redfern's *Puns*[2] demonstrates that it is possible to be fascinated with the pun and yet have no idea why the world is ready for a book-length study of punning (or for a line of 'punny bears' – Humphrey Beargart, Lauren Bearcall, William Shakesbear, and so on – manufactured by North American Bear Company). In the middle of a survey of everything ever said about or done with the pun Redfern complains about the tendency in recent French theory to reduce the analytical method to punning, the worst offender being that manic punster, Jacques Lacan. Taking the side of the concept, Redfern insists that any theory based on gratuitous puns that anyway work only in French is self-refuting. But if an authority on the pun such as Redfern fails to understand what has happened in (post)modern thinking it is likely that the topic would benefit from some review.

One place to begin is with the story that has become the emblem of contemporary sensibility, Borges' 'Pierre Menard, Author of the Quixote'.[3] Borges has been nominated several times for emblem of the era – by Edward Said and Michel Foucault, for example. Gerard Genette said that he found

---

[1] Thomas Kuhn, *The Structure of Scientific Revolutions* (Chicago, 1970), p. 150.
[2] Walter Redfern, *Puns* (Oxford, 1982).
[3] Jorge Luis Borges, *Labyrinths* (New York, 1962).

more truth in this story than in the whole science of criticism. The selection of 'Pierre Menard' as the opening text in the influential collection, *Art After Modernism: Rethinking Representation*, devoted to making intelligible the culture of the 1980s, attests to the continuing value of Borges as a model for current thinking.

Several features of 'Menard' recommend it – that it violates generic boundaries (story/essay), and that it is a parody (alluding in part to T. S. Eliot's famous 'Tradition and the Individual Talent'). Most important in our context is the central joke by means of which Borges reformulates Eliot's insight into tradition – that the reading of earlier texts is altered by the reading of later ones. The joke, of course, is the scenario in which, first, Menard recomposes several short sections of *Don Quijote* word for word, and second, the commentator argues that Menard's version, although identical to the original, is better.

Here we have the lesson of our epoch, the one that most fascinates us just now – that, unlike physics, in which two bodies may not occupy the same space, language is a material in which the same names are capable of supporting several mutually exclusive meanings simultaneously. Because Borges couched this point in a parody rather than directly asserting it, most critics are able to acknowledge that the story dramatizes a legitimate insight into hermeneutics, without necessarily concluding that Menard's methodology of deliberate anachronism and the erroneous attribution constitute a basis for practical criticism. But when Jacques Derrida takes up the practice of punning the experiment is no longer so easily assimilated, since it is a joke applied in earnest.

The difference between an archivist of the pun such as Redfern and a Derrida who refunctions the pun into the philosopheme of a new cognition may be seen in this statement in which Derrida explains the attitude to the pun at work in *Glas*:

The new glossary and the new grammar no longer leave any place for the *pun*, at least if – but this is obviously the whole question – one persists in understanding by this word, as is often done in certain socio-ideological situations and to defend certain norms, the free play, the complacent and slightly narcissistic relation to language, the exercise of virtuosity to no profit, without economy of sense or knowledge, without any necessity but that of enjoying one's mastery over one's language and the others. Here, on the contrary, the pun is analyzed as much as practiced. The possibility of its economy, the mastery it seems to secure finds itself submitted to a *curious* X-ray.... How is a pun possible? How in the pun does the aleatory cut across a necessity each time proper name or a family genealogy is the law there?[4]

[4] Jacques Derrida, 'Proverbs: "He that would pun ..." ', in John Leavey, *Glassary* (Lincoln, Neb., 1986), p. 18.

How is a pun possible? Derrida's most economical answer to this question is: 'If I had to risk a single definition of deconstruction, one as brief, elliptical, and economical as a password, I would say simply and without overstatement: *plus d'une langue* – both more than a language and no more of *a* language.'[5] He is very interested, that is, in the macaronic pun, the pun across languages, of the kind practiced by Joyce in *Finnegans Wake*: for example, 'He War'. 'It *was* written *simultaneously* in both English and German. Two words in one (*war*). . . . *War* is a noun in English, a verb in German, it resembles an adjective (*wahr*) in that same language, and the truth of this multiplicity returns, from the attributes (the verb is also an attribute), towards the subject, *he*, who is divided by it right from the origin. In the beginning, difference, that's what happens.'[6]

What is at stake in such puns is not simply a problem of style, even the style of what many take to be the definitive text of the twentieth century, but the generalization of this possibility into a new relation between and among thought, language and writing, and hence a renegotiation of the functions of truth and history in a new paradigm. Derrida's name for this refunctioning is 'programmatology', concerned with the sur-vival, the life and growth of texts and language, based on the material role played by the pun in the history of language change. In the new paradigm meaning arises dialogically, in Bakhtin's sense of the heterological word, according to a mode of reception pragmatics. Derrida's version of this operation is 'open to a different sense of the dispatch (*envoi*) and of dispatches (*envois*), programmatology should always take the situation of the marks into account; in particular that of utterances, the place of senders and addressees, of framing and of the socio-historical circumscription. It should therefore take account of the problematics of randomness in all fields where it evolves: physics, biology, game theory, and the like'.[7]

Practicing and analysing the pun at once, Derrida approaches programmatology as an alternative to more traditional models of reading and writing formulated in terms of communication. Against the emphasis on utterance as a performative *enunciation*, Derrida imagines comprehension in terms of the *annunciation* as it is couched in the apocalyptic mode, in the Biblical tradition of apocalyptic prophecy and forecasts. To perform writing in terms of annunciation, for a mind listening with a psychoanalytic or dialogical ear, requires a shift away from signifieds to tone. 'By what is a tone marked, a change or rupture of tone? And how do you recognize a tonal difference

[5] Derrida, *Memoires: For Paul de Man* (New York, 1986), p. 15.

[6] Derrida, 'Two Words for Joyce', in *Post-Structuralist Joyce*, eds Derek Attridge and Daniel Ferrer (Cambridge, 1984), p. 155.

[7] Derrida, 'My Chances/*Mes Chances*', in *Taking Chances: Derrida, Psychoanalysis, Literature*, eds Joseph Smith and William Kerrigan (Baltimore, 1984), pp. 27–8.

within the same corpus?'[8] What is written, uttered as annunciation, comes to the receiver as a gift/ *Gift* (present/poison).

The case of Nietzsche best illustrates why Derrida wants to write in this mode of 'sending on'. In trying to think what is specific in writing, and to work within this specificity, Derrida continually reminds the theorists of intention, from Plato to Searle, that writing functions in the absence of the author (a death that is constantly denied). 'To begin with, he [Nietzsche, but the same is true in another session of Paul de Man] is dead, *himself*, a trivial fact but at bottom incredible enough and the genius or genie of the name is there to make us forget that.'[9] Nothing, neither for good or evil, then, can ever return to the bearer of that name, but only to 'Nietzsche' (or to 'de Man'), signifiers detached now from that trajectory in which the letter is said to always arrive. And 'Nietzsche' *is the homonym of the other one*, Nietzsche – the relation of living or dead persons to their names is that of the pun. Here we encounter the full force of the consequences, political and moral as well as aesthetic and epistemological, of the pun as philosopheme. The contemporary defense of Nietzsche coming from the left, insisting that Nietzsche never intended any of the things the Nazi theorists found there, in his texts, fails to confront a fundamental issue: 'one wonders why and how that which one calls so naively a falsification was possible, why and how the "same" statements, if they are the same, could serve over again in senses and contexts that one deems different, even incompatible.'[10] The same colossal pun that opened Schreber's madness (he started listening to the homophones reverberating in his speech and thought they were addressed to him by God, as an annunciation) allowed Hitler to be the *Führer* Nietzsche spoke of. And any Marxist who condemns the poststructuralist Nietzscheans on the basis of such a pun must be held accountable for another such pun that put Stalin's Gulag in the texts of Marx and Lenin.

The future of a text is never closed. It survives everything while programming the possibility of left and right Marxists, left and right Nietzscheans, left and right Derrideans. 'The most important thing, with respect to the difference of the ear, is that the signature will not be effective, performed, performing, not at the moment when it apparently takes place, but only later, when ears have been able to receive the message. It is on the side of the addressees, or of an addressee who will have an ear sufficiently fine to hear/understand my name, for example, my signature, that with

[8] Derrida, 'Of an Apocalyptic Tone Recently Adopted in Philosophy', *Oxford Literary Review* 6:2 (1984), p. 6.

[9] Derrida, 'Otobiographie de Nietzsche', in *L'Oreille de l'autre*, eds Claude Lévesque and Christie McDonald (Montreal, 1982), p. 18.

[10] Ibid., p. 39.

which I sign, that the signature will take place.'[11] The pun is the philosopheme of this ear tuned to the other.

My purpose will not have been to counter-sign for Derrida, but to review
if not the question of how the pun is possible, then the problematic of the
puncept: who or what is responsible for making it seem desirable, necessary,
to think in another way?

Joyce's *Wake*

I noted in *Applied Grammatology* that the aspect of Derrida's work that most
astonishes me is the fully developed homonymic program at work in
Derrida's style, a program as different from traditional academic discourse
and assumptions as it is productive in its own terms of knowledge and
insight. I say I was astonished because it is one thing to engage in wordplay,
but another thing to sustain it and extend it into an epistemology, into a
procedure that is not just a tour de force but that is functional, replicable.
This Writing, however, is not a method of analysis or criticism but of
invention (and here Writing departs from deconstruction). Writing is the
inventio of a new rhetoric, with 'invention' – or even 'creativity' – being the
'mana' word of the new pedagogy associated with Writing.

The other major innovation of Writing is its reliance on images. Again,
Derrida's contribution is not simply the use of images, but his sustained
expansion of images into models. Thus he gives considerable attention in
his texts (much to the frustration of normal readers trained to look for
arguments, concepts, evidence, and theses – all of which are included, but
seemingly obscured by ornament) to the description of quotidian objects –
an umbrella, a matchbox, an unlaced shoe, a post card – whose functioning
he interrogates as modeling the most complex or abstract levels of thought.
In the process he reveals a simplicity, an economy, underlying the so-called
esotericism of intellectual discourse which, if properly tapped, could
eliminate the gap separating the general public from specialists in cultural
studies.

The two elements – homophones and models – supplement one another
in that the vocabulary associated with the model is scrutinized, as well as its
operation as an object, for double inscriptions joining the sensible with the
intelligible realm. The world of Western thought is investigated at the levels
of both words and things, giving fresh insight into the ancient problem of
motivation in language. The resultant achievement could be described as
non-Euclidean – the humanities equivalent of non-Euclidean geometry – in

[11] Ibid., p. 71.

that it builds, in defiance of the axioms of dialectics, a coherent, productive procedure out of the elements of writing considered traditionally to be mere ornament, not suitable for fostering true knowledge. The ultimate deconstruction of the logocentric suppression of writing is not to analyze the inconsistency of the offending theories, but to construct a fully operational mode of thought on the basis of the excluded elements (in the way that the non-Euclideans built consistent geometries that defied and contradicted the accepted axioms).

We in the humanities are only just beginning to grasp the radicality of Derrida's experiment, only just beginning to realize the opportunities it opens to us or even to comprehend the exact nature of the lesson he offers to us. One way to think this lesson is to dwell upon its filiation with the legacy of James Joyce. Although only recently venturing to write on Joyce, Derrida reminds us that in his earliest published work he stated the choice confronting modern writers between two paradigms of thought and langauge. From Plato to the present, most philosophers had chosen to write in the paradigm exemplified by Husserl who 'proposes to render language as transparent as possible, univocal, limited to that which, by being transmittable or able to be placed in tradition, thereby constitutes the only condition of a possible historicity'.[12] But Derrida chose the other possibility, the one followed by many artists in all eras but rarely if ever adopted as a model for cognitive, theoretical, even scientific application, the model exemplified in *Finnegans Wake*.

He repeats and mobilizes and babelizes the (asymptotic) totality of the equivocal, he makes this his theme and his operation, he tries to make outcrop, with the greatest possible synchrony, at great speed, the greatest power of the meanings buried in each syllabic fragment, subjecting each atom of writing to fission in order to overload the unconscious with the whole memory of man: mythologies, religion, philosophies, sciences, psychoanalysis, literatures. This generalized equivocality of writing does not translate one language into another on the basis of common nuclei of meaning; it talks several languages at once, parasiting them as in the example *He war*. ('Two Words for Joyce', p. 149)

Two points need to be made at once: first, the fact *that* Derrida decided to do philosophy (if that term still applies) with Joyce's rather than with Husserl's model of language. At a stroke he transformed with this move the status of aesthetic discourse in the hierarchy of the university apparatus from *object* of study (powerless) to a *subject* of knowledge – to a *source* of cognition to be applied directly to problem-solving across the divisions of knowledge from anthropology to zoology. Herman Rapaport points out (in a forthcoming book) that Derrida's poetic epistemics extends a turn already

[12] Derrida, 'Two Words for Joyce', p. 149.

taken by Heidegger in his reading of Hölderlin and Trakl, with the key device transposed from aesthetics to epistemics being none other than paronomasia. Heidegger did not explain or interpret poetry, he learned from the poet's relation to language how to think and write about the questions posed in his own discipline.

The more precedents the better, for with this turn the entire agenda of the humanities has been changed. The new agenda at one level is a reversal of the old one. Instead of importing from other divisions of knowledge the methodologies used to explicate the arts, humanists are beginning to use the aesthetic inventions of our time to articulate the problems of the day, regardless of 'competence'. Indeed, one of Derrida's major targets recently has been the myth of competence (the intractability of certain world problems has begun to expose the limitations of expertise). The task of the humanities today, in other words, includes the representation (drawing on all the styles invented in the history of the avant-garde) of the interaction of the human and natural sciences with everyday life.

Which brings me to the second point with respect to Derrida's Joycean gamble. Why does Derrida believe Joyce's paradigm of language has a better chance of success in formulating the solutions to our problems than has the conventional model of univocal transparency? The answer, which you are not going to like if you do not yet share the paradigm, has to do with the 'great speed' of Joyce's textual 'machine', faster than any computer yet built.

Ulysses, *Finnegans Wake* – beside which the current technology of our computers and our micro-computerified archives and our translating machines remains a *bricolage* of a prehistoric child's toys. And above all its mechanisms are of a slowness incommensurable with the quasi-infinite speed of the movements on Joyce's cables. How could you calculate the speed with which a mark, a marked piece of information, is placed in contact with another in the same word or from one end of the book to the other? (p. 147).

One of the obstacles to problem-solving in the information age is the knowledge explosion itself. We are buried in data which by its sheer quantity impedes comprehension. Moreover, having tended to concentrate more on data processing than on understanding, we are in need of some new ideas, or *moiras*, as the event to which the puncept gives rise is called (as I will explain in a moment). Speed, then, is essential, but not only the algorithmic speed of calculation. The history of invention suggests that however valuable the analytical model may be for exploiting discoveries, the discovery process itself works with the poetic device of analogy, or rather, with the association of elements previously thought to be unrelated.

At the level of language the pun is precisely the device capable of relating elements with the least motivation, hence with the greatest economy or speed. Even Redfern notes that the pun is a kind of linguistic collage. One way to understand Derrida's project is as an extension to the level of discourse of this logic of least motivation (the structuralists started this line of thinking by suggesting the homology between linguistics and literature). Thus for example Derrida has observed that two of our greatest problems world-wide involve 'speed' – the arms race and the race problem (apartheid). I would add that speed, to the extent that it serves as a metonym for the drug problem, actually names three world difficulties. The puncept that gathers these three issues into a single set suggests a new way to think about them as organized by a single cause. The anagram of 'race' – 'care' – already tells us one solution for our hurry. 'Care' is one of Heidegger's existentalia, but not yet part of the punceptual procedure. Derrida has written several articles on these races, but at this stage of the research I can do no more than outline the strategy for thinking out politics in a new way.

The point to stress for now is that the legitimation of the puncept, as I explained in my account of applied grammatology (AG), derives from the importance of *Finnegans Wake* as the touchstone for thinking about language (and hence everything else) in the new paradigm. David Hayman has identified the principal lesson of the *Wake* as having to do with its being 'open' or 'writeable': 'The *Wake* belongs to a class (not a genre) of works which invite the reader to perpetuate creation.'[13] Eco agrees: 'The search for "open" models capable of guaranteeing and founding the mutation and the growth and, finally, the vision of a universe founded on possibility, as contemporary philosophy and science suggest to the imagination, encounters perhaps its most provoking and violent representation – perhaps its anticipation – in *Finnegans Wake*.'[14] Eco believes that works constructed in accord with an open aesthetic are inherently didactic, are 'epistemological metaphors': 'It has to do with elaborating models of relations in which ambiguity finds a justification and acquires a positive value. ... Contemporary art attempts to find – anticipating science and social structures – a solution to our crisis, and encounters it in the only mode possible, with an imaginative guise, offering images of the world which amount to epistemological metaphors' (p. 11).

Contemporary art, with its 'continuous exercise of free selection and of conscious and continuous breaks with established methods', may well represent, Eco suggests, an 'instrument of liberation', providing us with an education in 'self-direction' (p. 127). Eco's discussion of avant-garde art in terms of 'information theory' provides a clue to the nature of an 'open'

---

[13] David Hayman, 'Some Writers in the Wake of the *Wake*', in *The Avant-Garde Tradition in Literature*, ed. Richard Kostelanetz (Buffalo, 1982), p. 177.

[14] Umberto Eco, *La Obra Abierta* (Barcelona, 1965), p. 12.

pedagogy. The clue is based on the homonym in 'information'. If traditional pedagogy attempted a transparent, univocal transmission of a body of information, understood as the content or signifieds of a discipline, an open pedagogy concerns itself with information as it is understood in General Systems Theory, cybernetics, and the like, defined in terms of the probability or improbability of a message within a rule-governed system. The more probable (banal) the message, the less information it conveys. 'Information' here is statistical, referring not to what one says but to what one *could* say, the extent of liberty of selection (p. 103). Ordinary languages, such as English, Eco notes, tend to be balanced at a statistical rate of fifty per cent redundancy.

AG, then, deals with information in this statistical sense, adopting a style from the experimental arts, which favor a high improbability, as opposed to the clarity (low information) favored in traditional pedagogy. While classic art introduced original movements within a linguistic system which substantially respected the basic rules, contemporary art realizes its originality in proposing a new linguistic system which carries within itself new laws' (p. 106). In the tension between form and possibility, the artists strive to augment the possibilities of information by means of an 'organized disorder'. 'In consequence, information associates itself not with order, but disorder, or at least with a certain type of order-not-habitual-forseeable. Could we say that the positive measure of such information (distinct from signification) be entropy?' (p. 101).

The pun or homophone acquires a new status with respect to the new sensibility, attuned no longer to the expectations of cause and effect, the logic of the excluded middle, but to the pleasure of surprise, in that homophones represent 'the bridge of least motivation', thus generating the greatest 'information'. Eco establishes the epistemological importance of the pun by identifying it as the principal figure of *Finnegans Wake*, understood itself to be an 'epistemological metaphor' of 'unlimited semiosis' (the *apeiron*, in Derrida's terms). 'In proposing itself as a model of language in general, *Finnegans Wake* [FW] focuses our attention specifically on semantic values. In other words, since FW is itself a metaphor for the process of unlimited semiosis, I have chosen it for metaphoric reasons as a field of inquiry in order to cover certain itineraries of knowledge more quickly.'[15] The crucial point of Eco's analysis for AG is his observations on how the *Wake* functions: 'We should be able to show that each metaphor produced in FW is, in the last analysis, comprehensible because the entire book, read in different directions, actually furnishes the metonymic chains that justify it. We can test this hypothesis on the atomic element of FW, *the*

[15] Eco, *The Role of the Reader* (Bloomington, Ind., 1979), p. 70.

pun, which constitutes a particular form of metaphor founded on subjacent chains of metonymies' (p. 72).

For specific examples of how the pun operates in the *Wake* ('meander-tale' is a key illustration of this 'nomadic' writing) I refer the reader to Eco's study. What interests me here, and what may serve as a model for this intelligibility of the puncept, is Eco's description of the homophonic system.

The pun constitutes a forced contiguity between two or more words: *sang* plus *sans* plus *glorians* plus *riant* makes 'Sanglorians'. It is a contiguity made of reciprocal elisions, whose result is an ambiguous deformation; but even in the form of fragments, there are words that nonetheless are related to one another. This *forced contiguity* frees a series of possible readings – hence interpretations – which lead to an acceptance of the terms as a metaphoric *vehicle* of different *tenors.* . . . We can in theory distinguish between two types of puns, in accordance with the reasons that established the contiguity of terms: contiguity of resemblance of signifiers. . . . contiguity of resemblance of signifieds. . . . As one can see, the two types refer to each other, even as contiguity seems to refer to the instituting resemblance, and vice versa. In truth, though, the force of the pun (and of every successful and inventive metaphor) consists in the fact that prior to it no one had grasped the resemblance. . . . The resemblance becomes necessary only after the contiguity is realized. Actually (FW is itself the proof), *it is enough to find the means of rendering two terms phonetically contiguous for the resemblance to impose itself*, at best, the similitude of signifiers is that which precedes, and the similitude of signifieds is a consequence of it. The exploration of the field of FW as a contracted model of the global semantic field is at once useful and derisive. It is useful because nothing can show us better than a reading of FW that, even when semantic kinship seems to precede the coercion to coexist in the pun, in point of fact a network of subjacent contiguities makes necessary the resemblance which was presumed to be spontaneous. It is derisive because, everything being given in the text already, it is difficult to discover the 'before' and the 'after'. (pp. 73–4)

Eco's account clarifies the epistemic foundations of Derrida's decision to experiment with a mimesis of signifiers.

Lalangue

What makes it difficult to accept the puncept as paradigm is its modality, its mood of re-joyce-ing and high spirits, its attempt to think through laughter, 'Qu'est-ce que ça veut dire, le rire? Qu'est-ce que ça veut rire?'

What does laughter want to say? Once one recognizes that in theory in *Ulysses* the virtual totality of experience, of meaning, of history, of the symbolic, of languages, and of writings, the great cycle and the great encyclopaedia of cultures, in sum, the sum total of all sum totals tends to be displayed and to reconstitute itself by taking advantage of all possible combinations, with writing seeking to occupy all the spaces, well then, the totalising hermeneutic which makes up the task of a world wide and eternal institution of Joyce studies will find itself in front of what I hesitate to call a dominant effect, a *Stimmung* or a *pathos*, a tone which crosses all others again and which does not participate in the series of others since it *re-marks* all of them. . . . And it is this yes in laughter (*oui-rire*) which overmarks not only the totality of writing, but all the qualities, modalities, types of laughter whose differences might be classified into some sort of typology.[16]

Another precedent for the puncept may be found in psychoanalysis, especially in the notion of *jouissance* elaborated by Jacques Lacan, whose discourse also rings with Joycean laughter. When he declared the special focus of psychoanalysis to be the desire of the subject of knowledge, accompanied by a pedagogy that introduced his own desire – the action of the unconscious, of his *bêtise* – into the scene of teaching, Lacan was not setting up an impasse nor an aporia for the research subject, but simply creating the conditions that constitute the starting point for the psycho-analytic mode of knowledge. This mode operates not according to the anamnesic principle of self-consciousness, 'living memory', or introspec-tion, but by means of hypomnesis and the repetition of the signifier. Lacan has his own formulation of it, as for example when he says that he is going to submit to the test of the signifier 'a certain number of *dires* [sayings] of the philosophical tradition' – to interrogate how the *dires* of Aristotle and Freud traverse one another on the question of bliss – with *dires* being the anagram of *désir* (desire).[17]

Following Freud's lead (the conjunction of science and pleasure in the formulation of the Pleasure Principle), Lacan sets in motion his own merger of love and knowledge by asking if the term '*jouissance*' itself knows something. At one level, he is asking if the Other knows – what the mystic knows, or what the woman knows. The problem, in fact, is less one of knowledge than of pedagogy – the transmission of knowledge, for the real issue is what the mystic or the woman is or is not able to *say* about what is known, keeping in mind always that Theresa, woman and mystic at once, is a metaphor finally for unconscious thought. Lacan is not researching mysticism, nor even (although this point is not as obvious) feminine sexuality, but the activity of the unconscious in language. Lacan offers a 'formula' with respect to this issue (his procedure often being to begin a lesson with an aphoristic or condensed formulation dealing with the matter of a given session): '*The unconscious is that the being* [l'être], *in speaking, delights, and*, I add, *wants to know nothing more about it.* I add that that means – *knows*

---

[16] Derrida, *Ulysse Gramophone: Deux Mots pour Joyce* (Paris, 1987), p. 116.
[17] Jacques Lacan, *Encore, Le Seminaire XX* (Paris, 1975), pp. 25, 27.

nothing at all' (p. 95). Freud's formula, Lacan says, was 'there where it speaks, it enjoys', recalling Lacan's own formula – the unconscious is structured like a language – both of which point to the way psychoanalysis cut the Gordian knot of the 'inaccessibility' of the unconscious – of dreams and all related phenomena – by focusing its investigation on the *parlêtre*, the speaking being (equating *l'être* with the letter, *la lettre*). Thus, when Lacan says that the unconscious knows nothing, he adds that 'the unconscious has revealed nothing to us about the physiology of the nervous system, nor about the functioning of binding, nor about premature ejaculation' (p. 104). Given this situation, in order sometimes to escape 'the infernal affair', Lacan jokingly notes that he resorts to certain techniques of Zen teaching – to respond to questions with a bark: 'ça!'.

But as a teacher, one of whose assumptions is that he says more than he knows, Lacan is not content to remain at the level of religion in any form. Rather, he adopts a manner of speaking ('Theoretical models', Max Black states, 'whether treated as real or fictitious, are not literally constructed: the heart of the method consists in *talking* in a certain way')[18] which allows language to say what it knows, or allows the unconscious to show itself in the play of language. The procedure is based on the discovery through analysis 'that there is a knowledge which does not know itself, a knowledge which supports itself in the signifier as such' (giving rise to the use of metaphors drawn from the experience of mystics to describe the effect of receiving these 'messages') (*Encore*, p. 88).

The locus of this knowledge is indeed the Other ('the unconscious, which I represent to you as that which is inside the subject, but which can be realized only outside, that is to say, in that locus of the Other in which alone it may assume its status',[19] from whence it must be taken: '*il est à prendre*'. In other words, the signifier teaches here that to learn (*apprendre*) requires this taking (*à prendre*) and also that this acquisition, as noted earlier, is more valuable the more it costs (joining *appris* with *mis à prix*). *Jouissance* (bliss) refers, then, to a fourth level of 'sense', the four levels being sense, non-sense, common sense, and '*jouis*-sense'.[20] The sense of psychoanalysis as it is usually understood is its critique of sex, Lacan explains. But this sense reduces to a 'non-sense' in the sweet nothings exchanged between lovers. At the level of 'common sense', this pleasure has to do with jokes, laughter, suggestive remarks, and the like. Still another level, the one that interests Lacan in *Encore*, carries the insistence of desire in the chain of signifiers, productive of homonyms and puns, and called, in this context, *jouis-sens*.

---

[18] Max Black, *Models and Metaphors* (Ithaca, 1962), p. 229.
[19] Lacan, *The Four Fundamental Concepts of Psychoanalysis* (New York, 1978), p. 147.
[20] Lacan, *Télévision* (Paris, 1973), pp. 19–21.

The technique, ultimately, is derived from this comment to Fliess in one of Freud's letters, anticipating his joke book: 'It is certainly true that the dreamer is too ingenious and amusing, but it is not my fault, and I cannot be reproached with it. All dreamers are insufferably witty, and they have to be, because they are under pressure, and the direct way is barred to them.'[21]

In alerting his class to the existence of this level of sense, Lacan makes liberal use of puns, the point being that the pun itself tells him, in a sense, how to proceed, as for example when he confronts the impossible question '*Was will das Weib?*': 'It is here that I play on the pun [*équivoque*]. The impossible knowledge is prohibited, censored, forbidden [*interdit*], but it is not if you write it conveniently *l'inter-dit*, it is said [*dit*] between [inter-, *entre*] the words, between the lines. ... It is a question of showing the tendency of this putting-into-form, this metalanguage that is not one, and which I make ex-sist. About that which may not be demonstrated, something true nonetheless can be said' (*Encore*, p. 108). This dimension of the between, this interdimension of reading between the lines, to be associated with Derrida's hymenal betweenness (*entre-antre*), opens up a new dimension of knowledge called the *dit-mension* (a pun on the *dit* – said, spoken – which could be rendered in English by means of the other syllable, the mention in di-mention, with the *di* suggesting the double inscription of the pun – di-mention). This di-mention, in which the signifier exercises its effect, is also the dimension of *bêtise*, the stupidities which may now be understood as referring to the incessant puns in the lectures. 'The signifier is stupid [*bête*],' Lacan remarks, and, in the pun, engenders 'a stupid smile' which, he hastens to add, is the grin of angels, at least those that can be seen in the cathedrals, including Bernini's angel. They smile so, he suggests, because they are 'swimming' in the supreme signifer (which is after all, the phallus). The angels, that is (like the one standing over Theresa in Bernini's statue) carry no messages, and to this extent, 'they are truly signifiers'. He stresses the signifier 'because it is the basis of the dimension ["which should be written *dit-mention*"] of the symbolic, which alone the analytic discourse enables us to isolate as such' [pp. 24–5). Bernini's statue, in short, provides no evidence for what is at issue in *Encore*, because, as an image, it exists at the level of the Imaginary, which is dependent on sense perception. But *Encore* is a seminar not about the Imaginary but about the Symbolic and the 'sense' of di-mention (what Derrida discussed as spacing). The association of this mode of knowledge, taken at the level of the pun, with bliss (like that pictured in the statue) is justified by Lacan's description of what takes place: 'It is because there is the unconscious, that is *lalangue* in as much as it is by

---

[21] Sigmund Freud, *The Origins of Psychoanalysis: Letters to Wilhelm Fliess* (New York, 1954), p. 297.

cohabitation with it that a being defines itself called the speaking being, that the signifier can be called to make a sign' (p. 130).

This cohabitation of the subject with *lalangue*, producing the speaking being called a human, is a kind of copulation productive of bliss. Something is touched, a dimension reached through the di-mention, which is akin to sexual bliss in its fundamental contribution to human reproduction (in the form of the repetition which constitutes identity), akin but supplementary – not sexual (the mystics, too, however, use sexual metaphors for what they know), but on the order of love, which, Lacan stresses, is a relationship having nothing to do with sex. The term introduced here to further the investigation is *lalangue*, written in one word, which Lacan uses to distinguish his interest in language from that of linguists and structuralists. *Lalangue* has nothing to do with communication or dialogue but is a presentational mode of a different sort: 'Lalangue presents all sorts of affects ["its effects are affects"] which remain enigmatic. These effects are those which result from the presence of lalangue to the degree that, as knowledge, it articulates things which go much further than what the speaking being supports in a stated knowledge. . . . The unconscious is a knowledge, a know-how of lalangue. And what one knows how to do with lalangue surpasses by far what one is capable of accounting for in terms of language' (p. 127).

Jean-Claude Milner has written a book on *lalangue*, based apparently on the paper he gave at a session of the *Encore* seminar (p. 92), student papers and guest lectures being as much a part of Lacan's practice as of any other professor.[22] Milner's topic is 'the love of language' – taking up Lacan's question of the scientist's desire by asking about the 'love' that motivates people to become linguists. He reminds us that not only is language teachable (indeed, linguistics has no social basis as an activity except in the university), but that it is the vehicle of all other possible teaching. Psychoanalysis supplements conventional pedagogy, which tends to forget language or assume its transparency and secondarity, by asking what language itself knows. Milner approaches this question, as does Lacan, by alluding to Saussure's study of the anagrams in 'saturnian' verse. Saussure, showing that the phonemes in these Latin poems are paired and selected according to the anagram of a name linked to the narrative sense of the verse, assumed that the ordering principle could be attributed to a secret knowledge. But, Milner remarks, Saussure was never able to prove his hypothesis (indeed, he never published any of these studies), partly because the anagrams turned up in every verse he examined, ancient or modern. In these anagrams, then, philology faced a phenomenon it could not account for, having to do with the material intersection of language with the real.

[22] Jean Claude Milner, *L'Amour de la langue* (Paris, 1978), pp. 92–3.

The anagram, that is, far from being illusory, touched precisely on a fundamental reality of language – the homophone. Because of the irreducible and material nature of its reality, the homophone (and all the odd figures of association it makes possible) has a function of excess, an '*en plus*', related to Derrida's chiasmatic plus: 'This function of excess we call lalangue' (Milner, pp. 92–3). 'It is always possible to valorize in any locution a dimension of the non-identical: it is the pun and all that it includes, homophony, homosemy, homography, everything that sustains double meaning and speaking in hints, incessant tissue of our interviews' (*Encore*, p. 18). Milner describes these figures of association (*lalangue*) as being those that linguistics excludes from language in order to achieve closure and establish itself as a science, representing only certain approved chains or sequences such as etymology, diverse paradigms, derivations, transformations, and so forth.

Why Lacan mentioned that *lalangue* is that which causes a language to be termed one's 'mother tongue' is explained in this comment: 'This register is nothing other than that which absolutely distinguishes one language from every other one: a singular mode of making puns, there you have what makes a specific language. By that, it becomes a collection of places, all singular and all heterogeneous. . . . By that it also makes itself substance, possible matter for fantasms, inconsistent ensemble of places for desire' (Milner, p. 22). Derrida's discussion of the difficulty and the importance of translation is based on this same feature of the particularity of the homophones to a given language, although both Derrida and Lacan (and psychoanalysis in general) take advantage of the macaronic possibility of using puns that cross between language – hence they both admire James Joyce: '*Finnegans Wake*,' Lacan says, 'is very much that which is closest to what we analysts, thanks to the analytic discourse, have to read – the slip' (*Encore*, p. 37).

As for the desire of the linguist, Milner defines it by reversing the 'scientific' explanation of *lalangue*, which suggests that it is caused by or is the effect of the 'Indo-European' origin of modern language. But Indo-European is itself an effect, generated by a speculative knowledge, Milner says, reflecting the desire of the linguists to write *lalangue* itself. This interaction between a 'real' and a 'fantasmatic' language is not a problem, from Milner's perspective, but a condition or necessity of research which we are only beginning to acknowledge and exploit. Following Lacan, Milner proposes the ideal of a new academic writing based on these points: 'that no one is master of lalangue, that the real insists therein, that finally lalangue knows. Then, if the linguist does not lack a certain tact, he could accomplish to a degree scholarly writing in which coincide rule and *Witz*' (Milner, p. 133).

Moira

The old paradigm concerned itself with the relation between concepts and ideas. In the new paradigm one thinks less with or about the *idea* – *eidos*, form, clear and distinct outline or shape, dependent on the sense of sight – and more by means of the *moira*, having to do with the way the aleatory cuts across a necessity in the event of the pun. I have been trying to persuade my colleagues that we should stop using the term 'idea' to characterize poststructuralist thinking and replace it with *moira*, in order to fully grasp the incommensurability of these alternative processes. Since this usage does not seem to be catching on I want to take this opportunity to reiterate some of the reasons why I think this switch would be a good moira. In 'White Mythology', Derrida allies his operation with Bachelard's 'psychoanalysis of objective knowledge'. Bachelard's most influential insight, dating back to the early thirties, was that the new physics rendered conventional thinking in philosophy obsolete. In order to overcome the obstacles to a new epistemology relevant to the new science, Bachelard argued that a pedagogy would have to be devised capable of reeducating human sensibility at its very root. One of his favorite examples dealt with the microphysics of Heisenberg and Bohr – the uncertainty principle and the complementarity principle – having to do with the nature of light, which behaves sometimes as a wave and sometimes as a particle. Keeping in mind that light is *the* philosophic metaphor, any change in our understanding of its nature should affect its analogical extensions in such concepts as form and theory. Thinking, in Einstein's universe, Bachelard stated, requires a new logic that breaks with all absolutes, whether Newtonian or Hegelian, but especially a logic that frees itself from the identity principle (the principle of noncontradiction and the excluded middle) of Aristotelian logic. The basic feature of this non-Aristotelian logic (to accomplish for the concept what non-Euclidean geometry and non-Newtonian physics accomplished for the object) would be a three-valued operation, including, in addition to the usual 'true' and 'false' values, a value labeled 'absurd'. Derrida's borrowing, by way of analogy (as he stresses), of Gödel's notion of undecidability to characterize his own 'quasi-concepts', not to mention the Einsteinian or fourth-dimensional (space–time synthesis) tone of differance itself, which at once 'differs' (spatial) and 'defers' (temporal), indicates his sympathy for Bachelard's project.

With Bachelard's surrationalism in mind, and remembering that the French 'non' and 'nom' (name) are homophones, Derrida's textuality may be understood as non-Aristotelian – his philosophy of the name as a philosophy of the 'non' – a context that is made explicit in 'White Mythology'. In Aristotle's system, of course, there is no place for differance:

For human language is not uniformly human in all its parts to the same degree. It is still the criterion of the noun which is decisive: its literal elements – vocal sounds without meaning – include more than letters alone. The syllable too belongs to *lexis*, but of course has no sense in itself. Above all there are whole 'words' which, though they have an indispensable role in the organization of discourse, remain nonetheless quite devoid of sense, in the eyes of Aristotle. Conjunction (*sundesmos*) is a *phone asemos*. The same goes for the article, and in general for every joint (*arthron*, everything which operates *between* significant members, between nouns, substantives, or verbs. A joint has no sense because it does not refer to an independent unit, a substance or a being, by means of a categorematic unit. It is for this reason that it is excluded from the field of metaphor as an onomastic field. From this point on, the anagrammatic, using parts of nouns, nouns cut into pieces, is outside the field of metaphor in general, as too is the syntactic play of 'joints'.[23]

Against Aristotle's influential doctrine that 'in non-sense, language is not yet born', Derrida builds an alternative onomastics based precisely on what Aristotle excludes from metaphor.

The extent of Derrida's non-Aristotelian inspiration may be seen in Aristotle's condemnation of homonymy as the figure that doubled and thus threatened philosophy. One of the first 'places' to check for the obscurity that characterizes bad metaphors, according to Aristotle, is to determine whether the term used is the homonym of any other term (pp. 53, 74). Derrida, with his interest in discerning and then transgressing the limits of philosophical discourse, takes his cue from Aristotle and builds an entire philosophical system on the basis of the homonym (and homophone). In this respect he resembles the nineteenth-century mathematicians who, challenged by the axiomatic absoluteness of Euclid's principles, were able to prove that it was possible to devise a geometry that Euclid's system held to be impossible. Considered at first to be playful monstrosities or abstract exercises, these non-Euclidean geometries provided eventually the mathematics of relativity.

Problem-solving must be approached otherwise, avoiding all dialectic, all confrontation or oppositional thinking. Instead, in the essays included in *Marges*, Derrida exposes the 'inner border' of philosophy (thus implying the outer border), which is constituted by the 'philosophemes', or founding ideas of philosophy. His strategy is to interrogate the relationship between sense and sense: 'This divergence between sense (signified) and the senses (sensible signifier) is declared through the same root (*sensus*, *Sinn*). One

[23] Derrida, 'White Mythology: Metaphor in the Text of Philosophy', *New Literary History* 6 (1974), pp. 40–1.

might, like Hegel, admire the generosity of this stock and interpret its
hidden sublation speculatively and dialectically; but before using a
dialectical concept of metaphor, it is necessary to investigate the double
twist which opened up metaphor and dialectic by allowing the term *sense* to
be applied to that which should be foreign to the senses' (pp. 28–9).

Derrida questions whether such defining tropes, productive of philosophemes, even should be called 'metaphors'. Metaphor assumes that one
of the terms in the comparison has a 'proper' meaning, but the philosophemes are produced by catachresis, 'the imposition of a sign on a sense
not yet having a proper sign in the language. And so there is no substitution
here, no transfer of proper signs, but an irruptive extension of a sign proper
to one idea to a sense without a signifier' (p. 57). Catachresis, Derrida
suggests, should be removed from its traditional placement as a 'phenomenon of abuse' and recognized as an irreducibly original production of
meaning. 'Catechresis does not go outside the language, does not create new
signs, does not enrich the code; yet it transforms its functioning: it produces,
with the same material, new rules of exchange, new meanings.' Deconstruction, in other words, is a form of catachresis, but one that must be
distinguished from the traditional use of this device, since philosophy
always interpreted its catechresis as 'a torque turning back to a sense already
present, a production (of signs, rather than of meanings), but this as
revelation, unveiling, bringing to light, truth' (pp. 59–60). Against philosophy's tendency to present 'forced metaphors' as 'natural and correct',
deconstruction uses catachresis openly to carry thought not forward to the
origin (teleology), but 'elsewhere'.

That the strategy is an explicit alternative to theory as *eidos*, the idea as
the sublation of the sensible into the intelligible, may be seen in Derrida's
allusion to the key of I-D itself (not an insignificant combination of letters in
this context, 'Id' suggesting the relation of Derrida's Mallarméan method to
'unconscious thought'). 'The reader is now invited to count the dots, to
follow the fine needlepoint pattern of *i*'s and *iques*'s [*-ic* or *-ical*] which are
being sprinkled rapidly across the tissue being pushed by another hand.
Perhaps he will be able to discern, according to the rapid, regular movement
of the machine, the stitches of Mallarmé's idea, a certain instance of *i*'s and
a certain scattering of dice [*d*'s].'[24] As the translator notes, 'The word *idée*
[idea] is composed of the two syllables in question here: *i* and *de* [de = the
letter "d" and the word "dice"].' The idea put to work hypomnemically (the
idea, *i-d*, operating according to the mechanical repetition of the signifier –
a sophistic technique of artificial memory, rather than the living memory
favored by Plato and dialectics) is not the signified concept, then, but the

[24] Derrida, *Dissemination* (Chicago, 1981), p. 238.

letters/phonemes of the word itself, which are set free to generate conceptual material *mechanically* (without the intention or presence of the subject) by gathering into a discourse terms possessing these letters (often using the pun or homophone).

Moiré-Moirae   Derrida gets his ideas from the systematic exploitation of puns, used as an *inventio* to suggest nondialectical points of entry for the deconstruction of the philosophemes. His best-known version of this strategy involves the deflation of proper names into common nouns (antonomasia), as in *Glas*, in which Genet's texts are discussed in terms of flowers (the flowers of rhetoric), beginning with *genêt* (a broomflower). Blanchot, Hegel, Kant and Ponge have all received similar treatment, described as research into the signature effect. Discussing this methodology in his essay on Ponge, Derrida exposes his mood: 'It is necessary to scandalize resolutely the analphabet scientisms, . . . before what one can do with a dictionary. . . . One must scandalize them, make them cry even louder, because that gives pleasure, and why deprive oneself of it, in risking a final etymological simulacrum.'[25]

The technique works as well for concepts, both for subverting old ones and for building new (pseudo-) concepts. Part of my discussion of the critique of theory as metaphor is to discern the homophone that (in retrospect, as an aftereffect at least) could be said to be the organizing articulation of Derrida's approach to this project. This search may result in the formulation of an aspect of deconstructive writing which as yet has found few, if any, imitators. The *idea* (*i-d*) accounting for the specific terms used to deconstruct *theoria* has its source in the 'constellation' O-I-R, originally discerned in Mallarmé. (It is worth nothing that *oir* is the Spanish equivalent of *entendre*, meaning to hear and to understand, a propos both of Derrida's Joycean macaronics and of his suggestion that the idea itself could not be seen but only heard.) The principle at work here involves 'a hymen between chance and rule. That which presents itself as contingent and haphazard in the *present* of language . . . finds itself struck out anew, retempered with the seal of necessity in the uniqueness of a textual configuration. For example, consider the duels among the *moire* [watered silk] and the *memoire* [memory], the *grimoire* [cryptic spell book] and the *armoire* [wardrobe]' (*Dissemination*, p. 277).

What especially interests Derrida is precisely the *articulation*: 'Rhyme – which is the general law of textual effects – is the folding-together of an identity and a difference. The raw material for this operation is no longer merely the sound of the end of a word: all "substances" (phonic and graphic)

[25] Derrida, 'Entre crochets', *Diagraphe* 8 (1976), p. 33.

and all "forms" can be linked together at any distance and under any rule in order to produce new versions of "that which in discourse does not speak" ' (p. 277). Derrida is interested in the way in which the arbitrarily rhyming terms have some motivated relationship. To perceive the motivation of the series of O-I-R words for the deconstruction of *theoria* requires that I add one more term to the sequence which Derrida himself neglects, thus imitating his own addition of *pharmakos* to the series set going in Plato's dialogues: 'Certain forces of association unite – at diverse distances, with different strengths and according to disparate paths – the words "actually present" in a discourse with all the other words in the lexical system' (pp. 129–30). The term, of course, is *Moira* (*Destiny* in Greek). Let us say that the antonomasia, the exchange between proper and common, governing this project involves *Moirae* – the fates – and *moiré* (not 'watered silk', but the visual illusion known as the moiré effect). *Grimoire* is drawn in with respect to the thirteenth-century fortune-telling book featured in *La carte postale* (whose wheel of fortune might be associated with Destiny); *memoire* with respect to the artificial memory (hypomnemics) associated with the mechanics of the *inventio*. This *inventio* (an aspect of Derrida's 'new rhetoric') functions on the assumption that language itself is 'intelligent', hence that homophones 'know' something. Derrida's deconstruction of *theoria* reveals what *Moirae—moiré* knows.

In 'Envois' Derrida states, 'no matter what I say, I seek above all to produce effects'.[26] The specific effect he seeks, in fact, is the textual equivalent of the moiré effect, whose pattern is woven into language on the loom of fate (*Moira*). As already noted in terms of his interest in the ideographic or nonphonetic features of writing, Derrida wants to restore to writing the balance between design and symbol it had in hieroglyphics. His pursuit of the moiré effect, as an attempt to write the structurality of structure, contributes to this project by assigning to ornamentation a generative role in text production.

The moiré effect manifests itself in the special functioning of Derrida's terminology, best illustrated by the term 'differance'. The verb 'to differ' (*différer*) differs from itself in that it conveys two meanings: 'On the one hand it indicates the difference as distinction, inequality, or discernbility; on the other, it expresses the interposition of delay, the interval of a *spacing* and temporalizing'. Derrida concludes that 'there must be a common, although entirely differant [*différante*] root within the sphere that relates the two movements of differing to one another. We provisionally give the name *différance* to this sameness which is not *identical*'.[27]

[26] Derrida, *La Carte postale* (Paris, 1980), p. 124.
[27] Derrida, *Speech and Phenomena* (Evanston, Ill., 1973), p. 129.

The articulation of 'differ' and 'defer' in 'differance' exemplifies the moiré effect in language. Constructivist artists in the 1960s, inspired by the work of Victor Vasarely, developed the style known as 'Op Art' – the creation of optical effects through the manipulation of geometric forms, color dissonance and kinetic elements, all exploiting the extreme limits of the psychology of optical effects or visual illusions. These 'optical illusions' provide a tangible model for comprehending the intellectual effects of conceptual illusions. One of Vasarely's chief techniques was the development of a 'surface kinetics' that set off a two-dimensional surface into an apparently three-dimensional pulsation, dubbed the 'moiré effect'.

Op Art provides a guide for appreciating, or for that matter for teaching, the 'trembling' or 'shaking' effect Derrida achieves in his *solicitation* of the *idea* as form (*eidos*). 'Structure then can be *methodically* threatened in order to be comprehended more clearly and to reveal not only its supports but also that secret place in which it is neither construction nor ruin but lability. This operation is called (from the Latin) *soliciting*. In other words, *shaking* in a way related to the *whole* (from *sollus*, in archaic Latin "the whole", and from *citare*, "to put in motion").'[28] In terms of the homonymic event, the destiny of language, its relation to *Moira* and the *Moirae*, may be solicited in the same way that structural engineers, using computer analyses of moiré patterns, examine buildings and bridges for defects. The cracks and flaws in the surface of philosophy, and in the systems of thought built with concepts, may be detected when the homophones of concept-names are sounded through the system, exposing the crossings of chance and necessity (destiny).

We see here why Derrida calls Hegel the first philosopher of writing as well as the last philosopher of the book, since the articulation of the undecidability in difference is a generalization of Hegel's speculative procedure (a generalization with anti- or non-Hegelian consequences):

Without naively using the category of chance, of happy predestination or of the chance encounter, one would have to do for each concept what Hegel does for the German notion of *Aufhebung*, whose equivocality and presence in the German language he calls *delightful*: '*Aufheben* has in the German language a double sense: that of preserving, *maintaining*, and that of leaving off, *bringing to an end* ... It is remarkable that a language comes to use one and the same word to express two opposed meanings. Speculative thought is delighted to find in language words which by themselves have a speculative sense.' (*Writing*, pp. 113–14)

Derrida, believing that 'since this equivocality [in ordinary language] is original and irreducible, perhaps philosophy must adopt it, think it and be thought in it', proposes not to follow Hegel's laborious analysis of each

[28] Derrida, *Writing and Difference* (Chicago, 1978), p. 6.

concept but to adopt a homonymic principle that, in a sense, automatically locates all possible equivocality.

As opposed to the clarity and distinctness that is part of philosophy's founding opposition between the sensible and the intelligible (themselves qualities of 'literality' suggested by the clarity and distinctness of the alphabetic letter), differance marks a *movement between two letters* – *e* and *a*, a 'marginal' difference – and between two 'differences', a movement that articulates a strange space '*between* speech and writing and beyond the tranquil familiarity that binds us to one and to the other, reassuring us sometimes in the illusion that they are two separate things' (*Speech*, pp. 133– 4). The strategy of paleonymy (the science of old names) extends this beat, or rhythm, set in motion by the proximity of two meanings, two spellings, that are the same and different, offset, *like the two overlapping but not quite matching grids that generate the flicker of the moiré effect*. Deconstruction, as a double science, is structured by the 'double mark', by means of which a term retains its old name while displacing the term (only slightly or marginally at first) toward a new family of terms: 'The rule according to which every concept necessarily receives two similar marks – a repetition without identity – one mark inside and the other outside the deconstructed system, should give rise to a double reading and a double writing. And, as will appear in due course: a *double science*' (*Dissemination*, p. 4).

Elsewhere Derrida not only characterizes differance as a movement, he actually describes the nature of this movement, understood to be 'virtual', like the moiré effect, while referring to the 'path' followed by thought, traced by a step (*pas*) which is not one (because the *pas* is also the negative in *ne pas*), which does not advance. The moiré effect in op writing, the movement between the disparate semantic domains of a homophonic series of terms, is the effect of *marginal* spelling differences: 'Each cited word gives an index card or a grid [*grille*] which enables you to survey the text. It is accompanied by a diagram which you ought to be able to verify at each occurrence.'[29] The term Derrida chooses to name this movement in *Glas* is '*la navette*' (shuttle, referring to the 'to and fro' motion which bears this name in weaving, sewing and transportation). In French, moreover, the term also names a type of seed, a plant in the family of crucifers. 'It is [the term] I sought earlier in order to describe, when a gondola has crossed the gallery, the grammatical to and fro between *langue* [language, tongue] and *lagune* [lagoon] (*lacuna*)' (p. 232).

In short, the grids involved are the two spellings, the paragram, with only one letter out of order between them. The shuttle motion between these two words is the binding necessity of their chance occupation of the same letters.

[29] Derrida, *Glas* (Paris, 1974), p. 223.

The motion is set up within the shuttle itself, joining its meanings or semantic domains, which in French ('*la navette*') include, besides those already mentioned, a liturgical sense (it is a small vessel for incense). 'To and fro woven in a warp [*chaîne*]. The woof [*trame* – also *plot*] is in the shuttle. You can see all that I could do with that. Elaboration, isn't it a weaver's movement?' (p. 233). But Derrida states that he distrusts this textile metaphor, however, because finally it retains a 'virtue' of the natural, the originary, of propriety. He decides instead to think of the motion of *Glas* as the interlacing stitching of *sewing*. In either case, the vibration or to and fro motion of articulation carries or displaces the sensorium only to the vicinity of handicrafts, evoking the hand (writing as a hand–eye relation rather than a voice–ear relation) and, in the textile metaphor, the sense of touch. But the hand has been the philosopheme of 'concept' from the beginning (to grasp and to hold), so that 'textuality', with its associations with textile and the sense of touch, only initiates the transition to the new notion of idea as *action by contact* (in place of the action as a distance which characterizes the idealizing senses), touch being the intermediate sense, which is both abstract and concrete.

Derrida is particularly interested in the way the shuttle motion (the soliciting vibration, whose homophonically overlapping terms offer an alternative metaphorics that challenges the logocentric structure of concept formation), is manifested in other systems of thought, especially in psychoanalysis (the science, along with geometry, that Derrida uses to think his way toward grammatology). It is not surprising, then, that Freud's famous anecdote of the game that his grandson played with a bobbin on a string (the bobbin itself being part of the apparatus of weaving and sewing, symbolizing in this moment of language acquisition the mother, whose loss is repaired with the *fort-da* stitch), should serve Derrida as the pretext or emblem guiding his reading of Freud's *Beyond the Pleasure Principle*.

For now it is important to note that the conceptual equivalent of the back and forth motion of sewing in the composition of the text is the undecidability of the fetish, the very topic being treated in the Hegel column of *Glas* next to the discussion of the shuttle in the Genet column: 'Here he [Freud] comes to recognize the "fetishist's attitude of splitting" and the oscillation of the subject between two possibilities' (p. 235). The oscillation or shuttle motion of the fetish enters the Genet column later: 'He oscillates like the beating of a truth which rings. Like the clapper in the throat, that is to say in the abyss of a bell' (p. 254). *Glas*, having found in the homophonic shuttle a different intonation of one of the philosophemes of logocentrism, sounds the death knell of dialectics.

As suggested by *antre* – the grotto, recalling the Italian grottoes in which the ancient decorations were discovered, hence their dubbing as grotes-query – the 'betweenness' of grammatological space is a zone of license. Part of the lesson of the grotesque genre for understanding Derrida, keeping in mind Gombrich's stress on the independence of grotesqueries – and all ornamentation, for that matter – from what it decorates, is that Derrida's writing deals only *marginally* with what it is 'about' (with what it surrounds or enframes, like a passe-partout). Nonetheless, the moiré effect of op writing, giving rise to grotesque etymologies, constitutes a new theory of mimesis (Derrida is opposed, he says, not to mimesis, but to a determined interpretation of mimesis, to 'mimetologism':[20] 'Here we are *playing* on the fortuituous *resemblance*, the purely simulated common parentage of *seme* and *semen*. There is no communication of meaning between them. And yet, by means of this floating, purely exterior collusion, accident produces a kind of *semantic mirage*: the deviance of meaning, its reflection-effect in writing, sets something off' (p. 45). The new mimesis, in short, is based on homophonic resemblance.

The metaphorics of non-Aristotelian articulation, I have argued, generate a discourse between the pulsating moiré effect (emblem of solicitation as vibration) and *Moira*, or destiny. The hinge joining these two domains may be found within the tympanum itself, whose meanings, as Derrida notes in 'Tympan', include of course the vibrating ear drum (sound and light being susceptible to the same effects, the beat of dissonance being the acoustic equivalent of the moiré blur – both effects of proximity), a part of the apparatus of printing presses, and a type of water wheel – suggesting an image of the wheel of fortune.[31] Derrida is redefining idea, working on its root metaphor of sight and light, analyzing it no longer in terms of its effect (the light bulb that lights up when we have an idea in cartoons and advertisements) but in terms of its physics, energy waves (the vibrations mediated by air, the level at which light and sound are equivalents, identified in relation to the body in terms of the 'objective senses' of sight and hearing). What electricity is to light, *Moira* is to language. To think grammatologically is not to have an idea, but to have a 'moira' (so to speak).

Derrida, against description theories, and also against phenomenological epistemologies dependent on perception, intuition, or experience, is developing a theory of naming that does not depend on intelligibility or prior knowledge. His procedure in *Glas*, with regard to the relation of flowers to rhetoric (representing the analogical process in general), exemplifies his alternative. *The principle underlying Derrida's method for*

[30] Derrida, *Positions* (Chicago, 1981), p. 70.
[31] Derrida, 'Tympan', *Margins of Philosophy* (Chicago, 1982), pp. ix–xxix.

researching the relation of metaphors to concepts is exactly the same one that governs the signature – a systematic exploitation of the chance–necessity effects produced by the event of homophony or homonymy. In order to discover how flowers take root in language, according to Derrida's theory of concept formation, *the place to look is in the discourses that describe flowers* – literature and botany. The initial step of the operation is 'mechanical' or 'objective' – a cross-referencing of an artistic and a scientific terminology. What this research reveals is that a number of botanical terms relate homophonically, and even etymologically, to certain rhetorical terms. At stake is a theory of creativity, classically stated in terms of an analogy between sexual and spiritual creation and conception, as well as a pedagogy, also classically posed in terms of husbandry (as in Rousseau's famous image in *Emile* of the seedling in the roadway).

The philosopher, and especially the teacher of applied grammatology, must learn like poets and revolutionary scientists to explore the frivolities of chance. The dehiscence of iteration, an economimesis that redistributes the property or attributes of names, is exemplified in its generalized mode in 'Dissemination', an essay that, as Derrida explains, is a systematic and playful exploration of the interval of the gap itself, leading from '*écart*' (gap) to '*carré, carrure, carte, charte, quatre, trace*'. He calls this play of the interval, set to work within the history of philosophy,

undecidables, that is, unities of simulacrum, 'false' verbal properties (nominal or semantic) that can no longer be included within philosophical (binary) opposition, but which, however, inhabit philosophical opposition, resisting and disorganizing it, *without ever* constituting a third term, without ever leaving room for a solution in the form of speculative dialectics (the *pharmakon* is neither remedy nor poison, neither good nor evil, neither the inside nor the outside, neither speech nor writing; the *supplement* is neither a plus nor a minus, neither an outside nor the complement of an inside, neither accident nor essence, etc.) (*Positions*, p. 43)

The puncept, we may now understand, is not a gathering or collecting of properties at all, as in the concept, but a scattering, a dissemination, a throwing of the dice. Against the form of the idea, the moira breaks a line shaping thought, hence Derrida's interest in the story of Babel and the diaspora, and his critique of gathering and dispersion in Heidegger's *Dasein*.

One direction for further research is now available – to test and validate the moira or puncept, to replicate its effects by soliciting other materials. In *Teletheory*, for example, I use this strategy with the moira of *program*, noun and verb, to examine the paradigm in which the prostheses of thinking are the technologies of video and computers. The procedure begins with the research-pun, juxtaposing the semantic domains of logic and electronics, and then giving them a good shake. What this solicitation reveals or suggests (such is my thesis) is that thinking in teletheory will rely less on deduction and induction (despite the electronic status of the latter) and more on conduction and transduction.

Index